THE SOCIAL HISTORY
OF ART

Naturalism, Impressionism, The Film Age

VOLUME FOUR

THE SOCIAL HISTORY
OF ART

Naturalism, Impressionism,
The Film Age

ARNOLD HAUSER

VOLUME IV

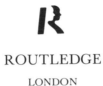

ROUTLEDGE

LONDON

First published in two volumes 1951
Reprinted 1952
This edition
Published in four volumes 1962
by Routledge & Kegan Paul plc
Reprinted four times
Reprinted 1989 by
Routledge
11 New Fetter Lane, London EC4P 4EE
Text printed in Great Britain
by Unwin Brothers Limited
The Gresham Press, Old Woking, Surrey, England
A member of the Martins Printing Group
Plates printed in Great Britain
by Headley Bros. Ltd., Ashford, Kent

Translated in collaboration
with the Author by
Stanley Godman

ISBN 0 415 04581 9

CONTENTS

CONTENTS

CONTENTS

ILLUSTRATIONS

ix

CHAPTER I

NATURALISM AND IMPRESSIONISM

---

1. THE GENERATION OF 1830

IF the purpose of historical research is the understanding of the present—and what else could it be?—then this enquiry is approaching its goal. What we are now to be concerned with is modern capitalism, modern bourgeois society, modern naturalistic art and literature, in short, our own world. Everywhere we are faced with new situations, new ways of life and feel as if we were cut off from the past. But the incision is probably nowhere so deep as in literature, where the frontier between the older works which are merely of historical interest to us and those that arise from now onwards and are still more or less topical today represents the most remarkable breach in the whole history of art. It is only the works produced on our side of the divide that constitute the living, modern literature directly concerned with our own contemporary problems. We are separated from all the older works by an unbridgeable gulf—to understand them, a special approach and a special effort on our part are necessary and their interpretation is always involved in the danger of misunderstanding and falsification. We read the works of the older literature differently from those of our own age; we enjoy them purely aesthetically, that is, indirectly, disinterestedly, perfectly aware of their fictitiousness and of our self-deception. This presupposes points of view and abilities which the average reader in no way has at his command; but even the historically and aesthetically interested reader feels there is an irreconcilable difference between works which have no immediate relationship to his own age, his own feelings and aims in life and such as have grown out of these very feelings and seek an answer to the

1

question: How can one, how should one, live in this present age?

The nineteenth century, or what we usually understand by that term, begins around 1830. It is only during the July monarchy that the foundations and outlines of this century are developed, that is to say, the social order in which we ourselves are rooted, the economic system, the antagonisms and contradictions of which still continue, and the literature in whose forms we on the whole still express ourselves today. The novels of Stendhal and Balzac are the first books concerned with our own life, our own vital problems, with moral difficulties and conflicts unknown to earlier generations. Julien Sorel and Mathilde de la Mole, Lucien de Rubempré and Rastignac are the first modern characters in Western literature—our first intellectual contemporaries. In them we meet for the first time the sensibility which throbs in our own nerves, in the delineation of their characters we find the first outlines of the psychological differentiation which for us is part of the nature of contemporary man. From Stendhal to Proust, from the generation of 1830 to that of 1910, we are witnesses of a homogeneous, organic intellectual development. Three generations struggle with the same problems, for seventy to eighty years the course of history remains unchanged.

All the characteristic features of the century are already recognizable around 1830. The bourgeoisie is in full possession and awareness of its power. The aristocracy has vanished from the scene of historical events and leads a purely private existence. The victory of the middle class is undoubted and undisputed. It is true that the victors form a thoroughly conservative and illiberal capitalist class adopting the administrative forms and methods of the old aristocracy often without alteration, but a class that is absolutely unaristocratic and untraditionalistic in its way of life and thought. Romanticism was, no doubt, already an essentially bourgeois movement, which would have been inconceivable without the emancipation of the middle classes, but the romantics often behaved rather aristocratically and flirted with the idea of appealing to the nobility as their public. After 1830 these whims come to an end entirely and it becomes obvious that there is in fact no massive public apart from the middle class.

But as soon as the emancipation of the middle class is accomplished, the struggle of the working class for its rights already begins. And that is the second of the decisively important movements which proceed from the July revolution and monarchy. Hitherto the class struggles of the proletariat had been fused with those of the middle class, and it had been mainly the political aspirations of the middle classes for which the working class had fought. The developments after 1830 first open its eyes and supply it with the proof that, in fighting for its rights, it can rely on no other class. Simultaneously with the awakening class-consciousness of the proletariat, socialist theory acquires its first more or less concrete form and there also arises the programme of an artistic activist movement which for radicalism and consistency surpasses all previous movements of a similar nature. 'L'art pour l'art' goes through its first crisis and has from now on to fight not only against the idealism of the classicists but also against the utilitarianism of both 'social' and 'bourgeois' art.

The economic rationalism which goes hand in hand with advancing industrialization and the total victory of capitalism, the progress of the historical and exact sciences and the general philosophical scientism connected with it, the repeated experience of an unsuccessful revolution and the political realism which results—all this paves the way for the great fight against romanticism which pervades the history of the next hundred years. The preparation and institution of this fight is a further contribution of the 1830 generation to the foundations of the nineteenth century. Stendhal's wavering between 'logique' and 'espagnolisme', Balzac's ambivalent relationship to the middle class, the dialectic of rationalism and irrationalism in both of them, shows the fight already in full swing; Flaubert's generation deepens the conflict, but finds it already under way. The artistic outlook of the July monarchy is partly bourgeois, partly socialistic, but unromantic on the whole. The public is, as Balzac remarks in the preface to *Peau de Chagrin* (1831), 'fed up with Spain, the Orient and the history of France à la Walter Scott', and, as Lamartine laments, the age of poetry, that is, of 'romantic' poetry, is past.[1] The naturalistic novel, the most original creation

3

of this period and the most important art form of the nineteenth century, gives expression, despite the romanticism of its founders, despite Stendhal's Rousseauism and Balzac's melodramatics, to the unromantic spirit of the new generation. Both economic rationalism and political thinking in terms of the class struggle refer the novel to the study of social reality and socio-psychological mechanisms. The subject and the point of view are both in full accord with the aspirations of the middle class and the result, the naturalistic novel, serves this rising class as a kind of textbook in its endeavour to secure complete control of society. The writers of the period turn it into an instrument for sounding man and dealing with the world and thereby conform to the taste and needs of a public that they hate and despise. They strive to satisfy their middle-class readers, no matter whether they are Saint-Simonites and Fourierites or not, and believe in social art or 'l'art pour l'art'—for there is no proletarian reading public, and even if there were, its existence would only embarrass them.

Until the eighteenth century, authors had been nothing but the mouthpiece of their public;[2] they looked after their readers' minds, just as servants and officials managed their material goods. They accepted and confirmed the generally recognized moral principles and criteria of taste; they did not invent them and they did not alter them. They produced their works for a clearly defined and clearly limited public and made no attempt whatsoever to gain new readers. Thus there was no tension of any kind between the real and an ideal public.[3] The writer knew neither the tormenting problem of having to choose between different subjective possibilities, nor the moral problem of having to choose between different strata of society. It is not until the eighteenth century that the public divides into two different camps and art into two rival tendencies. From now on every artist stands between two opposing orders, between the world of the conservative aristocracy and that of the progressive bourgeoisie, between a group that holds fast to the old, traditional, allegedly absolute values and one based on the view that even, and above all, these values are historically conditioned and that there are other, more up-to-date values, more in accordance with the general good. The

4

middle class renounces its aristocratic models and the aristocracy itself begins to doubt the validity of its own standards; partly it goes over to the bourgeois camp, in order to promote a literature which is hostile and pernicious to its own interests. For writers an absolutely new situation develops; those who continue in the service of the conservative classes, the Churches, the court and the court nobility, betray their own social compeers; those, on the other hand, who represent the world-view of the rising bour- geoisie fulfill a function never before discharged by representa- tive writers, apart from isolated individuals—they fight for an oppressed class, or at least for a class that is not yet in possession of power.[4] They no longer find the ideology of this public ready and waiting for them, they have themselves to contribute to its conceptual system, its philosophical categories and standards of value. They are, therefore, no longer merely the mouthpiece of their readers, they are at the same time their advocates and teachers, and even regain something of that long-lost priestly dignity which neither the poets of antiquity nor of the Renais- sance had enjoyed, least of all the clerics of the Middle Ages, whose readers were themselves merely clerics and who came into no contact at all with the lay public. During the Restoration and the July monarchy the littérateurs lose the unique position they had occupied in the eighteenth century; they are no longer either the protectors or the teachers of their readers, they are, on the contrary, their unwilling, constantly revolting, but none the less very useful, servants. Once again they proclaim a more or less ready-made, prescribed ideology, namely, the liberalism of the victorious middle class, derived from the enlightenment, but falsifying it in many ways. They are compelled to base them- selves on this philosophy, if they want to find readers and sell their books. The peculiar thing is, however, that they do it with- out identifying themselves with their public. Even the authors of the enlightenment counted only a part of the literary public among their supporters; they, too, were surrounded by a hostile and dangerous world, but at least they were in the same camp as their own readers. Even the romantics still felt themselves re- lated to one or other stratum of society, in spite of their home- lessness, and were always able to say which group, which class

5

they were supporting. But to what section of the public does Stendhal feel himself related? At best to the 'happy few'—the outsiders, the outlaws, the defeated. And Balzac? Does he identify himself with the nobility, with the bourgeoisie, or the proletariat?—with the class for which he has certain sympathies, but which he abandons without turning an eyelash, or with the class whose inexhaustible energy he recognizes, but for which he feels a loathing, or with the masses by whom he is as frightened as he is by fire? The writers who are not merely the 'maîtres de plaisir' of the bourgeoisie have no real public—Balzac, the successful, no more than Stendhal, the failure.

Nothing reflects the tense, discordant relationship between the literarily productive and the receptive sections of the 1830 generation more sharply than the new type of novel hero appearing in Stendhal and Balzac. The disillusionment and *Weltschmerz* of the heroes of Rousseau, Chateaubriand and Byron, their remoteness from the world and their loneliness, are transformed into a forgoing of the realization of their ideals, into a contempt for society and often into a desperate cynicism concerning current norms and conventions. The romantic novel of disillusionment becomes the novel of hopelessness and resignation. All the tragic and heroic characteristics, the self-assertiveness, the belief in the perfectibility of one's own nature, yield to a readiness to compromise, to the readiness to live aimlessly and die obscurely. The romantic novel of disillusionment still contained something of the idea of the tragedy which allows the hero fighting against trivial reality to be victorious even in defeat; in the nineteenth-century novel, on the other hand, he appears inwardly defeated even, and often precisely, when he has reached his actual goal. Nothing was further from the minds of the young Goethe, Chateaubriand or Benjamin Constant than to let their heroes doubt the *raison d'être* of their own personalities and aims in life; the modern novel first creates the bad conscience of the hero in conflict with the bourgeois social order, and demands that he accept the customs and conventions of society at least as the rules of the game. Werther is still the exceptional personality to whom the poet grants the right to revolt against the unappreciative and prosaic world from the very outset; Wilhelm Meister, on the other hand, ends his years of apprenticeship with the realization that one has to adapt oneself to the world as one finds it. External reality is more bereft of meaning and more soulless, because it has become more mechanical and self-sufficient; society, which had hitherto been the individual's natural milieu and only field of activity, has lost all significance, all value from the point of view of his higher aims, but the requirement that he should comply with society, live in and for it, has become more imperative.

The politicization of society, which began with the French Revolution, reaches its climax under the July monarchy. The quarrel between liberalism and reaction, the struggle for the reconciliation of the achievements of the Revolution with the interests of the privileged classes, continues and embraces every sphere of public life. Finance capital triumphs over landed property, and both the feudal aristocracy and the Church cease to play a leading rôle in political life; the progressive elements are opposed by the bankers and industrialists. The old political and social antagonism has not become any less, but the positions have shifted. The deepest antitheses are now between industrial capitalism, on the one side, and the wage-earning workers with the petty bourgeoisie, on the other. The aims of the class struggle are clarified and the methods of warfare intensified; everything seems to point to the imminence of a new revolution. In spite of constant setbacks, liberalism gains ground and the way for Western European democracy is gradually prepared. The electoral law is altered and the number òf electors is increased from some 100,000 to two and a half times its previous size. The rudiments of the parliamentary system and the foundations of the coalition of the working class come into being. In parliament, in spite of the electoral reforms, the possessing classes continue to be represented exclusively, and the liberalism that comes to power represents merely a liberalism within the bounds of the upper middle class. The July monarchy is, in brief, a period of eclecticism, of compromise, of the middle way—if not precisely the period of the 'right' middle way, as Louis-Philippe calls it and as it is now called by everyone, sometimes approvingly, sometimes ironically. It is outwardly a period of moderation and tolerance,

7

but inwardly one marked by the most severe struggle for existence, an epoch of moderate political progress and economic conservatism after the English pattern. The Guizots and the Thiers
extol the idea of the constitutional monarchy, desire that the
king should merely reign, not rule, but they are the instrument
of a parliamentary oligarchy, of a small government party which
keeps the broader strata of the middle class spellbound with the
magic formula of 'Enrichissez-vous!'. The July monarchy is a
period of glorious prosperity, a flowering time for all industrial
and commercial undertakings. Money dominates the whole of
public and private life; everything bows before it, everything
serves it, everything is prostituted—exactly, or almost, as Balzac
described it. It is true that the rule of capital does not in any
sense begin now, but hitherto the possession of money had been
only one of the means by which a man had been able to gain a
position for himself in France, and neither the most refined nor
the most effective method either. Now, on the other hand, all
rights, all power, all ability, are suddenly expressed in terms of
money. In order to be understood, everything has to be reduced
to this common denominator. From this point of view, the whole
previous history of capitalism seems no more than a mere prelude. Not only politics and the higher strata of society, not only
parliament and the bureaucracy, are plutocratic in character,
France is dominated not merely by the Rothschilds and the other
'juste-millionaires', as Heine called them, but the king himself is
a wily and unscrupulous speculator. For eighteen years the
government represents, as Tocqueville says, a kind of 'trading
company'; the king, the parliament and the administration share
the tasty morsels amongst themselves, exchange information and
tips, make each other a present of transactions and concessions,
speculate in shares and rents, bills of exchange and mortgages.
The capitalist monopolizes the leadership of society and gains a
position for himself that he had never had before. Hitherto, in
order to play this part, the man of property had to have some
kind of ideological halo; the rich man had to come forward as a
patron of the Church, the Crown or the arts and sciences, but now
he enjoys the highest honours simply because he is rich. 'From
now on the bankers will rule!'—Laffitte prophesies after Louis-

Philippe has been elected king. And: 'No society can continue without an aristocracy'—a deputy says in parliament in 1836.— 'Do you want to know who the aristocrats of the July monarchy are? The captains of industry; they are the basis of the new dynasty.' But the bourgeoisie is still fighting for its position, for the social prestige that the nobility concedes to it reluctantly and hesitantly. It is still a 'rising class' and still has the dashing offensive spirit and unbroken self-consciousness of the disfranchised. But it is so certain of victory that its self-consciousness already begins to turn into self-satisfaction and self-righteousness. Its good conscience is based partly on self-deception and develops into a state of mind in which the exposures of socialism will later break its self-confidence. It becomes more and more intolerant and illiberal, and takes for the foundations of its philosophy its worst inadequacies, its narrow-mindedness, its shallow rationalism and its idealistically disguised striving for profit. It suspects all real idealism and laughs at all unworldliness; it struggles against all intransigence and radicalism, persecutes and suppresses all opposition to the spirit of the 'juste-milieu' and the prudent concealment of antagonisms. It trains its satellites to be hypocrites, and shelters all the more desperately behind the fictions of its idealogy the more dangerous the attacks of socialism become.

The basic tendencies of modern capitalism, which had been becoming increasingly apparent ever since the Renaissance, now emerge in all their blatant and uncompromising clarity, unmitigated by any tradition. The most conspicuous of these tendencies is the attempt to withdraw the whole mechanism of an economic undertaking from all direct human influence, that is, from all consideration for personal circumstances. The undertaking becomes an autonomous organism, pursuing its own interests and aims, conforming to the laws of its own internal logic, a tyrant turning everyone who comes into contact with it into its slave.[6] The absolute devotion to business, the self-sacrifice of the entrepreneur in the interest of the competitive system, the prosperity and extension of the firm, his abstract, ruthless, self-centred striving for success, acquires an alarming monomaniacal character.[7] The system becomes independent of those who sustain it,

9

and transformed into a mechanism whose progress no human power is able to restrain. This automobility of the apparatus is the uncanny thing about modern capitalism; it gives it that demonism which Balzac described so terrifyingly. To the extent that the means and presuppositions of economic success are withdrawn from the individual's sphere of influence, the feeling of insecurity, the feeling of being at the mercy of a despotic monster, becomes ever stronger. And as economic interests become intertwined and interwoven, the struggle becomes more and more wild, more and more desperate, the monster more and more multiform, and ultimate ruin more and more inescapable. In the end, people find themselves surrounded on every side by rivals and enemies, everyone fights against everyone else, everyone stands in the front line of an unremiting, universal, really 'total' war.[8] All property, all position, all influence, have to be newly acquired, conquered and enforced from day to day; everything seems provisional, unreliable and unstable.[9] Hence the general scepticism and pessimism, hence the feeling of choking anxiety which fills the world of Balzac and remains the predominant characteristic of the literature of the capitalist era.

Louis-Philippe and his financial aristocracy are faced by a powerful and extensive opposition which embraces, in addition to the aristocratic and clerical legitimists, all the elements who feel that the hopes they placed in the July revolution have been disappointed, that is, it embraces, on the one hand, the patriotic and Bonapartist but fundamentally liberal-minded petty bourgeoisie, on the other hand, the left wing consisting of the bourgeois republicans and the socialists, with the progressive intelligentsia in one camp or the other. The so-called 'liberal' government party is therefore surrounded by a whole circle of opposition and revolutionary groups, whilst Louis-Philippe, the 'citizen king', is opposed by the overwhelming majority of his people.[10] The radical tendencies are expressed and discharge themselves in the formation of democratic associations, parties and sects, in strikes, hunger revolts and attempted murders, in brief, in what has been rightly described as a state of permanent revolution. These disturbances are by no means simply the continuation of the earlier revolutions and revolts. Even the Lyons rising of 1831 is different

10

from the older revolutionary movements by reason of its non-political character;[11] it is the prelude and beginning of that mass movement whose symbol, the red flag, first appears in the year 1832. The change begins with a discovery typical of socialistic thinking. 'The bourgeois economic doctrine of the identity of the interests of capital and labour, of universal harmony and universal national prosperity as the results of free competition, is', as Engels remarks, 'confounded more and more conclusively by the facts.'[12] Socialism as a theory develops from the recognition of the class character of this economy. Of course, we already come across socialistic ideas and tendencies in the great French Revolution, especially in the Convention and the Babeuf conspiracy, but there can be no question of a proletarian mass movement and a corresponding class-consciousness until after the victory of the Industrial Revolution and the introduction of the large-scale, completely mechanized factory. The human contacts in these factories are the origin of working-class solidarity and of the whole modern labour movement.[13] The modern proletariat, as the integration of the hitherto dispersed small labour-units, is first created by the nineteenth century and industrialism; nothing similar had been known to former ages.[14] The socialistic theory, founded by isolated philanthropists and Utopians, which arose from the economic sufferings of the people, from the desire to relieve this suffering and find a way to distribute wealth more equitably, only becomes an effective weapon with the consolidation of the urban factory and the social struggles which take place from 1830 onwards; now it first begins to tread the path described by Engels as its development 'from Utopia to science'. The social criticism of Saint-Simon and Fourier had already sprung from the experience of industrialism and the recognition of its devastating effects, but the realism of these thinkers was still combined with a good deal of romanticism and the right questions with fantastic attempts to achieve a solution. The religious tendencies appearing after the Restoration, indeed, to some extent as soon as the Concordat, and which become deeper after 1830, determined the character of their whole reforming and missionary activity. From Saint-Simon to Auguste Comte a romantic goal hovers before the mind of the socialists and social philosophers: they would all like

11

to put a new order, a new organization of society in the place of the medieval Church as an organic, synthetic form, and set up the 'new Christianity' with the aid of the poets and artists.

Along with the advancing politicization of life, between 1830 and 1848, the political tendency in literature is also intensified. During this period there are hardly any works without some political interest; even the quietism of 'l'art pour l'art' has, of course, a political tinge. The new trend is expressed most strikingly in the fact that politics and literature are now combined by the same men, and that it is usually the members of the same social stratum who practise politics or literature as a profession. Literary abilities are regarded as the obvious precondition of a political career and political influence is often the reward for literary services. The literary politicians and the political littérateurs of the July monarchy—men like Guizot, Thiers, Michelet, Thierry, Villemain, Cousin, Jouffroy, Nisard—are the last descendants of the 'philosophes' of the eighteenth century; the writers of the next generation have no political ambitions and its politicians no longer have any intellectual influence. Until the February revolution, however, political life absorbs all the intellectual forces of the time. The gifted young people who are barred from a political career owing to lack of means devote themselves to journalism; that is now the usual beginning and the typical form of a literary career. As a journalist, one not only builds oneself a bridge to the world of politics and the world of real literature, one often secures a considerable influence, income and reputation through journalism itself. Bertin, the chief editor of the *Journal des Débats*, is, with his complacency and self-confidence, the very embodiment of the July monarchy. He is the incarnation of the bourgeois littérateur and the literary bourgeois. But literary activity not only becomes a business for men like Bertin, but, as Sainte-Beuve remarks, it develops into an 'industry' for all concerned in its production.[15] It becomes simply a means of acquiring advertisements and subscribers. The connection of literature with the daily press has, according to one contemporary, just as revolutionary an effect as the use of steam for industrial purposes; the whole output of literature changes its character.[16] Even if this analogy is exaggerated and the indus-

12

trialization of literature is only a symptom of a universal intellectual development, that is, only expresses a general trend to which the artistic production of the period inclines in any case, nevertheless, it must be described as an historical event, when Émile de Girardin, an unimportant writer but an imaginative business man, adopts the idea of the previously completely unknown Dutacq and founds the newspaper *La Presse* in 1836. The epoch-making innovation is that he fixes the subscription at forty francs per annum, that is, at half the usual rate, and plans to cover the loss with the income from announcements and advertisements. In the same year, Dutacq founds the *Siècle* with the same programme, and the rest of the Paris newspapers follow his example. The number of subscribers grows and amounts to 200,000 in 1846, compared with 70,000 ten years before. The new undertakings force the editors to compete with each other in improving the contents of their papers. They have to offer their readers as tasty and varied fare as possible, in order to increase the attraction of their papers, above all with an eye on the income from advertisements. From now on everyone is to find in his paper articles in accordance with his taste and interests; it is to become everyman's private library and encyclopaedia.

Apart from specialist contributions, the newspapers carry articles of general interest, particularly travel descriptions, scandal stories and law reports. But serial novels are their greatest attraction. Everyone reads them, the aristocracy and the bourgeoisie, polite society and the intelligentsia, young and old, men and women, masters and servants. The *Presse* opens the series of its 'feuilletons' with the publication of works of Balzac, who supplies it with a new novel every year from 1837 to 1847, and of Eugène Sue, who lets it have most of his works. The *Siècle* plays off Alexandre Dumas against the authors of the *Presse*, the Dumas whose *Three Musketeers* is enormously successful and brings considerable profit to the paper. The *Journal des Débats* owes its popularity above all to the *Mystères de Paris* by Eugène Sue, who is, after the publication of this novel, one of the best-paid authors and one of those most in demand. The *Constitutionnel* offers him 100,000 francs for his *Juif Errant*, and henceforth this amount is regarded as his standard fee. But Alexandre

13

Dumas still has the biggest income, earning roughly 200,000 francs yearly and receiving an annual sum of 63,000 francs for 220,000 lines from the *Presse* and the *Constitutionnel*. To satisfy the enormous demand, popular authors now join forces with the literary hacks who give them invaluable help in turning out standardized products. Whole factories of literature are set up and novels are produced almost mechanically. In a court action it is proved that Dumas publishes more under his own name than he could write even if he were to work day and night without a break. In fact, he employs seventy-three collaborators, and amongst them one August Maquet, whom he allows to work quite independently. Literary work now becomes a 'commodity' in the fullest sense of the word; it has its price tariff, is produced according to a pattern and delivered on a day fixed in advance. It is a commercial article for which one pays the price it is worth— the price it returns. It does not occur to any editor to pay Mr. Dumas or Mr. Sue any more than he must and can. The authors of the newspaper serials are therefore no more 'overpaid' than the filmstars of today; their prices conform to the demand and have nothing to do with the artistic value of what they produce.

The *Presse* and the *Siècle* are the first daily papers to print serials, but the idea of publishing a novel in serial form is not their property. It comes from Véron, who already puts it into practice in his *Revue de Paris* founded in 1829.[17] Buloz takes the idea over from him in the *Revue des Deux Mondes* and in this form publishes, amongst other things, novels by Balzac. The 'feuilleton' in itself is, however, older than these periodicals; we come across it as early as 1800. The newspapers, which are very scanty during the Consulate and the first Empire, owing to the censorship and the other restrictions on the press, publish a literary supplement, in order to offer something to their readers. To begin with, this represents a kind of chronicle of the social and artistic worlds, but develops into a real literary supplement during the Restoration. From 1830 stories and travel descriptions are its main contents and after 1840 it only carries novels. The Second Empire, which imposes a tax of one centime on every copy of a paper with a 'feuilleton', soon brings the serial novel to an end. It is true that the genre is revived later on, but it has no further influence on the development of literature, compared with the deep tracks which it leaves behind in the literature of the 'forties.

The serial novel is intended for just as mixed and recently constituted a public as the melodrama or the vaudeville; it conforms to the same formal principles and aesthetic criteria as the contemporary popular stage. The fondness for exaggeration and raciness, for the crude and the eccentric, is just as decisive an influence on its style of presentation; the most popular subjects revolve around seductions and adulteries, acts of violence and cruelty. Here, too, as in the melodrama, the characters and the plot are stereotyped and constructed in accordance with a set pattern.[18] The interruption of the story at the end of each instalment, the problem of creating a climax every time and making the reader curious for the next instalment, induces the author to acquire a kind of stage technique and to take over from the dramatist the discontinuous method of presentation in separate scenes. Alexandre Dumas, the master of dramatic tension, is also a brilliant exponent of the technique of the serial; for the more dramatic the development of a serial novel, the stronger the effect it has on its public. But the continuation of the plot from day to day, the publication of the separate parts usually without an exact plan and without the possibility of altering what has already appeared and bringing it into harmony with the later instalments, produces, on the other hand, an 'undramatic', episodic and improvising narrative style, a never-ending stream of events and an unorganic, often contradictory portrayal of the characters. The whole art of 'preparation', the technique of seemingly natural, unforced, unintentional motivation, is lost. The turns in the plot and the changes of purpose in the characters often seem to be far-fetched, and the secondary characters, who turn up in the course of the story, often appear much too suddenly, as the author has failed to 'introduce' them in time. Even Balzac is often guilty of introducing characters without preparing the reader for them in advance, although it is precisely this improvising technique that he finds fault with in the *Chartreuse de Parme*. With Stendhal, however, the careless, loose construction is the result of an intrinsically episodic, picaresque and essentially undramatic

15

narrative method,[19] whereas with Balzac, whose ideal is a novel with a dramatic form, it is an inadequacy ensuing from his journalistic mode of writing, from his hand-to-mouth existence. Whether the industrialization of literature is a consequence of journalism, however, and the light novel owes its rigid, stereotyped character entirely to the newspaper serial, must be left an open question; for, as the Empire and Restoration style proves, the conventionalization of this form had already been in progress for a long time past.[20]

The serial novel signifies an unprecedented democratization of literature and an almost complete reduction of the reading public to one level. Never has an art been so unanimously recognized by such different social and cultural strata and received with such similar feelings. Even a Sainte-Beuve praises the author of the *Mystères de Paris* for qualities that he regrets to find missing in Balzac. The spread of socialism and the growth of the reading public go hand in hand, but Eugène Sue's democratic approach and his belief in the social purpose of art only partly explain the success of his novels. It is, on the contrary, peculiar to hear the favourite of a very largely bourgeois public waxing enthusiastic about the 'noble labourer' and storming furiously about the 'cruelties of capitalism'. The humanitarian aim that he pursues, the revelation of the wounds of the diseased social body that he sets himself in his works, explains at most the sympathy with which he is treated by the progressive press, the *Globe*, the *Démocratie pacifique*, the *Revue indépendante*, the *Phallange* and their followers. The majority of his readers probably merely take his socialistic tendencies into the bargain. But there is no doubt that even this section of the public takes for granted the literary treatment of the social problems of the day. The idea emphasized by Mme de Staël, that literature is the expression of society, finds universal recognition and becomes an axiom of French literary criticism. From 1830 onwards it is quite normal to judge a literary work from the point of view of its relation to topical political and social problems, and, with the exception of the comparatively small group behind the 'l'art pour l'art' movement, no one is annoyed at seeing art subordinated to political ideals. There was probably never a time when so little purely formal, non-utilitarian art criticism was practised as now.[21]

Until 1848 the most important and the major part of the works of art belong to the activistic, after 1848 to the quietistic school. Stendhal's disillusionment is still aggressive, extroverted, anarchistic, whereas Flaubert's acquiescence is passive, egocentric and nihilistic. Even within the romantic movement, the 'l'art pour l'art' of Théophile Gautier and Gérard de Nerval is no longer the leading tendency. The old unworldly, mystical and mystifying kind of romanticism is dead. Romanticism is continued, but transformed and reinterpreted. The anti-clerical and anti-legitimist tendency which makes itself felt at the end of the Restoration develops into a more revolutionary philosophy. Most of the romantics fall away from 'pure art' and go over to the Saint-Simonites and Fourierites.[22] The leading personalities— Hugo, Lamartine, George Sand—profess an artistic activism and place themselves at the disposal of the 'popular' art demanded by the socialists. The people has triumphed, and the call is now to give expression to the revolutionary change in art as well. Not only George Sand and Eugène Sue become socialists, not only Lamartine and Hugo become enthusiastic about the people, even writers like Scribe, Dumas, Musset, Mérimée and Balzac flirt with socialistic ideas.[23] This flirtation soon comes to an end, however; for, just as the July monarchy turns away from the democratic ideals of the revolution and becomes the régime of the conservative bourgeoisie, the romantics also fall away from socialism and return to their former conception of art, though in a modified form. In the end not a single important writer remains loyal to the socialist ideal and, for the moment, the cause of 'popular art' seems to be lost. Romantic art quietens down, becomes more disciplined and more middle-class. Under the leadership of Lamartine, Hugo, Vigny and Musset, there arises, on the one hand, a conservatively academic, on the other, an elegant salon romanticism. The wild and violent rebelliousness of earlier days is subdued and the bourgeoisie takes an enthusiastic interest in this new romanticism, now partly subject to academic restraints and almost 'classical' in its outlook, partly fused with the dandyism of Byron's disciples.[24] Sainte-Beuve, Villemain, Buloz, are the highest authorities, the *Journal des Débats* and the *Revue des Deux Mondes* the official organs of the new, romantically tinged, but academically-minded bourgeois literary world.[25]

To some sections of the public, however, romanticism still seems too wild and despotic. A new, matter-of-fact, strictly bourgeois classicism is put in its place, the art of the so-called 'école de bon sens' and the aesthetic 'juste-milieu'. Ponsard's success, the revival of the 'tragédie classique' and the Rachel vogue are the most striking expression of this new school of taste. After the 'morbid' exaggerations and overheated atmosphere there is a desire to breathe fresh air again. There is a desire for balanced, measured, exemplary characters, for normal, universally understandable feelings and passions, for a philosophy of balance, order and the middle way, in short, for a literature that forgoes the piquancy, bizarre ideas and eccentric style of romanticism. 1843 is the year in which *Lucrèce* is a success and the *Burgraves* a fiasco; and this implies not only the victory of Ponsard over Hugo, but also that of Scribe, Dumas and Ingres and their ilk over Stendhal, Balzac and Delacroix. The middle class does not expect to get violent shocks but entertainment from art; it does not see a 'vates' in the poet but a 'maître de plaisir'. Ingres is followed by the endless succession of orthodox but drearily academic painters, Ponsard by the reliable but unimportant caterers for the state and municipal theatres. Amusement and peace and quiet are what is wanted and there is a corresponding change in the attitude to 'pure', non-political art.

'L'art pour l'art' sprang from romanticism and represents one of the weapons in its struggle for freedom; it is the result and to some extent the sum-total of romantic aesthetic theory. What was originally merely a revolt against the classical rules has become a revolt against all external ties, an emancipation from all non-artistic, moral and intellectual values. For Gautier artistic freedom already means independence from the criteria of the middle class, a lack of interest in its utilitarian ideals and the refusal to co-operate in the realization of these ideals. For the romantics 'l'art pour l'art' becomes the ivory tower in which they shut themselves off from all practical affairs. They buy the peace and superiority of a purely contemplative attitude at the price of an understanding with the prevailing order. Until 1830 the middle class hoped that art would promote its ideals, it therefore accepted art as a vehicle of political propaganda. 'Man is not created only to sing, believe and love . . . Life is no exile, but a call to action . . .'—writes the *Globe* in 1825.[26] After 1830, however, the bourgeoisie becomes suspicious of the artist, and prefers neutrality to the former alliance. The *Revue des Deux Mondes* is now of the opinion that it is not necessary, that it is in fact undesirable for the artist to have his own political and social ideas; and that is the standpoint represented by the most authoritative critics, amongst others Gustave Planche, Nisard and Cousin.[27] The middle class makes 'l'art pour l'art' its own; it stresses the ideal nature of art and the high, superpolitical status of the artist. It locks him up in a golden cage. Cousin goes back to the idea of autonomy in Kant's philosophy and revives the theory of the 'disinterestedness' of art, and here the tendency to specialization which becomes ascendant with capitalism proves very useful. 'L'art pour l'art' is, in fact, partly the expression of the division of labour which advances hand in hand with industrialization, partly the bulwark of art against the danger of being swallowed up by industrialized and mechanized life. It signifies, on the one hand, the rationalization, disenchantment and contraction of art, but simultaneously the attempt to preserve its individual quality and spontaneity, in spite of the universal mechanization of life.

'L'art pour l'art' indubitably represents the most involved problem in the whole field of aesthetics. Nothing expresses so acutely the dualistic, spiritually divided nature of the artistic outlook. Is art its own end or only the means to an end? This question will be answered differently, not only according to the particular historical and social situation in which one happens to find oneself, but also according to which element in the complex structure of art one concentrates on. The work of art has been compared to a window through which life can be seen without the necessity of accounting for the structure, transparency and colour of the window-pane itself.[28] According to this analogy, the work of art appears to be a mere vehicle of observation and knowledge, that is, a pane of glass or an eye-glass of no consequence in itself and merely serving as a means to an end. But just as one can concentrate one's attention on the structure of the window-pane, without paying any attention to the picture displayed on the other side of the window, so the work of art can be thought of as an independent formal structure existing for its own sake, as a coherent and significant entity, complete and perfect in itself, and in which all transgressing interpretations, all 'looking through the window', prejudices the appreciation of its spiritual coherence. The purpose of the work of art constantly wavers between these two points of view, between an immanent being, detached from all reality beyond the work itself, and a function determined by life, society and practical necessity. From the standpoint of the direct aesthetic experience, autonomy and self-sufficiency appear to be the essence of the work of art, for only by cutting itself off from reality and putting itself completely in the place of reality, only by forming a total, self-contained cosmos, is it able to produce a perfect illusion. But this illusion is in no way the whole content of art and often has no share in the effect it produces. The greatest works of art forgo the deceptive illusionism of a self-contained aesthetic world and point beyond themselves. They stand in an immediate relationship to the great problems of their age and are always searching for an answer to the questions: How can a purpose be gained from human life? and: How can we participate in this purpose?

The most inexplicable paradox of the work of art is that it seems to exist for itself and yet not for itself; that it addresses itself to a concrete, historically and sociologically conditioned public, but seems, at the same time, to want to have no knowledge at all of a public. The 'fourth wall' of the stage seems at times the most natural premise, at others the most arbitrary fiction of aesthetics. The destruction of the illusion by a thesis, a moral purpose, a practical intention, which prevents, on the one hand, the pure and perfect enjoyment of art, first leads, on the other hand, to the real participation of the beholder or the reader in the work, taking hold of his whole being. This alternative has, however, nothing to do with the actual intention of the artist. Even the politically and morally most tendentious work can be regarded as pure art, that is, as a mere formal structure, provided it is a work of art at all; on the other hand, every artistic product, even one with which its creator has connected no practical intention of any kind, can be considered the expression and instrument of social causality. Dante's activism no more excludes a purely aesthetic interpretation of the *Divine Comedy*, than Flaubert's formalism a sociological explanation of *Madame Bovary* and the *Éducation sentimentale*.

The main artistic trends around 1830—'social' art, the 'école de bon sens' and 'l'art pour l'art'—are correlated to one another in complicated and usually contradictory ways. The Saint-Simonites and the Fourierites are conditioned by these contradictions both in their relationship to romanticism and to bourgeois classicism. They reject romanticism because of its fondness for the Church and monarchy, its unreal, romanesque outlook, its selfish individualism, but chiefly on account of its quietistic principle of 'l'art pour l'art'. On the other hand, they sympathize with romanticism on account of its liberalism, its principle of artistic freedom and spontaneity, its revolt against the classical rules and authorities. But they also feel strongly drawn by the naturalistic efforts of romanticism; they recognize in this naturalism an affinity with their own positive, affirmative, open-minded disposition. The affinity between socialism and naturalism explains above all their sympathetic attitude to Balzac, whose works they judge very kindly especially at the beginning of his career.[29] An equally contradictory attitude to bourgeois classicism is connected with these conflicting feelings about romanticism. The acknowledgement of the liberalism in the romantic conception of art implies the simultaneous condemnation of the return to classical models in bourgeois art, whereas the dislike for the caprices and extravagances of romantic poetry, above all of the romantic theatre, expresses itself in a partial approval of Ponsard's classicism.[30] Corresponding to this indecision of the socialists, we find, on the one hand, the favours of the bourgeoisie divided between academic romanticism and Ponsard's drama, and, on the other hand, the wavering of the romantics themselves between activism and 'l'art pour l'art'. These three tendencies are crossed by yet a fourth and historically the most important of them all: the naturalism of Stendhal and Balzac. The relationship of this naturalism to romanticism is also ambivalent. The ambivalence here corresponds above all to the rift which usually exists between two successive generations or two consecutive intellectual trends. Naturalism is both the continuation and the dissolution of romanticism; Stendhal and Balzac are its most legitimate heirs and its most violent opponents.

Naturalism is not a homogeneous, clear-cut conception of art, always based on the same idea of nature, but changes with the times, always aiming at a particular and immediate goal, always concerned with a concrete task and confining its interpretation of life to particular phenomena. One professes a belief in naturalism, not because one considers a naturalistic representation more artistic *a priori* than a stylizing, but because one discovers a trait, a tendency in reality on which one would like to put more emphasis, which one would like either to promote or fight against. Such a discovery is not itself the result of naturalistic observation, on the contrary, the interest in naturalism is the result of such a discovery. The 1830 generation begins its literary career with the recognition that the structure of society has completely changed; partly it accepts, partly it opposes this change, but, in any case, it reacts to it in an extremely activistic fashion and its naturalistic approach is derived from this activism. Naturalism is not aimed at reality as a whole, not at 'nature' or 'life' in general, but at social life in particular, that is, at that province of reality which has become specially important for this generation. Stendhal and Balzac make it their task to portray the new and changed society; the aim of giving expression to its novelties and peculiarities leads them to naturalism and determines their conception of artistic truth. The social consciousness of the generation of 1830, its sensitiveness to phenomena in which social interests are at stake, its quick eye for social changes and revaluations, make its writers the creators of the social novel and modern naturalism.

The history of the novel begins with the medieval epic of chivalry. It is true that this has little to do with the modern novel in general, but its cumulative structure, its continuative narrative method stringing together one adventure and one episode after another, are the source of a tradition which is maintained not only in the picaresque novel, the heroic and pastoral novels of the Renaissance and the baroque, but even in the adventure novel of the nineteenth century and, to some extent, in the representation of the stream of life and experience in the novels of Proust and Joyce. Apart from the general tendency, characteristic of the whole Middle Ages, towards the cumulative form, and apart from the Christian conception of life as a non-tragic phenomenon which does not come to a head in isolated dramatic conflicts, but is more in the nature of a journey with many stages, this structure is connected, above all, with the recitation of medieval poetry and the medieval public's naïve hunger for new material. Printing, that is, the direct reading of books, and the more concentrated Renaissance conception of art bring it about that the expansive narrative style of the Middle Ages begins to yield to a more compact, less episodic method of presentation. In spite of its still essentially picaresque structure, *Don Quixote* constitutes a criticism of the extravagant novel of chivalry even from a purely formal point of view. But the decisive change towards a unification and simplification of the novel is first brought about by French classicism. It is true that the *Princesse de Clèves* is an isolated example, for the heroic and pastoral novels of the seventeenth century still belong to the category of the medieval adventure stories with their avalanche-like cumulation of episodes; but in Mme de Lafayette's masterpiece the idea of the love novel, with a uniform plot and a dramatic climax, and of the psychological analysis of a single conflict had been realized and had become a possibility capable of realization at any time. The adventure novel now represents a second-rate literary genre; it stands outside the frontiers of representative art and enjoys the advantages of insignificance and irresponsibility. The *Grand Cyrus* and *Astrée* form the main reading of the court aristocracy, but people read them, so to say, in their private capacity and indulge in them as it were in a vice, or, at any rate, a weakness of which there is no reason to be proud. In his funeral oration on Henriette d'Angleterre, Bossuet mentions it as praiseworthy in the deceased that she cared little for fashionable novels and their silly heroes; that is enough to show how this genre was judged in public. Where their private amusements were concerned, the aristocracy did not allow themselves, however, to be guided by the classicistic rules of art, but indulged in the enjoyment of adventures and extravaganzas as unrestrainedly as ever.

The novel of the eighteenth century still belongs very largely to the diffuse, picaresque genre. Not only *Gil Blas* and the *Diable boiteux* but also Voltaire's novels, in spite of their limited size, are constructed episodically, and *Gulliver* and *Robinson* are a complete embodiment of the cumulative principle. Even *Manon Lescaut*, the *Vie de Marianne* and the *Liaisons dangereuses* still represent transitional forms between the old adventure stories and the love novel, which gradually becomes the leading genre and begins to dominate the literature of pre-romanticism. With *Clarissa Harlowe*, the *Nouvelle Héloïse* and *Werther*, the dramatic principle triumphs in the novel and a development begins which is to reach its climax in works like Flaubert's *Madame Bovary* and Tolstoy's *Anna Karenina*. Attention is now concentrated on the psychological movement of the story; the external events are only taken into consideration in so far as they produce spiritual reactions. The psychologization of the novel is the most striking evidence of the spiritualization and subjectivization through which the culture of the age is passing. The novel of character-formation (*Bildungsroman*), which represents the next stage in the development and the stylistically most important literary form of the century, gives even stronger expression to the spiritualizing tendency. The story of the hero's development now becomes the story of the formation of a world. Only an age in which individual culture had become the most important source of culture altogether could have produced this form of the novel, and it had to arise in a country like Germany where the roots of a common culture were shallowest. At any rate, Goethe's *Wilhelm Meister* is the first *Bildungsroman* in the strict sense of the word, even if the origins of the genre are to be found in earlier works, mainly of a picaresque character, such as Fielding's *Tom Jones* and Sterne's *Tristram Shandy*.

The novel becomes the leading literary genre of the eighteenth century, because it gives the most comprehensive and profound expression to the cultural problem of the age—the antithesis between individualism and society. In no other form do the

antagonisms of bourgeois society make themselves felt so intensely, in none are the struggles and defeats of the individual
described so thrillingly. It was not without reason that Friedrich
Schlegel called the novel the romantic genre par excellence.
Romanticism sees in it the most satisfactory representation of the
conflict between the individual and the world, dreams and real
life, poetry and prose, and the deepest expression of the acquiescence which it regards as the only solution of this conflict. In
Wilhelm Meister, Goethe finds a solution diametrically opposed
to the romantic; and his work is not only the culmination of the
history of the novel in the eighteenth century, not only the
prototype from which the most representative creations of the
genre, the *Rouge et Noir*, the *Illusions perdues*, the *Éducation
sentimentale* and the *Gruene Heinrich*, can be derived directly or
indirectly, but also the first important criticism of romanticism as
a way of life. Goethe here points, and this is the real message of
the work, to the absolute sterility of the romantic turning away
from reality; he emphasizes that one can only do the world justice if one is spiritually bound up with it, and that one can only
reform it from inside. He by no means conceals and glosses over
the discrepancy between the inner spirit and the outer world,
between the spiritual self and conventional reality, but he recognizes and proves that the romantic contempt for the world is an
evasion of the real problem.[31] The Goethean demand that man
should live with the world and in accordance with the rules of
the world was trivialized by later bourgeois literature and turned
into a summons to co-operate unconditionally with the world.
The peaceable, but by no means absolute adaptation of the individual to the given situation was transformed into a cringing
spirit of indiscriminate tolerance and a utilitarian secularism.
Goethe had a share in this development only in so far as he did
not perceive the impossibility of a peaceful reconciliation of the
antitheses and only in so far as his somewhat frivolous optimism
offered itself automatically as the ideology of the bourgeois policy
of appeasement. Stendhal and Balzac saw the prevailing tensions
much more acutely and judged the situation with a greater sense
of reality than Goethe. The social novel, in which they recorded
their insights, was a step which not only led beyond the romantic

novel of disillusionment but also beyond Goethe's *Bildungs-roman*. In their attitude both the romantic contempt for the world and Goethe's criticism of romanticism were quashed. Their pessimism resulted from an analysis of society which was quite clear of illusions about the possibility of solving the social problem.

The realism with which Stendhal and Balzac described the situation, their understanding of the dialectic which was moving society, was unparalleled in the literature of their time, but the idea of the social novel was in the air. Sub-titles like 'Scenes from polite society' or 'Scenes from private life' are met with long before Balzac.[32] 'Many young people describe things just as they happen daily in the provinces . . . Not much art but a good deal of truth results,' writes Stendhal with reference to the society novel of his day.[33] There had long been omens and experiments everywhere, but with Stendhal and Balzac the social novel becomes *the* modern novel and it now appears quite impossible to portray a character in isolation from society and to allow him to develop outside a definite social milieu. The facts of social life make their way into the human consciousness and can no longer be displaced from it. The greatest literary creations of the nineteenth century, the works of Stendhal, Balzac, Flaubert, Dickens, Tolstoy and Dostoevsky, are social novels, whatever other category they may belong to. The social definition of the characters becomes the criterion of their reality and credibility and the social problems of their life first make them suitable subjects for the new naturalistic novel. It is this sociological conception of man that the writers of the 1830 generation discovered for the novel and which was what most interested a thinker like Marx in the works of Balzac.

Stendhal and Balzac are both stern, often malicious critics of the society of their time; but the one criticizes it from the liberal, the other from the conservative standpoint. In spite of his reactionary views, Balzac is the more progressive artist; he sees the structure of middle-class society more acutely and describes the tendencies at work in it more objectively than the politically more radical but in his whole thinking and feeling more contradictory Stendhal. There is probably no other example in the whole history of art which makes it so clear that the service an artist renders to progress depends not so much on his personal convictions and sympathies as on the power with which he portrays the problems and contradictions of social reality. Stendhal judges his age according to the already out-of-date concepts of the eighteenth century, and fails to recognize the historical significance of capitalism. It is true that Balzac considers even these concepts much too progressive, but he cannot help describing society in his novels in such a way as to make a return to pre-revolutionary conditions and ideas appear absolutely unthinkable. Stendhal regards the culture of the enlightenment, the intellectual world of Diderot, Helvétius and Holbach, as exemplary and immortal; he considers its decline a passing phenomenon and dates its future revival from the day when he expects his own rehabilitation as an artist to take place. Balzac, on the other hand, sees that the old culture has already broken up, recognizes that the aristocracy itself has furthered the process and regards this in itself as a sign of the irresistible progress of capitalism. Stendhal's outlook is essentially political and, in his descriptions of society, he concentrates his attention on the 'mechanism of the state'.[34] Balzac, on the other hand, bases his social structure on economics, and, to some extent, anticipates the doctrines of historical materialism. He is perfectly aware that the actual forms of science, art and morality, as well as of politics, are functions of material reality and that bourgeois culture, with its individualism and rationalism, has its roots in the economic structure of capitalism. The fact that feudal conditions are more in accordance with his ideal than bourgeois-capitalist conditions does not in any way affect the fruitfulness of this insight. In spite of his enthusiasm for the old monarchy, the Catholic Church and aristocratic society, the realism and materialism of this world-view acts as one of the intellectual ferments by which the last remains of feudalism are dissolved.

Stendhal's novels are political chronicles: *Rouge et Noir* is the story of French society during the Restoration, the *Chartreuse de Parme* a picture of Europe under the rule of the Holy Alliance, *Lucien Leuwen* the socio-historical analysis of the July monarchy. Novels with a historical and political background had also existed in earlier times, of course, but it would never have occurred to anyone before Stendhal to make the political system of his own age the real subject of a novel. No one before him had been so conscious of the historical moment, no one felt so strongly as he did that history is made up purely and simply of such moments and constitutes a continuous chronicle of the generations. Stendhal experiences his own age as a time of unfulfilled promise and expectations, of unexploited energies and disappointed talents. He experiences it as an awful tragi-comedy, in which the parvenu middle class plays just as pitiable a rôle as the conspiring aristocracy, as a cruel political drama, in which all the players are only intriguers, no matter whether they are called ultras or liberals. He asks himself whether in a world like this, in which everyone lies and plays the hypocrite, any means is not good enough, provided it leads to success? The main thing is not to be the deceived, that is, to lie and simulate better than the others. All Stendhal's great novels revolve around the problem of hypocrisy, around the secret of how to deal with men and how to rule the world; they are all in the nature of text-books of political realism and courses of instruction in political amoralism. In his critique of Stendhal, Balzac already remarks that the *Chartreuse de Parme* is a new *Principe*, which Machiavelli himself, if he had lived as an émigré in the Italy of the nineteenth century, would not have been able to write any differently. Julien Sorel's Machiavellian motto, 'Qui veut les fins veut les moyens', here acquires its classical formulation, as used repeatedly by Balzac himself, namely that one must accept the rules of the world's game, if one wants to count in the world and to take part in the play.

For Stendhal the new society differs from the old above all by reason of its forms of government, the shift of power and the change in the political significance of the classes; for him the capitalistic system is the result of the political reconstruction. He describes French society at a stage of development where the middle class has already achieved economic supremacy, but still has to fight for its position in society. Stendhal portrays this struggle from a subjective, personal point of view, in the way that it presents itself to the rising intelligentsia. Julien Sorel's homelessness is the leitmotif of his whole work, the theme that he merely varies and modulates in his other novels, above all in the *Chartreuse de Parme* and in *Lucien Leuwen*. The social problem consists for him in the fate of those ambitious young people, rising from the lower classes and uprooted by their education, who find themselves without money and without connections at the end of the revolutionary period, and who, deluded, on the one hand, by the opportunities of the Revolution, on the other, by Napoleon's good fortune, want to play a rôle in society in accordance with their talents and ambitions. But they now discover that all power, all influence, all important posts are held by the old nobility and the new financial aristocracy and that superior gifts and greater intelligence are being displaced everywhere by mediocrity. The principle of the Revolution, that everyone is the architect of his own fortune, an idea that was absolutely foreign to the *ancien régime* but all the more familiar to the revolutionary youth of the time, loses its validity. Twenty years earlier the fate of Julien Sorel would have shaped itself quite differently; at twenty-five he would have become a colonel, at thirty-five a general—that is what we are told again and again. He was born too late or too early, and stands between the times, just as he stands between the classes. Where does he belong, whose side is he really on? It is the old familiar question, the problem of romanticism, coming up again and it remains as unsolved as ever. The romantic source of Stendhal's political ideas is probably revealed most clearly in the fact that he bases his hero's claim to success and position merely on the prerogative of talent, intelligence and energy. In his criticism of the Restoration and in his apologia for the Revolution, he bases his argument on the conviction that it is only in the people that real vitality and energy are still to be found. He regards the circumstances of the notorious murder committed by the seminarist Berthet, which he uses as a motif in *Rouge et Noir*, as evidence that the great men will henceforth proceed from those vigorous lower classes which are still capable of real passion, and to which not only Berthet, but also, as he now stresses, Napoleon, belonged.

In this way, the conscious class struggle is now ushered into literature proper. The conflict between the various strata of

29

society had already been described by great writers in earlier ages, of course; to be true to life, no portrayal of social realities could omit to consider it. But the real meaning of the struggle was not realized either by the literary characters or even by their creators. The slave, the serf and the peasant even appeared comparatively frequently in the older literature—usually as comic figures—and the plebeian was described not only as the representative of a sluggish element of society, but also, as for example in Marivaux's *Paysan parvenu*, as an upstart; a representative of the lower classes, that is, of the classes below the middle section of the bourgeoisie, never came forward, however, as the pioneer of a disfranchized class. Julien Sorel is the first hero in a novel to be constantly aware of his plebeian birth, and to regard every success as a victory over the ruling class and every defeat as a humiliation. He cannot even forgive Mme de Rênal, the one woman he really loves, for being rich and belonging to the class against which he imagines he must for ever be on his guard. In his relation to Mathilde de la Mole the class conflict can no longer be distinguished at all from the conflict between the sexes. And the speech which he addresses to his judges is nothing but a proclamation of the class war, a challenge to his enemies with his neck already under the axe: 'Gentlemen,' he says, 'I have not the honour to belong to your social class. You see in me a peasant in revolt against the baseness of his fate . . . I see men who would like in my person to punish and dishearten for ever that class of young people who, born in a lowly and poverty-stricken class, had the chance to educate themselves and the courage to associate with those circles which the arrogance of the rich calls society . . .' And yet, the author is not only and perhaps not even primarily concerned with the class struggle; his sympathy is bestowed not simply on the poor and the disfranchised, but on society's brilliantly gifted, sensitive stepchildren, on the victims of the heartless, unimaginative ruling class. Hence Julien Sorel, the peasant's son, Fabrice del Dongo, the descendant of an age-old aristocratic family, and Lucien Leuwen, the heir of a fortune of millions, appear as allies, as fellow-combatants and fellow-sufferers sharing a feeling of strangeness and homelessness in this common and prosaic world. The Restoration created conditions in which conformity is the only way to success and in which no one can any longer breathe and move about freely, whatever his descent.

The common destiny of Stendhal's heroes does not, however, alter the fact that the class struggle is the sociological source of the new type of hero and that Fabrice and Lucien are nothing but ideological transcriptions of Julien, variations of the 'indignant plebeian', species of the 'unfortunate who wages war against the whole of society'. The figure of Fabrice del Dongo would be no more conceivable than that of Julien Sorel without the existence of a middle class threatened by reaction and of that intelligentsia condemned to passivity, to which Stendhal himself belongs. Henri Beyle, the functionary of the Imperial army, is placed on half-pay in 1815; for years he applies for a new position, but cannot even get a job as librarian. He lives in voluntary exile far away from France and the possibilities of a career, as one whose life has been shipwrecked. He hates reaction, but always, whenever he speaks of freedom, thinks only of himself, always of the right to 'pursue his happiness'. The happiness of the individual, happiness in a purely epicurean sense, is for him the aim of all political endeavour. His liberalism is the result of his personal destiny, of his education, of the antagonism to society bred by childhood experiences, of his lack of success in life, not of a genuinely democratic feeling. He is an 'enfant de gauche'[35]— partly as the victim of his Oedipus complex, but also as the pupil of his grandfather who, as a faithful disciple of the eighteenth-century 'philosophes', transmits the spirit of the enlightenment to him. His failures keep this spirit alive in him, turn him into a rebel; but emotionally he is an individualist and an aristocrat, a stranger to all herd instincts. His romantic hero-worship, his glorification of the strong, gifted, extraordinary personality, his conception of the 'happy few', his morbid aversion to everything plebeian, his aestheticism and dandyism are all expressions of a supersensitive, complacently aristocratic taste. He is afraid of the republic, refuses to have anything to do with the masses, loves comfort and luxury, and sees the ideal political state of affairs in a constitutional monarchy which assures the intellectual of a carefree existence. He loves the cultured salons, a life of leisure and enjoyment, well-bred, frivolous and intelligent people. He fears that the republic and democracy will impoverish and shed a pall of gloom over life, lead to the victory of the coarse, uncultivated masses over refined, cultured society with its sophisticated pleasure in the beauties of life. 'I love the people and hate the oppressors,' he said, 'but it would be torture for me always to have to live with the people.'

Despite the sympathy that Stendhal feels for Julien Sorel, he follows him with a strictly critical eye, and, for all his admiration for the genius and purity of the young rebel, does not allow us to overlook his reservations concerning his plebeian nature. He understands his bitterness, he shares his contempt for society, he approves his unscrupulous hypocrisy and his refusal to co-operate with the people surrounding him, but what he in no way understands and approves of is the 'folle méfiance', the morbid degrading suspicions of the plebeian tormented by inferiority complexes and feelings of resentment, his impotent, blind vindictiveness, his ugly, disfiguring jealousy. The description of Julien's feelings after the letter with Mathilde's declaration of love shows most unmistakably the distance separating Stendhal from his hero. It actually constitutes the key to the whole novel and reminds us that the story of Julien Sorel is no mere personal confession on the part of the author. Confronted with this monomaniacal suspicion, the writer is overcome rather by a feeling of strangeness, awe and horror. 'Julien's look was cruel, his countenance hideous,' he says quite unsympathetically, without the slightest attempt to excuse him. Can it never have occurred to Stendhal that society's greatest sin against Julien was precisely that it made him so suspicious, and so unhappy, so inhuman in his suspiciousness?

Stendhal's political views are just as full of contradictions as the circumstances of his life. By descent he belongs to the upper middle class, but, as a result of his education, he becomes its antagonist. He holds quite an important official position under Napoleon, takes part in the Emperor's last campaigns, is perhaps deeply impressed but by no means enthusiastic—he still has his reservations about the violent despot and the ruthless conqueror.[36] For him, too, the Restoration at first means peace and the end of the long, restless, uncertain period of the Revolution; to begin with, he feels in no way strange and uncomfortable in the new France. But as he gradually becomes aware of the hopelessness of his existence on half-pay and the Restoration reveals its true face, his hatred and loathing of the new régime grows and, at the same time, his enthusiasm for Napoleon. His weakness for the good, comfortable life makes him an apponent of social levelling, but his poverty and lack of success keep alive his mistrust and hostility towards the prevailing order and prevent him from coming to terms with reaction. These two tendencies are constantly present in Stendhal's mind and, according to the particular circumstances of his life, now one, now the other comes into the foreground. During the period of the Restoration, which is unsuccessful for him, his dissatisfaction and political radicalism grow; but as soon as his personal circumstances improve, he calms down and the rebel becomes the champion of order and a moderate conservative.[37] *Rouge et Noir* is still the confession of an uprooted rebel, whereas the *Chartreuse de Parme* is already the work of a man who has found inward peace and quiet strength in renunciation.[38] A tragedy has turned into a tragi-comedy, the genius of hatred into a philanthropic, almost conciliatory wisdom and frank, superior sense of humour, surveying everything with relentless objectivity, but recognizing at the same time the relativity of all things and the weakness of everything human. There is no doubt that this results in a note of frivolity creeping into his writing, something of the tolerance of 'to understand all is to forgive all'; but how remote Stendhal is from the conformity of the later bourgeoisie that forgives everything within and nothing outside its conventions. What a difference of values! What enthusiasm in Stendhal for youth, courage, intellect, the need for happiness, for the talent to enjoy and to create happiness, and what weariness, what boredom, what fear of happiness in the successful and established bourgeoisie! 'I should be happier than the others, because I possess everything that they have not . . .' says Count Mosca. 'But let us be honest, this idea must disfigure my smile . . . must give me an expression of selfishness and self-satisfaction . . . How charming, on the other hand, is his smile! [He means Fabrice.] He has the expression of the easy happiness

33

of early youth and creates it in others.' And yet Mosca is by no means a scoundrel. He is only weak and he has sold himself. But Stendhal makes a great effort to understand him. Indeed, he already asked himself in *Rouge et Noir*: 'Who knows what one goes through on the way to a great deed?'—'Danton stole, Mirabeau sold himself. Napoleon stole millions in Italy, without which he would hardly have made any progress . . . Only Lafayette never stole. Must one steal, must one sell oneself?' Stendhal is here obviously not merely worried about Napoleon's millions: he discovers the inexorable dialectic of actions conditioned by material reality, the materialism of all existence and all practical life. A shattering discovery for a born, though inhibited, romantic.

In no representative of the nineteenth century are the seductions of romanticism and resistance to it distributed so equally as in Stendhal. This is the origin of the lack of harmony in his political philosophy. Stendhal is a strict rationalist and positivist; he finds all metaphysics, all mere speculation and idealism of the German kind, strange and loathsome. For him the embodiment of morality, the essence of intellectual integrity, consists in the effort 'to see clearly in that which is', that is to say, it consists in resistance to the temptations of superstition and self-deception. 'Her fiery imagination sometimes veiled things from her eyes,' he says of one of his favourite characters, the Duchess Sanseverina, 'but the arbitrary illusions prompted by cowardice were foreign to her.' In his eyes, the highest ideal in life is that cherished by Voltaire and Lucretius: to live free from fear. His atheism consists in the fight against the despot of the Bible and mythology, and is only one form of the passionate realist's constant struggle against lies and deception. His loathing for all rhetoric and emotionalism, for big words and phrases, for the colourful, luxuriant, emphatic style of Chateaubriand and de Maistre, his fondness for the clear, objective, dry style of the 'civil code', for 'good definitions', for short, precise, colourless sentences, all this is the expression of his stern, uncompromising and, as Bourget says, 'heroic' materialism—of the desire to see clearly and to make others see clearly in that which is. All exaggeration and ostentation is suspect and alien to him, and even though he is

34

often enthusiastic, he is never bombastic. It has been noted, for example, that he never says 'freedom' but always merely 'the two chambers and the freedom of the press';[39] this, too, is a sign of his dislike for everything that is unreal and sounds over-excited and it is also part of his fight against romanticism and his own romantic feelings.

For, emotionally, Stendhal is a romantic; 'it is true that he thinks like Helvétius, but he feels like Rousseau'.[40] His heroes are disillusioned idealists, passionate dare-devils and unspoilt children, unsullied by the filth of life. They are, like their famous ancestor Saint-Preux, lovers of solitude and secluded heights, where they can dream in peace and devote themselves to their memories. Their dreams, their recollections, their most secret thoughts, are filled with tenderness. That is the great power counter-balancing reason in Stendhal, the source of the purest poetry and the deepest magic in his work. But his romanticism is by no means always pure poetry and pure, unmixed art. It is, on the contrary, full of romanesque, fantastic, morbid and macabre traits. His cult of genius does not in any way consist merely in an enthusiasm for greatness and the superhuman, but at the same time in a joy in the extravagant and the strange; his glorification of the 'dangerous life' does not signify merely a reverence for fearlessness and heroism, but also a toying with wickedness and crime. *Rouge et Noir* is, if you like, a thriller with a spicy and creepy ending, the *Chartreuse de Parme* an adventure novel full of surprises, miraculous rescues, cruelties and mélodramatic situations. 'Beylism' is not merely a religion of power and beauty, but also a cult of pleasure and a gospel of force—a variant of romantic satanism. The whole of Stendhal's analysis of present-day culture is romantic; it is inspired by Rousseau's enthusiasm for the state of nature, but it constitutes, at the same time, an exaggerated and a negative Rousseauism, lamenting, as it does, not only the loss of spontaneity in modern civilization but also the drying up of the courage needed to commit great and pic-turesque crimes. Stendhal's Bonapartism is the best illustration of the complex and to some extent still very romantic character of his mind. Apart from the aestheticising glorification of the genius, this cult of Napoleon consists, on the one hand, in an

35

appreciation of the upstart and the will to rise in society, on the other, in a sense of solidarity with the defeated, with the victim of reaction and the powers of darkness. For Stendhal, Napoleon is partly the little lieutenant who becomes the ruler of the world, the youngest son of the fairy tale, who solves the riddle and obtains the king's daughter, partly the eternal martyr and spiritual hero who is too good for this corrupt world and perishes as its victim. The immoralism and satanism of the romantic attitude are also intermingled in this cult of Napoleon and transform it from an apotheosis of greatness in good and evil, from an admiration of greatness, in spite of the evil that it is often forced to cause, into a cult of greatness precisely because of its readiness to commit evil and even crime. Stendhal's Napoleon is, like his Sorel, one of the ancestors of Raskolnikov; they are the embodiment of what Dostoevsky understood by Western individualism and made the cause of his hero's ruin.

Stendhal's resignation, too, has many romantic characteristics and is more directly connected with the romantic novel of disillusionment than Balzac's cold, clear-headed pessimism. But Stendhal's novels end just as badly as Balzac's; the difference lies in the manner, not in the degree, of the resignation. His heroes are also defeated: they, too, perish miserably or, what is still worse, are forced to capitulate and compromise; they die young or withdraw in disillusionment from the world. But in the end they are all tired of life, exhausted, worried to death, burnt out, they all give up the struggle and come to terms with society. Julien's death is a kind of suicide, and the end of the *Chartreuse de Parme* is just as melancholy a defeat. The note of renunciation is already sounded in *Armance*, where the motif of impotence is the unmistakable symbol of the estrangement from which all Stendhal's heroes suffer. The motif has its after-effect in the conviction of the young Fabrice that he is incapable of real love and in Julien's doubts as to his talent for love. In any case, he is a stranger to the bliss and self-extinguishing power of the erotic, the complete absorption in the moment and perfect self-forgetfulness of devotion to the beloved. For Stendhal's heroes the present has no blessedness; happiness always lies behind them and they think of it only when it is already past. There is no

36

more moving evidence of Stendhal's tragic conception of life than the grief that lies in Julien's realization that the days of Vergy and Verrières, which were lived through unconsciously and unappreciated, which have vanished inevitably and for ever, were the most beautiful, the best and the most precious thing that life had to offer. Only the passing of things makes us aware of their value; only in the shadow of death does Julien learn to value life and the love of Mme de Rênal, and only in prison does Fabrice discover genuine happiness and real, spiritual freedom. Who knows, Rilke once asked in front of a lion's cage, where freedom is—in front of or behind the railings?—a genuinely Stendhalien and extremely romantic question.

In spite of his dislike for the colourful and emphatic style, Stendhal is an heir of romanticism even from a formal point of view, and in a much stricter sense than more or less every modern artist. The classical ideal of unity, concentration and subordination of the parts under the control of a leading idea and of the steady development of the theme, free from subjective arbitrariness and always taking the reader into consideration, is completely displaced in his work by a conception of art which is dominated entirely by self-expression and which strives to reproduce the material of experience as directly, as genuinely and as authentically as possible. Stendhal's novels seem like a collection of entries in a diary and sketches, attempting above all to hold fast the motions of the mind, the mechanism of the feelings and the intellectual labour of the author. Expression, confession, subjective communication, is the real aim, and the stream of experience, the rhythm of the stream of experience itself, the real subject of the novel; what the stream carries and drags along with it seems almost immaterial.

Practically all modern, post-romantic art is the fruit of improvisation; it is all contingent on the idea that feelings, moods and inspirations are more fruitful and more directly related to life than artistic intelligence, critical deliberation and the preconceived plan. Consciously or unconsciously, the whole modern conception of art is based on the belief that the most valuable elements of the work of art are the product of windfalls and flights of fancy, in a word, gifts of a mysterious inspiration, and

37

that the artist does best to allow himself to be carried along by his own power of invention. That is why the invention of details plays such a pre-eminent part in modern art, and why the impression that it arouses is dominated by the wealth of unexpected turns and unanticipated secondary motifs. Compared with those of his predecessors, Beethoven's works already seem the product of improvisation, although the creations of the older masters, and above all those of Mozart, arose more unconcernedly, more easily and more in accordance with direct inspiration than the carefully prepared compositions of Beethoven, which are often based on numerous preliminary sketches. Mozart always seems to be guided by an objective, inevitable and unalterable plan, whereas in Beethoven's work every theme, every motif and every note sounds as if the composer were saying 'because I feel it like this', 'because I hear it like this' and 'because I wish to have it so'. The works of the older masters are well-articulated and well-constructed compositions, with plain, neat, well-rounded melodies, whereas the creations of Beethoven and later composers are recitatives, outcries from the depths of a troubled heart.

In his *Port-Royal*, Sainte-Beuve remarks that in the age of classicism that writer was regarded as the greatest, who created the most finished, the clearest and the most pleasant work, whereas we, the moderns, look in a writer above all for stimulation, that is, for opportunities to join in the writer's dreams and creative activity.[41] Our most popular writers are those who only hint at many things and always leave something unsaid that we have to guess, explain and complete for ourselves. For us the uncompleted, inexhaustible, indefinable work is the most attractive, the most profound and the most expressive. Stendhal's whole psychological art is aimed at stimulating the reader to co-operate, to take an active part in the author's observations and analyses. There are two different methods of psychological analysis. French classicism is based on a uniform conception of character, and develops the various spiritual attributes from an inherently invariable substance. The convincing force of the resulting portrait is due to the logical consistency of the features, but the picture itself represents more the 'mythos' than the portrait of the person. The characters of classical literature do not gain in interest and probability from the reader's self-observation; they are impressive on account of the greatness and acuteness of their lines, they are intended to be looked at and admired, not to be verified and interpreted. Stendhal's psychological method, which is equally described as analytical, although it is diametrically opposed to the classical method, is not based on the unity of the personality, but on his or her various manifestations, and does not stress the outlines, but the shades and valeurs of the picture. The portrait is here made up of a mass of details which, in association, usually make such a contradictory and unfinished impression on the reader that he is constantly directed to add the traits of his self-observation and to interpret the complex and chaotic picture in his own way. For the age of classicism the uniformity and clarity of a character was the criterion of its authenticity, whereas now the impression made by a character is all the more live and convincing, the more complicated and rhapsodic it is, the more scope it leaves for the reader to add details from his own experience.

The Stendhalien technique of 'petits faits vrais' does not imply that spiritual life is made up of a mass of small, ephemeral, intrinsically irrelevant phenomena, but that human character is incalculable and indefinable, and that it contains innumerable features apt to modify the abstract idea of its nature and to break up its unity. To stimulate the reader to join in the process of observation and composition, and to admit the inexhaustibility of the subject, signifies one and the same thing, namely, doubt in the ability of art to master the whole of reality. The complexity of modern psychology is merely a sign of our impotence to understand the modern man in the way that classicism understood the man of the seventeenth and eighteenth centuries. But to exclaim in the face of this inadequacy, as Zola did, 'life is simpler',[42] would amount to sheer blindness to the complex nature of modern life. For Stendhal, the psychological complication results from the growing self-consciousness of contemporary man, from his passionate self-observation, from the vigilance with which he follows all the motions of his heart and mind. When it is said, in Rouge et Noir, that 'man has two souls within

39

himself', the author does not yet mean, however, the discord and self-estrangement of Dostoevsky, but simply the dualism which consists in the fact that the intellectual of our day is both a man of action and an observer, an actor and also his own audience. Stendhal knows the source of his greatest happiness and his worst misery: the reflexivity of his spiritual life. When he loves, enjoys beauty, feels free and unconstrained, he realizes not only the bliss of these feelings but, at the same time, the happiness of being aware of this happiness.[43] But now that he ought to be completely absorbed by his happiness and feel redeemed from all his limitations and inadequacies, he is still full of problems and doubts: Is that the whole story?—he asks himself. Is that what they call love? Is it possible to love, to feel, to be delighted and yet to observe oneself so coolly and so calmly? Stendhal's answer is by no means the usual one, which assumes the existence of an insurmountable gulf between feeling and reason, passion and reflexion, love and ambition, but is based on the assumption that modern man simply feels differently, is enraptured and enthusiastic differently from a contemporary of Racine or Rousseau. For them, spontaneity and reflexivity of the emotions were incompatible, for Stendhal and his heroes they are quite inseparable; none of their passions is so strong as the desire to be constantly calling themselves to account for what is going on inside them. Compared with the older literature, this self-consciousness implies just as profound a change as Stendhal's realism, and the overcoming of classical-romantic psychology is just as strictly one of the preconditions of his art as the abolition of the alternative between the romantic escape from the world and the anti-romantic belief in the world.

Balzac's characters are more coherent, less contradictory and problematical than Stendhal's; they signify to some extent a return to the psychology of classical and romantic literature. They are monomaniacs ruled by a single passion, who seem, with every step they take and with every word they speak, to follow an absolute command. But it is curious that their credibility is not in any way prejudiced by this compulsion and that they are more real than Stendhal's characters, despite the fact that the latter correspond, with their antinomies, much more exactly to our psychological ideas. We are here, as everywhere in Balzac, faced by the mystery of an art the overwhelming influence of which is, in view of the absolutely unequal value of its constituent elements, one of the most inexplicable phenomena in the history of literature. Incidentally, Balzac's characters are by no means always so simple as they are usually described; their maniacal one-sidedness is often connected with an extraordinary wealth of individual traits. They are certainly less complex and 'interesting' than Stendhal's heroes, but they make a more lively, more unmistakable and unforgettable impression.

Balzac has been called the literary portraitist par excellence, and the incomparable effect of his art has been attributed to the power of his character descriptions. In fact, one thinks, in speaking of Balzac, above all of the human jungle of his novels, of the abundance and variety of the characters he sets in motion; but he is not interested primarily in the psychological aspect. If one attempts to explain the sources of his world, one is forced constantly to revert to his sociology and to speak of the material presuppositions of his intellectual cosmos. For him, in contrast to Stendhal, Dostoevsky or Proust, there is something more essential and irreducible than spiritual reality. For him a character in itself is unimportant; he only becomes interesting and significant as the agent of a social group, as the bearer of a conflict between antithetical, class-conditioned interests. Balzac himself always speaks of his characters as of natural phenomena, and when he wants to describe his artistic intentions, he never speaks of his psychology, but always of his sociology, of his natural history of society and of the function of the individual in the life of the social body. He became, anyhow, the master of the social novel, if not as the 'doctor of the social sciences', as he described himself, yet as the founder of the new conception of man, according to which 'the individual exists only in relation to society'. In the *Recherche de l'absolu*, he says that just as one can reconstruct a whole world from a geological find, so every monument of culture, every dwelling house, every mosaic, is the expression of a whole society; everything is an expression of and bears witness to the great universal social process. He is overcome by a transport of ecstasy, as he considers this social causality, this inescapable

41

conformity to law, which is his only clue to the meaning of the present age and the only solution of the problems around which his whole work revolves. For the *Comédie humaine* owes its inner unity not to the intertwinements of its plot, not to the recurrence of its characters, but to the predominance of this social causality and to the fact that it is actually one single great novel, namely the history of modern French society.

Balzac frees the narrative from the limitations of the auto-biography and mere psychology to which it had been subject since the second half of the eighteenth century. He breaks through the framework of individual destinies to which both the novels of Rousseau and Chateaubriand and those of Goethe and Stendhal were confined, and liberates himself from the con-fessional style of the eighteenth century, even though he is, naturally, unable all at once to strip away everything lyrical and autobiographical. Balzac discovers his style very slowly in any case; to begin with, he merely continues the fashionable litera-ture of the Revolution, Restoration and romanticism, and even his most mature work still suffers from reminiscences of the trashy novels of his predecessors. He can no more deny the descent of his art from the mystical novel of terror and the melo-dramatic 'roman-feuilleton' than from the romantic love and historical novel, and his style presupposes the works of Pigault-Lebrun and Ducray-Duminil just as much as those of Byron and Walter Scott.[44] Not only Ferragus and Vautrin but also Mon-triveau and Rastignac are among the rebels and outlaws of romanticism and not only the lives of adventurers and criminals but also bourgeois life is, as has been said, treated by him as material for a thriller.[45] Modern middle-class society, with its politicians, bureaucrats, bankers, speculators, men about town, cocottes and journalists, seems to him like a nightmare, like the relentless procession of a *danse macabre*. He regards capitalism as a social disease and toys for some time with the idea of treating it from a medical point of view in a 'Pathologie de la vie sociale'.[46] He diagnoses it as a hypertrophy of the striving for profit and power and attributes the evil to the egoism and irreligiosity of the age. He sees it all as the consequence of the Revolution and traces back the dissolution of the old hierarchies, especially that of the monarchy, the Church and the family, to individualism, free competition and inordinate, unrestrained ambition. Balzac describes with astonishing acuteness the symptoms of the boom period in which he finds himself with his generation, he sees through the fateful internal contradictions of the capitalistic system, but he presupposes too many arbitrary circumstances in its origins, and even he himself does not really believe in the cure which he prescribes. Gold, the Louis d'or and the five-franc piece, shares, bills of exchange, lottery tickets and playing cards are the idols and fetishes of the new society; the 'golden calf' has become a more frightening reality than it was in the Old Testament and the millions sound more seductively in the ears than the call of the apocalyptic woman. Balzac considers his tragedies of bourgeois life, although they merely revolve around money, more cruel than the drama of the Atridae, and the words of the dying Grandet to his daughter, 'You will give me an account of this down there', are indeed more dreadful than the gloomiest notes sounded in Greek tragedy. Numbers, sums, balances, are here the formulae of exorcism and the oracles of a new mythology, of a new world of magic. Millions spring from nothing and vanish, melt away again like the gifts of evil spirits in fairy tales. Balzac easily falls into the fairy-tale style, when the subject under discussion is money. He likes to play the part of the genii who give presents to beggars and is always ready to escape with his heroes into the world of day-dreams. But he never hides from himself the ultimate effect of gold, the devastation it causes and the poisoning of human relationships to which it leads; on this point his sense of reality never forsakes him.

The pursuit of money and profit destroys family life, estranges wife from husband, daughter from father, brother from brother, turns marriage into a mutual benefit society, love into a business and chains the victims one to another with the bonds of slavery. Can one imagine anything more sinister than the way old father Grandet is bound to his daughter as the inheritress of his fortune! Or the Grandet characteristics in Eugénie which emerge as soon as she becomes mistress of the house. Is there anything more uncanny than this power of nature, this mastery of matter over human souls! Money alienates men and women from them-

43

selves, destroys ideals, perverts talents, prostitutes artists, poets and scholars, turns geniuses into criminals and born leaders into adventurers and gamblers. The social class which bears the heaviest responsibility for the relentlessness of money economy and which makes the biggest profit out of it, is, of course, the bourgeoisie, but all classes are involved in the wild, bestial struggle for existence which it unleashes, the aristocracy, its bloodiest victim, no less than the other classes. Nevertheless, Balzac finds no other way out of the anarchy of the present than by reviving this aristocracy, educating it to the rationalism and realism of the middle class and opening its ranks to the talents striving up from below. He is an enthusiastic supporter of the feudal classes, he admires the intellectual and moral ideals which they embody and regrets their decline, but he describes their degeneration with an all the more merciless objectivity, above all their deference to the money-bags of the bourgeoisie. Balzac's snobbery is certainly very embarrassing, but his political capers are perfectly harmless, for, however zealous the interest he takes in the cause of the aristocracy, he is, nevertheless, no aristocrat and, as has been pointed out, the difference is fundamental.[47] His aristocratism is a speculative idea; it does not come from the heart or the instincts.

Balzac is not only a thoroughly bourgeois writer, all of whose spontaneous feelings are rooted in the outlook of his class, he is at the same time the most successful apologist of the bourgeoisie and he in no way conceals his admiration for the achievements of this class. He is only full of a hysterical fear and scents disorder and revolution everywhere. He attacks everything that threatens the stability of the status quo and defends everything that appears to protect it. He sees the strongest bulwark against anarchy and chaos in the monarchy and the Catholic Church; he regards feudalism as merely the system which follows from the dominion of these powers. He is not in any way concerned with the forms which the monarchy, the Church and the nobility have assumed since the Revolution, but only with the ideals which they represent, and he attacks democracy and liberalism only because he knows that the whole structure of the hierarchies of society must collapse, once they begin to be criticized. He is of the opinion that 'a power that is a subject for discussion is non-existent'.

Equality is a chimera; it has never been realized anywhere in the world. And just as every community, above all the family, is based on authority, so the whole of society must be founded on the principle of sovereign rule. Democrats and socialists are un-realistic dreamers, not merely because they believe in freedom and equality, but also because they idealize the common people and the proletariat inordinately. Men are, however, fundament-ally all the same; they are all out for their own advantages and pursue only their own interests. Society is entirely dominated by the logic of the class struggle; the conflict between rich and poor, strong and weak, the privileged and the underdog, knows no limits. 'Self-preservation is the aim of all power' (*Le Médecin de campagne*), and the destruction of its oppressors that of every suppressed class—these are unalterable facts. But Balzac is not only familiar with the concepts of the class struggle, he is already in possession of the method of exposure of historical materialism. 'They send a criminal to the galley,' says Vautrin in the *Illusions perdues*, 'whereas a man who ruins whole families by fraudulent bankruptcy gets a few months. . . . The judges who sentence a thief are guarding the barriers dividing rich and poor . . . they know, of course, that the bankrupt causes at most a shift in the distribution of wealth.'

But the fundamental difference between Balzac and Marx lies in the fact that the writer of the *Comédie humaine* judges the struggle of the proletariat in just the same way as that of the other classes, that is to say, as a struggle for benefits and privi-leges, whereas Marx sees in the proletariat's fight for power and in its victory the beginning of a new epoch in the world's history, the realization of an ideal and final situation.[48] Balzac discovers before Marx, and in a form which Marx himself can accept as authoritative, the ideological nature of all thinking. 'Virtue begins with prosperity,' he says in the *Rabouilleuse*, and in the *Illusions perdues*, Vautrin speaks of the 'luxury of honourable conduct', which one can only afford when one has reached a suitable position and acquired the money that goes with it. In his *Essai sur la situation du parti royaliste* (1832), Balzac already refers to the way ideologies are formed: 'Revolutions take place', he maintains, 'first of all in material things and interests, then they extend to ideas and finally become transformed into principles.' He already discovers the material ties which condition our ideas and the dialectic of being and consciousness in *Louis Lambert*, the hero of which becomes, as he remarks, more and more aware, after the spiritualism of his youth, of the material texture of all thinking. It was, obviously, no coincidence that Balzac and Hegel recognized the dialectical structure of history almost simultaneously. Capitalistic economy and the modern bourgeoisie were full of contradictions and gave clearer expression to the antithetical definition of historical developments than earlier cultures. But the material foundations of bourgeois society were not only intrinsically more transparent than those of feudalism, the new upper class also attached, for the time being, less importance to putting an ideological disguise on the material precondition of its power. In any case, its ideology was still far too recent to be able to hide its origin.

The outstanding feature in Balzac's world-view is his realism, his sober and honest examination of the facts. His historical materialism and his theory of ideologies are merely the applications of his sense of reality. And Balzac maintains his realistic, critical standpoint even when considering those phenomena to which he has an emotional attachment. Thus, in spite of his conservative outlook, he emphasizes the irresistibility of the development which has led to modern, bourgeois-capitalist society, and never lapses into the provincialism which conditions the idealists' approach to technical culture. His attitude to modern industry, as the new world-uniting power, is thoroughly positive.[49] He admires the modern metropolis with its standards, its dynamism and its élan. Paris enchants him; he loves it, despite its viciousness, indeed perhaps precisely because of the monstrosity of its vices. For when he speaks of the 'grand chancre fumeux, étalé sur les bords de la Seine', he betrays in every word the fascination that lies hidden behind his strong language. The mythos of Paris, as the new Babylon, the city of light and secret paradises, the home of Baudelaire and Verlaine, Constantin Guys and Toulouse-Lautrec, the mythos of dangerous, seductive, irresistible Paris, has its origins in the *Illusions perdues*, the *Histoire des Treize* and *Père Goriot*. Balzac is the first writer to speak about a modern metropolis with enthusiasm and to find pleasure in an industrial plant. It had never occurred to anyone before him to describe such a plant in the midst of a charming valley as a 'délicieuse fabrique'.[50] This admiration for the new, creative, albeit mercilessly impetuous life of the industrial age is the compensation for his pessimism and the awakening of his hope and confidence in the future. He knows that it is quite impossible to return to the patriarchal and idyllic life of the small town and village; but he also knows that this life was by no means so romantic and poetic as it is usually made out to be, and that its 'naturalness' meant nothing but ignorance, disease and poverty (*Le Médecin de campagne*, *Le Curé de village*). In spite of his own romanesque inclinations, Balzac is a complete stranger to the 'social mysticism' of the romantics,[51] and as for the 'moral purity' and 'unspoilt nature' of the peasants in particular, he indulges in no illusions on that score. He judges the good and the bad qualities of the common people with the same objectivity as the virtues and vices of the aristocracy, and his relation to the masses is just as undogmatic and full of contradictions as his mingling of hatred and affection for the bourgeoisie.

Balzac is a revolutionary writer without wanting to be and without knowing that he is. His real sympathies make him an ally of the rebels and nihilists. Most of his contemporaries recognize his political unrealiability; they know that he is essentially an anarchist who always feels in absolute agreement with the enemies of society, with those who have come off the rails and the uprooted. Louis Veuillot remarks that he defends the throne and altar in such a way as to make the enemies of these institutions grateful to him.[52] Alfred Nettement writes in the *Gazette de France* (February, 1836) that Balzac wanted to take revenge on society for all the wrongs he had suffered in his youth, and that his glorification of antisocial natures is simply one expression of this revenge. In his memoirs (October, 1833), Charles Weiss emphasizes that, although Balzac passed himself off for a legitimist, he always spoke as a liberal. Victor Hugo asserts that whether he wanted to or not he was a revolutionary writer, and that his works revealed the heart of a genuine democrat. Finally, Zola establishes the antithesis between the manifest and the latent elements in his outlook on life and notes, anticipating the Marxist interpretation, that a writer's talent may well be in conflict with his convictions. Engels is the first, however, to discover and define the real significance of this antagonism. He is the first to treat in a scientifically exploitable way the contradiction between the political views and the artistic creations of the writer and he thereby formulates one of the most important heuristic principles in the whole sociology of art. It has since become quite clear that artistic progressiveness and political conservatism are perfectly compatible and that every honest artist who describes reality faithfully and sincerely has an enlightening and emancipating influence on his age. Such an artist helps involuntarily to break up those conventions and clichés, taboos and dogmas on which the ideology of the reactionary, anti-liberal elements is based. In his famous letter to Miss Harkness of April, 1888, Engels writes as follows:

'The realism I allude to may creep out even in spite of the author's views. . . . Balzac, whom I consider a far greater master of realism than all the Zolas, past, present, or future, gives us in his *Comédie humaine* a most wonderfully realistic history of French "society", describing, chronicle fashion, almost year by year from 1816 to 1848, the ever-increasing pressure of the rising bourgeoisie upon the society of nobles that established itself after 1815 and that set up again, as far as it could, the standard of the *vieille politesse française*. He describes how the last remnants of this, to him, model society gradually succumbed before the intrusion of the vulgar moneyed upstart or was corrupted by him. . . . Well, Balzac was politically a legitimist; his great work is a constant elegy on the irreparable decay of good society; his sympathies are with the class that is doomed to extinction. But for all that, his satire is never keener, his irony never more bitter, than when he sets in motion the very men and women with whom he sympathizes most deeply—the nobles. . . . That Balzac was thus compelled to go against his own class sympathies and political prejudices, that he *saw* the necessity of the downfall of his favourite nobles and described them as people deserving no better fate; that he *saw* the real men of the future where, for the time being, they alone were to be found—that I consider one of the greatest triumphs of realism, and one of the greatest features in old Balzac.'[53]

Balzac is a naturalist who concentrates on the enrichment and differentiation of his experience. But if one understands by naturalism the absolute levelling of all the data of reality, the same criterion of truth in all the parts of an artist's work, then one will hesitate to call him simply a naturalist. One will rather be forced to face the fact that he is carried away by his romantic imagination and his inclination to melodrama again and again, and that he not only often goes out of his way to find the most eccentric characters and the most improbable situations, but also builds up the settings of his stories so that they are impossible to imagine in the concrete and only contribute by the colours and tones of the description to the atmosphere intended. To pronounce Balzac a naturalist pure and simple can only lead to disappointments. It is meaningless and useless to compare him as a psychologist or as a painter of milieu with the masters of the later naturalistic novel, with Flaubert or Maupassant, for example. If one cannot enjoy his works as descriptions of reality and, at the same time, as the most audacious and wildest visions, and if one expects to get from them anything but the indiscriminate mixture of these elements, one will never get to like them at all. Balzac's art is dominated by the passionate desire to be completely surrendered to life, but it owes almost nothing to direct observation; its most fundamental qualities are invented, the product of conscious thought and fictitious feeling.

Every work of art, even the most naturalistic, is an idealization of reality—a legend, a kind of Utopia. Even with the most unconventional style we accept certain characteristics, as for example the bright colours and blobs of impressionistic painting or the incoherent and inconsistent characters of the modern novel, as true and accurate *a priori*. But Balzac's portrayal of reality is much more arbitrary than that of most naturalists. He awakens the impression of truth to life mainly by the despotism

49

with which he subjects the reader to his own mood and the microcosmic totality of his fictitious world, from which the possibility of competition with the world of empirical reality is excluded from the very outset. His characters and settings do not seem so genuine, because their individual features correspond to real experience, but because they are drawn so sharply and circumstantially as if they had in fact been observed and copied from reality. We feel as though we were being confronted by a closely packed reality, because the individual elements of this microcosm all cohere in an indivisible unity, because the figures are inconceivable without their environment, the characters without their physical constitution and the bodies without the objects by which they are surrounded.

Classical and classicist works of art are cut off from the outside world and stand beside each other in strict isolation within their own aesthetic sphere. Naturalism in all its forms, that is to say, all art that is obviously dependent on a real model, breaks through the immanence of this sphere, and all cyclic forms which embrace a variety of artistic representations abolish the autocracy of the individual work of art. Most of the creations of medieval art arose in this cumulative fashion comprising several independent unities. With their lengthy, never-ending stories and their partly recurring characters, the epics of chivalry and the novels of adventure belong to this category no less than the cycles of medieval painting and the innumerable episodes of the mysteries. When Balzac discovered his system and came on the idea of the *Comédie humaine* as a framework embracing the individual novels, he returned to some extent to this medieval method of composition and adopted a form for which the self-sufficiency and crystalline definiteness of the classical works of art had lost their meaning and value. But how did Balzac alight on this 'medieval' form? How could it again become a matter of urgent topical interest in the nineteenth century?—The artistic method of the Middle Ages was completely displaced by the classicism of the Renaissance, by the idea of the unity and formal concentration of the work of art. As long as this classicism was alive, the cyclical method of composition could never regain its old position, but it remained alive only so long as men were con-

fident of their ability to master material reality. The predominance of classicistic art gradually comes to an end as the feeling of
dependence on the material conditions of life grows. In this
respect, too, the romantics are Balzac's direct predecessors.

Zola, Wagner and Proust mark the further stages in this
development and give more and more currency to the cyclic,
encyclopedic, world-embracing style, in contrast to the principle
of unity and selection. The modern artist wants to participate in
a life that is inexhaustible and cannot be reduced to a single
work. He can express greatness only by size, and power only by
boundlessness. Proust was obviously conscious of his relationship
to the cyclical form of Wagner and Balzac. 'The musician (that
is, Wagner)', he writes, 'inevitably felt the same intoxication as
Balzac, when he looked at his creations with the eyes of a stranger
and at the same time with those of a father. . . . He then observed
that they would be much more beautiful if united by recurring
figures into a cycle, and he added a final stroke of the brush,
the most sublime of them all, to his work . . . an additional but
by no means artificial . . . an unrecognized but all the more real,
all the more vital unity. . . .'[54]

Of the two thousand characters of the *Comédie humaine* four
hundred and sixty recur in several novels. Henry de Marsay, for
example, appears in twenty-five different works, and in the
Splendeurs et misères des courtisanes alone one hundred and fifty-
five figures appear, who also play a more or less prominent rôle
in other parts of the cycle.[55] All these characters are broader and
more substantial than the individual works, and we always feel
that Balzac is not telling us everything he knows about them and
could tell. When Ibsen was once asked why he gave the heroine
of his *Doll's House* such a foreign-sounding name, he answered
that she was named after her grandmother who was Italian. Her
real name was Eleonora, but she had been pampered as a child
and called Nora. To the objection that all this played no part in
the play itself, he replied in amazement: 'But facts are still facts.'
Thomas Mann is perfectly right, Ibsen belongs to one and the
same category as the two other great theatrical talents of the
nineteenth century, Zola and Wagner.[56] With him, too, the
individual work lost the microcosmic finality of classicistic form.

51

There is an extraordinary number of anecdotes about Balzac's relationship to his characters, similar to the one about Ibsen. The best known is the incident with Jules Sandeau who, while telling him about his sister's illness, was interrupted by Balzac saying: 'That's all very well, but let's get back to reality: to whom are we going to marry Eugénie Grandet?' Or there is the question with which he surprises one of his friends: 'Do you know whom Félix de Vaudeville will marry? A de Grandville. That's quite a good match, isn't it?' But the most beautiful and the most characteristic is Hofmannsthal's anecdote, in which Balzac is made to say in an imaginary dialogue: 'My Vautrin considers it (the *Venice Preserved* by Otway) the most beautiful of all plays. I set great store by the judgement of such a man.'[57] His characters' existence outside the novels is such an unmistakable reality for Balzac, and one which he takes so much for granted, that he would have been able to say of any play or book what Vautrin or de Marsay or Rastignac would think of it. The transcending of the immediate sphere of the work itself goes so far with Balzac that he often refers to individual characters in the *Comédie humaine* even when they do not appear at all in the work in question and quotes the titles of certain parts of the total work simply as references.

It is well known how fond Paul Bourget was of browsing in the 'Répertoire' of the *Comédie humaine*, this 'Who's Who' of Balzac's characters.[58] His hobby is regarded today almost as the passport of a real 'Balzacien'; it is, at any rate, the sign of an appreciation of the fact that the conception and effect of the *Comédie humaine* are only partly aesthetic and that it is inseparable from real life. Balzac represents a passing moment in the development leading from the pure artistic quality of classicistic and romantic writing to the aestheticism of Flaubert and Baudelaire—the brief hour of an art completely absorbed by the topical problems of the day. There is no nineteenth-century writer further removed from 'l'art pour l'art' and who was less concerned with artistic purism than he. Balzac's works can never be enjoyed in peace and with a good conscience, if the fact is not faced from the very outset that they are an ill-balanced, partly crude mixture with nothing in common with the classicistic

52

principles of 'no more and no less' and the transference of the data of experience on to a single level. The idea of the work of art as a perfect whole is always a fiction—even the most accomplished works are full of chaotic and disparate elements, but Balzac's novels are simply the classical example of a successful evasion of all the rules of aesthetics. If one takes the classical works of literature as a standard, one will be bound to find in them the most flagrant transgressions of even the most liberal rules of art. Still completely under their spell, with the self-destructive ravings of their characters, the terrible words of their rebels and desperados still burning in one's soul, one will be compelled to admit that in these works practically everything open to rational analysis has been 'bungled'; that Balzac can neither construct not develop a plot tidily; that his characters are often just as vaguely and heterogeneously put together as his milieus and settings; that his naturalism is not only incomplete, but also clumsy and summary. And, above all, one will be forced to confess that hair-raising examples of bad taste are concomitant with all these inadequacies; that the writer lacks all power of self-criticism and is prepared to go to any lengths to surprise and overwhelm the reader; that he no longer has anything of the aesthetic culture of the eighteenth century, its reserve, its elegant, playful casualness; that his taste is on the same level as the serial-reading public, and the worst serials at that; that nothing can be too overladen, exaggerated and exuberant for him; that he is incapable of expressing without emphasis and without superlatives anything that is near to his heart; that he always has his mouth full; that he brags and swindles; that he is a loathsome charlatan the moment he tries to give the impression of being a scholar and a philosopher; and that he is certainly greatest as a thinker, when he is least conscious of being one, when he thinks and reasons spontaneously, in accordance with his personal interests and historical situation.

The most embarrassing evidence of his bad taste are the lapses of his style: his confused torrent of words, his thickly laid-on solemnity, his affected and pompous metaphors, his raving enthusiasm and pseudo-sublime emotions. Not even his dialogues are irreproachable; here, too, there are dead passages and notes that sound 'wrong', just as one can sing wrong notes. The train of thought with which Taine attempts to explain and justify Balzac's stylistic peculiarities is well known. He remarks that there are different styles in literature, all entitled to the same rights, and he emphasizes that the author of the *Comédie humaine* no longer addresses himself to the public of the seventeenth- and eighteenth-century *salons*, to a public that reacted to the slightest hints and did not need loud colours and shrill sounds to have its attention attracted, but that, on the contrary, he writes for people who are impressed only by novelties, sensations and exaggerations, that is to say, for the readers of the serialized novels.[59] This is, no doubt, a splendid example of sociological literary criticism; for, although many of the writers of Balzac's generation had avoided his stylistic mistakes, few of them were so intimately engrossed in their own time as he. But should we not, instead of justifying Balzac's weaknesses, rather attempt to understand the abrupt proximity of the great and the inferior in his work? And for a sociological explanation should we not attribute the peculiarities of his style above all to the fact that he himself was a plebeian and the intellectual expression of the new, comparatively uncultivated but extraordinarily active and efficient middle class?

It has repeatedly been remarked that, in his works, Balzac draws more the picture of the succeeding than of his own generation and that his 'nouveaux riches' and parvenus, his speculators and adventurers, his artists and cocottes, are more typical of the Second Empire than the July monarchy. In his case it certainly seems as if life had imitated art. Balzac is one of the literary prophets in whom vision was stronger than observation. 'Prophet' and 'visionary' are, of course, mere words used in an attempt to cloak the dilemma presented by an art the magical influence of which seems only to increase with every fresh inadequacy. But what else can one say about a work like the *Chef-d'œuvre inconnu*, which combines the deepest insight into the meaning of life and the present age with an incredible naïvety?—Frenhofer, we read there, is the greatest pupil of Mabuse, the only one to whom the master has transmitted his art of infusing life into painted figures. He has been labouring for ten years on a work, the picture of a woman, in a struggle to achieve the highest object of all art, the secret of Pygmalion. He feels that every day is bringing him nearer to his goal, but there always remains something invincible, something insoluble and unattainable. He believes that reality is keeping it back from him, that he has not yet found the right model. Then, one day Poussin, in his enthusiasm for art, brings him his mistress, who is supposed to have the most perfect body ever painted. Frenhofer is carried away by the girl's beauty, but his eyes pass from her young body back to the uncompleted and uncompletable picture. Reality no longer holds him fast, he has killed the life within himself. But the picture, his life-work, that, more jealous than Poussin of his mistress, he had never wanted to reveal to any stranger's eyes, contains nothing but an un-intelligible muddle of curling lines and blobs, which he has painted one over the other and piled up one upon the other in the course of the years, and among which only the forms of a perfectly shaped leg- are still discernible. Balzac' foresaw the fate of the art of the last century and described it incomparably. He recognized the results of its estrangement from life and society, and understood the aestheticism, the nihilism, the danger of self-destruction which threatened it, and which was to become a dreadful reality under the Second Empire, more perfectly than even the most learned and sharp-sighted of his contemporaries.

2. THE SECOND EMPIRE

The romantics were perfectly aware of the loss of prestige which writers had suffered since the Revolution and sought a refuge from the unfriendly public in individualism. Their feeling of homelessness expressed itself in an embittered mood of conten-tion; but they did not consider their fight against society by any means hopeless. The writers of the generation of 1830 were the first to lose the pugnacious attitude of their predecessors and begin to resign themselves to their isolation; their only protest consisted in emphasizing the difference between themselves and the public they served. The writers of the next generation then became so arrogant that they forewent even this demonstration of independence and shrouded themselves in an ostentatious impersonality and insensitiveness. Their reserve was, however, quite different from the objectivity of the seventeenth and eighteenth centuries. The writers of the classicistic age wanted to amuse or instruct their readers or converse with them about certain problems of life. But since the advent of romanticism, literature had developed from an entertainment and a discussion between the author and his public into a self-revelation and self-glorification of the author. When, therefore, Flaubert and the Parnassiens try to hide their personal feelings, their reserve does not in any way imply a return to the spirit of pre-romantic literature; it represents rather the most overbearing and arrogant form of individualism—an individualism which does not even consider it worth while to unbosom itself to others.

1848 and its consequences completely estranged the real artists from the public. As in 1789 and 1830, the revolution again followed a period of supreme intellectual activity and productivity and ended, like the earlier revolutions, with the ultimate defeat of democracy and intellectual freedom. The victory of reaction was accompanied by an unprecedented intellectual decline and a complete brutalization of taste. The conspiracy of the bourgeoisie against the revolution, the denunciation of the class struggle as high treason, as having split the ostensibly peaceful nation into two camps,[60] the suppression of the freedom of the press, the creation of the new bureaucracy as the strongest support of the régime, the establishment of the police state as the most competent judge in all questions of morals and taste, brought about a cleavage in French culture, such as no previous age had known. This was also the beginning of that conflict between meekness and the spirit of revolt in the intelligentsia which has still not been settled today and that opposition to the state which made a part of the intelligentsia into an element of demoralization.

Socialism fell victim to the newly restored order without resistance of any kind. In the first ten years after the *coup d'état* there is no labour movement in France worth mentioning. The proletariat is exhausted, intimidated, confused, its unions have been dissolved, its leaders locked up, expelled or reduced to silence.[61] The elections of 1863, which lead to a considerable increase in the opposition, are the first sign of a change. The working class again combines in associations, strikes multiply and Napoleon III sees himself forced to make more and more new concessions. But socialism would not have reached its goal for a long time, if it had not found an involuntary aid in the liberal upper middle class which saw in Napoleon's caesarism a threat to its own power. This conflict at the heart of the régime explains the political development after 1860, the decay of the authoritarian government and the decadence of the Empire.[62] Napoleon III's rule was based on finance capital and big industry; the army was very useful in the struggle against the proletariat, but all the more useless against the bourgeoisie as its very life depended on the favour of this class. The Second Empire is unthinkable without the wave of economic prosperity with which it coincided. Its strength and its justification were in the wealth of its citizens, in the new technical inventions, the development of the railways and waterways, the consolidation and speeding up of goods traffic, the spread and growing flexibility of the credit system. During the July monarchy it was still politics that most attracted the younger talents, now commerce absorbs the best men. France becomes capitalistic not merely in the latent conditions, but also in the outward forms of its culture. It is true that capitalism and industrialism develop on long familiar lines, but it is only now that they exert their full influence, and from 1850 onwards daily life, the homes of the people, means of transport, the techniques of illumination, food and clothing undergo more radical changes than in all the centuries since the beginning of modern urban civilization. Above all, the demand for luxury and the mania for amusement become incomparably greater and more widespread than ever before.

The bourgeois becomes self-confident, fastidious, arrogant, and imagines he can hide the humbleness of his origins and the hybrid constitution of the new fashionable society, in which the *demi-monde*, actresses and foreigners play an unprecedented rôle, by mere externals. The dissolution of the *ancien régime* enters its final stage and, with the disappearance of the last representatives of the good old society, French culture goes through a more severe crisis than when it received its first violent shock. In art, above all in architecture and interior decoration, bad taste had never set the fashion so much as now. For the newly rich, who are wealthy enough to want to shine, but not old enough to shine without ostentation, nothing is too expensive or pompous. They have no discrimination in the choice of means, in the use of genuine and false materials, and none in the styles which they adopt and mix up. Renaissance and baroque are just as much merely means to an end as marble and onyx, satin and silk, mirror and crystal. They imitate Roman palaces and the castles on the Loire, Pompeian atriums, baroque salons, the furniture of the Louis-Quinze cabinet-makers and the tapestries of the Louis-Seize manufactories. Paris acquires a new splendour, a new metropolitan air. But its grandeur is often only an outward appearance, the pretentious materials are often only a substitute, the marble only stucco, the stone only mortar; the magnificent façades are merely splashed on, the rich decoration is unorganic and amorphous. An unreliable element comes into architecture, corresponding to the parvenu set-up of the prevailing society. Paris again becomes the capital of Europe, not, however, as formerly, the centre of art and culture, but the metropolis of the world of entertainment, the city of opera, operetta, balls, boulevards, restaurants, department stores, world exhibitions, and cheap, ready-made pleasures.

The Second Empire is the classical period of eclecticism— a period without a style of its own in architecture and the industrial arts, and with no stylistic unity in its painting. New theatres, hotels, tenement-houses, barracks, department stores, market-halls, come into being, whole rows and rings of streets arise, Paris is almost rebuilt by Haussmann, but apart from the principle of spaciousness and the beginnings of iron construction, all this takes place without a single original architectural idea. Even in earlier ages different competing styles had, of course, existed side by side and the discrepancy between the historically important style, which was not in accordance with the taste of the leading classes of society, and an inferior, historically insignificant but popular style was a well-known phenomenon. The artistically important tendencies had, however, never met

58

with so little approval as now, and in no other period do we feel so strongly that the art and literary history, which speaks only of the aesthetically valuable and historically significant phenomena, gives an inadequate picture of the real art life of the age; that, in other words, the history of the progressive trends which point to the future and the history of the tendencies which predominate on account of their momentary success and influence refer to two absolutely different sets of facts. An Octave Feuillet or a Paul Baudry, who are given ten lines in our textbooks, occupied incomparably more space in the consciousness of the contemporary public than Flaubert or Courbet, to whom we devote as many pages. The art life of the Second Empire is dominated by easy and agreeable productions, destined for the comfortable and lazy-minded bourgeoisie. The bourgeoisie which calls into being the pretentious architecture of the period, based on the greatest models but usually empty and unorganic, and which fills its homes with the most expensive but often completely superfluous, pseudo-historical articles, favours a style of painting that is nothing more than a pleasant decoration for the walls, a literature that is nothing more than a leisurely entertainment, a music that is easy and ingratiating, and a drama that celebrates its triumphs with the tricks of the 'pièce bien faite'. A bad, uncertain, easily satisfied taste now sets the fashion, whilst real art becomes the possession of a stratum of connoisseurs, who are not in a position to offer the artists any adequate compensation for their achievements.

The naturalism of the period, which contains the whole later development in the bud and can claim the most important artistic creations of the century, remains the art of an opposition, that is to say, the style of a small minority both among the artists themselves and in the public. It is the object of a concentrated attack on the part of the Academy, the University and the critics, in fact, of all official and influential parties. And the hostility becomes more intense as the aims and principles of the movement become more specific and the so-called 'realism' develops into 'naturalism'. In view of the fact that their boundaries are quite fluid, to separate the two phases of the development in this way proves, however, to be absolutely useless from a practical point of view, if not directly misleading. At any rate, it is more expedient to call the whole artistic movement under discussion here naturalism and to reserve the concept of 'realism' for the philosophy opposed to romanticism and its idealism. Naturalism as an artistic style and realism as a philosophical attitude are perfectly clear-cut, but the distinction between naturalism and realism in art only complicates the situation and presents us with a pseudo-problem. Furthermore, the antithesis to romanticism is given too much stress in the concept of 'realism', and both the fact that what we are dealing with here is the direct continuation of the romantic approach, and the fact that naturalism represents more a constant wrestling with the spirit of romanticism than a victory over it, are neglected. Naturalism is a romanticism with new conventions, with new, but still more or less arbitrary, presuppositions of verisimilitude. The most important difference between naturalism and romanticism consists in the scientism of the new trend, in the application of the principles of the exact sciences to the artistic portrayal of facts. The predominance of naturalistic art in the second half of the nineteenth century is altogether only a symptom of the victory of the scientific outlook and of technological thought over the spirit of idealism and traditionalism.

Naturalism derives almost all its criteria of probability from the empiricism of the natural sciences. It bases its concept of psychological truth on the principle of causality, the proper development of the plot on the elimination of chance and miracles, its description of milieu on the idea that every natural phenomenon has its place in an endless chain of conditions and motives, its utilization of characteristic details on the method of scientific observation in which no circumstance, however trifling, is neglected, its avoidance of pure and finished form on the inevitable inconclusiveness of scientific research. But the main source of the naturalistic outlook is the political experience of the generation of 1848: the failure of the revolution, the suppression of the June insurrection and the seizure of power by Louis Napoleon. The disappointment of the democrats and the general disillusionment caused by these events finds its perfect expression in the philosophy of the objective, realistic, strictly empirical natural sciences. After the failure of all ideals, of all Utopias, the tendency is now to keep to the facts, to nothing but the facts. The political origins of naturalism explain in particular its anti-romantic and ethical features: the refusal to escape from reality and the demand for absolute honesty in the description of facts; the striving for impersonality and impassibility as the guarantees of objectivity and social solidarity; activism as the attitude intent not only on knowing and describing but on altering reality; the modernism which keeps to the present as the sole subject of consequence; and, finally, its popular trend both in the choice of subject and in the choice of public. Champfleury's saying, 'le public du livre à vingt sous, c'est le vrai public',[63] shows the direction in which the Revolution of 1848 had influenced literature, and how different the new concept of popularity is from that of the old serial writers. The latter wrote for the broad masses, because they wanted to write for everyone, whereas the naturalists, that is, Champfleury and his circle, want to write above all for the masses. Nevertheless, there are two different trends within naturalistic literature: the naturalism of the writers who come from the bohemian circle, Champfleury, Duranty and Murger, and the naturalism of the 'rentiers', the Flauberts and the Goncourts.[64] The two camps confront each other as absolute adversaries; the bohemians hate all traditionalism, whilst Flaubert and his friends suspect any writer who strives for popular favour.

Naturalism begins as a movement of the artistic proletariat; its first master is Courbet, a man of the people, and an artist lacking all feeling for bourgeois respectability. After the old bohème had broken up and its members had become the favourites of the romanticizing bourgeoisie or the occupants of good bourgeois positions themselves, a new circle forms around Courbet, a second bohemian cénacle. The painter of the 'Stone-breakers' and the 'Burial at Ornans' owes his position as leader chiefly to human, not to artistic qualities, above all to his descent, to the fact that he describes the life of the common people and appeals to the people or, at any rate, to the broader strata of the public, that he leads the uncertain and unrestrained life of the artistic proletariat, despises the bourgeois and bourgeois ideals, and is a

61

convinced democrat, a revolutionary and the victim of persecution and contempt. Naturalistic theory arises directly in defence of his art against traditionalistic criticism. On the occasion of the exhibition of the 'Burial at Ornans' (1850), Champfleury declares: 'From now on the critics must decide for or against *realism*.' The great word had now been spoken.[65] Intrinsically, neither the concept nor the practice of this art is new, even if everyday life had perhaps never been portrayed with such directness and brutality; but its political bias, the social message which it contains, the representation of the people with a complete lack of condescension and any supercilious interest in folkways and customs—all this is new. But however new this social outlook is, and however much talk there is in Courbet's circle about the humanitarian aims and political tasks of art, bohemianism is and remains an heir of aestheticizing romanticism. It often ascribes a significance to art which it did not have even in the most exalted theories of the romantics and makes a prophet out of a confusedly chattering painter and a historical event out of the exhibition of an unsaleable picture.

The passion which fills Courbet and his supporters is, however, fundamentally political; their self-assurance comes from the conviction that they are the pioneers of truth and the forerunners of the future. Champfleury asserts that naturalism is nothing more than the artistic trend corresponding to democracy, and the Goncourts simply identify bohemianism with socialism in literature. In the eyes of Proudhon and Courbet, naturalism and political rebellion are different expressions of the same attitude, and they see no essential difference between social and artistic truth. In a letter of 1851, Courbet declares: 'I am not only a socialist, but also a democrat and a republican, in a word, a partisan of revolution and, above all, a realist, that is, the sincere friend of the real truth.'[66] And Zola merely continues Courbet's idea, when he says: 'La République sera naturaliste ou elle ne sera pas.'[67] By rejecting naturalism, the ruling classes, therefore, only give expression to their instinct of self-preservation: their perfectly correct feeling that every art that describes life without bias and without restraint is in itself a revolutionary act. In reference to this danger, conservatism has clearer ideas at its disposal than the opposition itself.[68] Gustave Planche declares quite frankly in the *Revue des Deux Mondes* that the resistance to naturalism is a confession of faith in the prevailing order and that by rejecting naturalism, one is also rejecting the materialism and democracy of the age.[69]

The conservative critics of the 'fifties already quote all the well-known arguments against naturalism and try to cloak the political and social prejudices which condition their anti-naturalistic attitude with aesthetic objections. Naturalism, they say, lacks all idealism and morality, luxuriates in ugliness and vulgarity, in the diseased and the obscene, and represents an indiscriminate, slavish imitation of reality. But what disturbs the conservative critics is, naturally, not the degree but the subject of the imitation. They know only too well that with the destruction of the classical-romantic kalokagathia and the abolition of the old ideal of beauty, which had survived almost unchanged until 1850, in spite of the revolutions and restratifications of society, Courbet is fighting for a new type of man and a new order. They feel that the ugliness of his peasants and workers, the corpulence and vulgarity of his middle-class women, are a protest against prevailing society and that his 'contempt for idealism' and his 'wallowing in filth' are all part of naturalism's revolutionary armoury. Millet paints the apotheosis of physical work and makes the peasant the hero of a new epic. Daumier describes the state-supporting bourgeois in his obtuseness and hardness of heart, scoffs at his politics, his justice, his amusements and uncovers the whole phantom-like comedy hidden behind bourgeois respectability. It is unmistakably clear that the choice of motifs is here conditioned more by political than by artistic considerations.

Even landscape painting becomes a demonstration against the culture of the prevailing society. The modern landscape arose from the very beginning as a contrast to the life of the industrial town, it is true, but romantic landscape painting still represented an autonomous world, the picture of an unreal, ideal existence, that did not need to be brought in any direct relationship to the life of the present and the life of everyday. This world was so different from the scenes of real, contemporary life that it was certainly understood as its antithesis, but hardly as a protest against it. The 'paysage intime' of modern painting, on the other hand, describes a milieu that, in its quietness and intimacy, is utterly different from the town, but is yet so close to it on account of its simple, unromantic, everyday character that we are inevitably prompted to compare them. The romantic mountain-tops and sea-levels and even Constable's woods and skies had something fabulous and mythical about them, whereas the forest clearings and forest fringes of the painters of Barbizon seem so natural and familiar, so easy to reach and so completely possessable, that the modern townsman must necessarily feel them as a warning and a reproach. In this choice of trivial, 'unpoetic' motifs the same democratic spirit is expressed as in the choice of the human types of Courbet, Millet and Daumier—with the sole difference that the landscape painters seem to say: nature is beautiful at all times and in all places, no 'ideal' motifs are necessary to do justice to its beauty, whereas the figure painters want to prove that man is ugly and pitiable no matter whether he is oppressing others or being oppressed himself. But, in spite of its sincerity and simplicity, the naturalistic landscape soon becomes just as conventional as the romantic had been. The romantics painted the poetry of the sacred grove, the naturalists paint the prose of rural life—the clearing with the grazing cattle, the river with the ferry, the field with the hayrick. Progress here consists, as so often in the history of art, more in the renewal than in the diminution of the stock motifs. The most radical changes follow from the principle of open-air painting, which is, incidentally, by no means put into practice all at once and hardly ever consistently, and is usually limited to creating the mere semblance that the picture has arisen in the open air. Apart from its obvious scientific elements, this technical idea also has a political and moral content and seems to be trying to say: Out into the open, out into the light of truth!

The social character of the new art is also expressed in the tendency towards a closer amalgamation of the painters, in their efforts to found artists' colonies and to adapt themselves to one another in their way of life. The 'School of Fontainebleau', which is no school at all and no coterie, but an incoherent group whose members go their own ways and are bound to one another merely by the earnestness of their artistic aims, already represents the collective spirit of the new age. And the later artist fraternities and settlements, the joint reformative efforts and *avant-garde* formations of the nineteenth century, all express the same tendency towards coalition and co-operation. The epochal consciousness, the awareness of the significance and the requirements of the hour, that came into the world with romanticism, now completely dominates the minds of artists. Courbet's dictum about 'faire de l'art vivant' and Daumier's alleged motto 'Il faut être de son temps' express one and the same idea, namely, the desire to break through the isolation of the romantic and redeem the artist from his individualism. The introduction of lithography as an artistic medium is likewise a symptom of this social aspiration. But it is not only in harmony with that democratization of the enjoyment of art which was attained in literature by the serial novel, it implies the victory of popular taste and journalism on an incomparably higher level. Daumier's 'journalistic' painting marks a culminating point in the art of his time, whereas Balzac's serial novel writing represents a lowering of his own level without a rise in the general standard.

But did the naturalists really represent the contemporary world, or at least an important part of the contemporary art public? They certainly did not represent the majority of the people who ordered, bought or publicly criticized pictures, who directed the art academies and had to decide which works were to be exhibited. The views of these people were fairly liberal on the whole, but their tolerance stopped short of naturalism. They liked and promoted the academic idealism of Ingres and his school, the romantic anecdotal painting of Decamps and Meissonier, the elegant portrait art of Winterhalter and Dubufe, the pseudo-baroque narrative painting of Couture and Boulanger, the mythological and allegorical decorations of Bouguereau and Baudry,[70] that is to say, large-scale, resplendent and empty form in all its varieties. But they had no room for the creations of naturalistic painting either in their homes crammed with furniture and draperies, nor in their official halls built in one or the other of the favourite historical styles. Modern art became homeless and began to lose all practical function. The same distance

65

that separated the naturalistic painting and the elegant 'wall decoration' of the time also divided serious and light literature, serious and light music, from each other. The literature or music which did not serve to entertain was just as devoid of function as the progressive painting of the time. Previously even the most valuable and most serious productions of literature, such as the novels of Prévost, Rousseau and Balzac, had formed the reading of relatively large strata of society, some of which were quite indifferent to literature as such. The dual rôle of literature as an art and an entertainment at the same time, and the satisfaction of the requirements of different levels of culture by means of the same works, now comes to an end. The artistically most valuable literary products are hardly any longer suitable for light reading and have no attraction at all for the general reading public, unless they draw public attention to themselves for some reason and become successful by creating a scandal, like Flaubert's *Madame Bovary*, for example. Only a quite small stratum of intellectuals appreciates such works adequately and therefore even this literature may be classed as 'studio art', like the whole school of progressive painting: it is intended for specialists, for artists and connoisseurs. The estrangement of the whole body of progressive artists from the contemporary world and their refusal to have anything to do with the public goes so far that they not only accept lack of success as something perfectly natural, but regard success itself as a sign of artistic inferiority and consider being misunderstood by their contemporaries a precondition of immortality.

Romanticism still contained a popular element appealing to the broader masses of society, whereas naturalism, at least in its most important productions, has nothing to attract the general public. The death of Balzac marks the end of the romantic age; Victor Hugo is still at the height of his artistic development, but as a literary movement romanticism has ceased to play any part in cultural life. The leading writers' renunciation of the romantic ideal also means a complete break with the most influential circles in the general public and the world of criticism. The 'partie de résistance', which in literature corresponds to the party of order in politics, takes up a more positive attitude to the

romantic school than naturalism, despite the latter's direct
historical connection with romanticism. It is true that conservative critics fight the spirit of rebellion in every form, romantic
as well as naturalistic, and put reasonableness above every kind of
spontaneity, but they demand that literature should express
'genuine feelings' and they regard the 'depth of the heart' as the
criterion of the real artist. This new aesthetic of the emotions is,
however, only a new, though not always entirely clear form of
the old kalokagathia; it is based on the alleged identity of the
emotionally spontaneous and the morally valuable elements of
the spiritual life, and postulates a mystical harmony between the
good and the beautiful. The moral effect of art is its most important axiom and the educational rôle of the artist its supreme
ideal. The bourgeois attitude to the principle of 'l'art pour l'art'
has changed once more. After its original rejection and later
recognition of 'pure', morally neutral art, its approach is now
relentlessly hostile. The rebelliousness of the artist has been
broken, there is no longer any cause to fear his intervention in
questions of practical life; 'l'art pour l'art' can be thrown over-
board and the competence of the artist as an intellectual leader
recognized again. Naturalism is the only surviving source of
possible danger; but since its representatives declare themselves
in favour, if not of 'l'art pour l'art' as such, at least of the unprejudiced and unsentimental treatment of moral questions, in other
words, of an a-moral approach in art, the rejection of 'l'art pour
l'art' is also directed against them. The government fits art and
artists into its educational and correctional system. The editors-
in-chief and the critics of the great periodicals and newspapers,
men like Buloz, Bertin, Gustave Planche, Charles Rémusat,
Arnauld de Pontmartin, Émile Montégut, are its highest authorities; Jules Sandeau, Octave Feuillet, Émile Augier and Dumas
fils its most respected authors; the University and the Academy
its teaching and research institutes for intellectual hygiene; the
public prosecutor and the prefect of the Paris police the guardians
of its moral principles. The representatives of naturalism have to
fight against the hostility of the critics until about 1860, and
against that of the University all their lives. The Academy remains barred to them and they are never able to count on help

from the state. Flaubert and the Goncourt brothers are impeached for offences against morality, and a considerable fine is imposed on Baudelaire.

The lawsuit against Flaubert and the sensational success of *Madame Bovary* (1857) decide the struggle for naturalism in favour of the new trend. The public shows itself interested and soon the critics also lay down their arms; only the most obstinate and short-sighted reactionaries remain in opposition. The progressive trend is this time forced on the critics by the reading public, although the reasons for the public's interest are by no means purely artistic. Sainte-Beuve, who has a very subtle feeling for changes in intellectual fashions, finds the way back to the liberalism of his youth. He joins the circle which includes Taine, Renan, Berthelot and Flaubert, criticizes the government and proclaims the victory of naturalism. The fact that his political and artistic conversion takes place at the same time is extremely symptomatic of the intellectual situation; it proves that, in spite of its internal division into the two camps of the bohemians and the 'rentiers', naturalism is rooted in liberalism. One cannot even maintain that Flaubert, whose political views are thoroughly conservative, represents a reactionary, anti-social and anti-liberal point of view. The opposition to the political system of the Second Empire and the opportunism of the bourgeoisie, as expressed above all in the *Éducation sentimentale*, is at any rate more characteristic of his way of thinking than the abusive references to democracy in his often all too impulsive and contradictory letters. Anti-government social criticism is common to all naturalistic literature, and Flaubert, Maupassant, Zola, Baudelaire and the Goncourts are, in spite of all the differences in their political outlook, in complete agreement as regards their nonconformity.[71] The 'triumph of realism' is repeated and its representatives all contribute to destroy the foundations of the prevailing society. In his letters, Flaubert complains repeatedly about the suppression of freedom and the hatred for the traditions of the great Revolution.[72] He is undeniably an opponent of the universal franchise and the rule of the uneducated masses,[73] but he is by no means an ally of the ruling bourgeoisie. His political views are often vague and childish, but they always express an honest endeavour to be rational and realistic, and manifest an attitude from which all Utopias, including those of the prophets of universal happiness and progress, are far removed. He rejects socialism not so much because of its materialistic as because of its irrational elements.[74] In order to be immune from all dogmatisms, all blind faiths and all ties, he refuses to accept any kind of political activism and fights against every temptation which might cause him to venture beyond the circle of purely private relationships and interests.[75] He becomes a nihilist for fear of self-deception. But he feels that he is the legitimate heir of the Revolution and the enlightenment and attributes the intellectual decline to the fateful victory of Rousseau over Voltaire.[76]

Flaubert clings to rationalism as the last relic of the unromantic eighteenth century, and one only needs to think of the anxiety neuroses of our own time, to understand the meaning of his warning about the irrational, self-destructive tendencies of Rousseauist romanticism. 'What is the offence for which men are supposed to be responsible' —he asks a neurotic woman correspondent tortured with religious hallucinations and self-reproach.[77] That sounds like a cry of distress and seems like the writer's last attempt to keep his equilibrium in the midst of a world in jeopardy on every side. Flaubert's wrestling with the spirit of romanticism, the constant changes in his attitude towards it, in the course of which he always has the feeling of being a traitor, are nothing but a manoeuvre to preserve this balance. His whole life and work consists in a wavering between two poles, between his romantic inclinations and his self-discipline, between his yearning for death and his desire to remain alive and sound. His very provincialism keeps him nearer to romanticism, already somewhat old-fashioned, than his contemporaries in Paris,[78] and right up to and beyond his twentieth year he lives in the fictitious world and overheated spiritual atmosphere of a youth without roots and behind the times. In later years he often refers to the terrible frame of mind, under the constant threat of madness and suicide, in which he found himself with his friends at that time,[79] and from which he was able to save himself only by an extraordinary exertion of the will, and a merciless self-discipline. Until the crisis which he goes through when he is twenty-two, he is a man tortured by visions, fits of depression, wild outbursts of emotion, a sick man whose irritability and sensibility contain the seeds of inevitable catastrophe. His life in and for art, the regularity and uncompromising character of his work, the in-humanity of his 'l'art pour l'art' and the impersonality of his style, in a word, the whole of his artistic theory and practice, is nothing but a desperate effort to save himself from certain destruction. In him aestheticism plays the same rôle psycho-logically as it had played in romanticism sociologically; it is a kind of escape from a reality that has become unbearable.

Flaubert writes himself free from romanticism; he overcomes it by giving it literary shape, and by developing from its lover and victim into its analyst and critic. He confronts the world of romantic dreams with the reality of everyday life and becomes a naturalist, in order to expose the mendacity and unwholesome-ness of these extravagant delusions. But he never tires of affirm-ing his hatred of humdrum everyday life, his loathing of the naturalism of *Madame Bovary* and the *Éducation sentimentale* and his contempt for the 'childishness' of the whole theory. Nevertheless, he remains the first real naturalistic writer, the first whose works give a picture of reality in harmony with the doctrines of naturalism. With a sure eye, Sainte-Beuve recognizes the results of the climacteric in the history of French literature represented by *Madame Bovary*. 'Flaubert wields the pen', he writes in his review, 'as others wield the scalpel,' and he describes the new style as the victory of the anatomist and physiologist in art.[80] Zola derives his whole theory of naturalism from the works of Flaubert and regards the author of *Madame Bovary* and the *Éducation sentimentale* as the creator of the modern novel.[81] Flaubert signifies above all, compared with the exaggerations and violent effects of Balzac, the complete renunciation of the melo-dramatic, adventurous and, in fact, of even the merely thrilling plot; the fondness for describing the monotony, flatness and lack of variety of everyday life; the avoidance of all extremes in the moulding of his characters, the refusal to lay any emphasis on the good or bad in them; the forgoing of all theses, propaganda, moral lessons, in brief, of all direct intervention in the proceed-ings and all direct interpretation of the facts.

70

But Flaubert's impersonality and impartiality by no means follow from the presuppositions of his naturalism, and do not correspond merely to the aesthetic requirement that the objects in a work of art should owe the impression they make to their own life, not to the author's recommendation; his 'impassibilité' in no way constitutes merely a reaction against Balzac's importunity and a return to the idea of the work of art as a self-contained microcosm, as a system in which 'the author, like God in the universe, should be always present but never visible';[82] it is also not merely the result of the knowledge, since repeated and confirmed so often by the Goncourts, by Maupassant, Gide, Valéry and others, that the worst poems are made from the most beautiful feelings and that personal sympathy, genuine emotion, twitching nerves and tear-filled eyes only impair the sharpness of the artist's vision—no, Flaubert's impassibility is not only a technical principle, it contains a new idea, a new morality of the artist. His 'nous sommes faits pour le dire, et non pour l'avoir' is the most extreme and most uncompromising formulation of that renunciation of life which was the starting point of romanticism as an aesthetic doctrine and a philosophy, but it is, in accordance with the ambivalence of Flaubert's feelings, at the same time the sharpest possible rejection of romanticism. For, when Flaubert exclaims that literature is not the 'dregs of the heart', he is trying to preserve both the purity of the heart and the purity of literature.

From the knowledge that the chaotic, eccentric, romantic disposition of his youth was on the point of destroying him both as an artist and as a human being, Flaubert derived a new way of life and a new aesthetic. 'There are children', he wrote in 1852, 'on whom music makes an adverse impression; they have great abilities, remember tunes after only hearing them once, get excited when they hear a piano being played, get palpitations, lose flesh, become pale, fall ill and their poor nerves are convulsed with agony, like the nerves of dogs when they hear music. One will search in vain for the Mozarts of the future amongst such children. Their talents have become deranged, the idea has worked its way into the flesh where it is sterile and where it also destroys the flesh itself . . .'[83] Flaubert did not realize how

71

romantic his separation of the 'idea' from the 'flesh' and his renunciation of life in favour of art was and never recognized that the real, unromantic solution of his problem can only grow out of life itself. Nevertheless, his own attempt at a solution is one of the great symbolical attitudes of Western man; it represents the last relevant form of the romantic outlook on life, the form in which it obliterates itself and in which the bourgeois intelligentsia becomes aware of its inability to master life and to make art an instrument of life. The self-disparagement of the middle class is actually part of the very nature of the bourgeois attitude to life, as Brunetière has pointed out,[84] but this self-criticism and self-denial only becomes a decisive factor in cultural life from Flaubert's time onwards. The bourgeoisie of the July monarchy still believed in itself and in the mission of its art.

Flaubert's criticism of the romantics, his loathing for the display and prostitution of their most personal experiences and most intimate feelings, is reminiscent of Voltaire's aversion to Rousseau's exhibitionism and crude naturalism. But Voltaire was still completely uncontaminated by romanticism and, in fighting against Rousseau, he did not have to fight against himself at the same time; his middle-classness was unproblematical and not exposed to any danger. Flaubert, on the other hand, is full of contradictions and his antithetical relationship to romanticism corresponds to an equally conflicting relationship to the middle class. His hatred of the bourgeois is, as has often been said, the source of his inspiration and the origin of his naturalism. In his persecution mania, he allows the bourgeois principle to expand into a metaphysical substance, into a kind of 'thing-in-itself', something unfathomable and inexhaustible. 'For me the bourgeois is something without definition', he writes to a friend—a saying in which, along with the idea of the indefinite, that of the infinite can also be heard. The discovery that the bourgeoisie itself had become romantic and in fact, to a certain extent, the romantic element in society par excellence, that romantic verse is declaimed by no one with so much feeling and emotion as by this class, and that the Emma Bovarys are the last representatives of the romantic ideal, contributed much to turning Flaubert away from his romanticism. But Flaubert himself is a bourgeois in

72

the very depths of his nature and he knows it. 'I refuse to be classed a man of letters,' he declares, ' . . . I am simply a bourgeois, living a quiet life in the country and occupying himself with literature.'[85] During the period when he stands accused on account of his book and is preparing his defence, he writes to his brother: 'It must be known at the Home Office that we in Rouen are what is called a *family* and that we have deep roots in the country.' But Flaubert's bourgeois character finds expression above all in his methodical and strictly disciplined habits of work, his distaste for the disorderly ways of the so-called genius-like creation. He quotes Goethe's words about the 'demands of the day' and makes it his duty to practise writing as a systematic, bourgeois profession, independent of likes and dislikes, moods and inspiration. His monomaniacal struggle to achieve formal perfection and his matter-of-fact philosophy of art originate in this bourgeois and workmanlike conception of artistic activity. 'L'art pour l'art' results, as we know, only partly from the romantic outlook and its estrangement from society and practical life; in some respects it is the direct expression of a genuinely bourgeois and workmanlike attitude, concentrated wholly on the efficient performance of the work in hand.[86] Flaubert's dislike for romanticism is closely connected with his aversion to the 'artist' as a type, with his loathing of the irresponsible dreamer and idealist. In the artist and the romantic he attacks the embodiment of a way of life by which he knows that his whole moral existence is threatened. He hates the bourgeois, but he hates the tramp even more. He knows that there is a destructive element in all artistic activity, an antisocial, disintegrating force. He knows that the artistic way of life tends to anarchy and chaos and that artistic work is apt to neglect discipline and order, perseverance and steadiness, if only because of the irrational factors involved in it. That which Goethe had already felt,[87] and Thomas Mann makes the central problem of his criticism of the artistic way of life, the artist's tendency to the pathological and the criminal, his shameless exhibitionism and his undignified trade of playing the fool, in a word, the whole histrion's and vagabond's existence that he leads, must have disturbed and depressed Flaubert deeply. The asceticism which he imposes on himself, his workmanlike

73

assiduity, the monastic seclusion in which he shelters behind his work, are intended, in the final analysis, to bear witness only to his seriousness, his bourgeois respectability and reliability, and to prove that he has absolutely nothing in common with Gautier's 'red waistcoat'. The artistic proletariat has become a social fact which it is impossible to neglect any longer; the bourgeoisie considers it a revolutionary danger and the bourgeois writers feel as unanimous with their own class about this danger as they do later, when faced with the Commune, which rouses into action all their suppressed bourgeois instincts.

A doctrine like Flaubert's aestheticism is, however, no clear-cut, unequivocal, final solution, but a dialectical force, altering its direction and questioning its own validity. Flaubert looks in art for reassurance and protection from the romantic impetuosity of his youth; but in fulfilling this function, it assumes fantastic proportions and a demonic power, it not only becomes a substitute for everything else that can satisfy and content the soul, but the basic principle of life itself. Only in art does there seem to be any stability, any fixed point in the stream of evanescence, corruption and dissolution. The self-surrender of life to art here acquires a quasi-religious, mystical character; it is no longer a mere service and a mere sacrifice, but an ecstatic, spellbound gazing at the only real Being, a total, self-denying absorption in the Idea. 'L'art, la seule chose vraie et bonne de la vie', Flaubert writes at the beginning of his career,[88] 'l'homme n'est rien, l'oeuvre tout', at the end.[89] The doctrine of 'l'art pour l'art' as the glorification of technical mastery, in contrast to romantic dilettantism, was originally the expression of a desire to adapt oneself to a firm social order, but the aestheticism to which Flaubert comes in the end, represents an antisocial and life-negating nihilism, an escape from everything connected with the practical, materially conditioned existence of ordinary human beings. It is the expression of mere contempt and absolute denial of the world. 'Life is so horrible', Flaubert groans, 'that one can only bear it by avoiding it. And that can be done by living in the world of art.'[90] The 'nous sommes faits pour le dire, et non pour l'avoir' is a cruel message, the acceptance of an unblessed and inhuman fate. 'You will only be able to describe wine, love, women and fame, if you are neither a drinker, neither a lover, neither a husband, nor a soldier', writes Flaubert and adds that the artist 'is a monstrosity, something standing outside nature'. The romantic was too intimately connected with life, that is to say, with a yearning for life; he was mere feeling, mere nature. Flaubert's artist no longer has any direct relationship to life; he is nothing but a puppet, an abstraction, something thoroughly inhuman and unnatural.

Art lost its spontaneity in its conflict with romanticism and became the prize in the artist's fight against himself, against his romantic origins, against his inclinations and instincts. Hitherto artistic activity had been regarded, if not as a process of letting oneself go, at any rate, as that of letting oneself be guided by one's own talent; now every work seems to be a 'tour de force', an achievement that has to be wrung from oneself, obtained by fighting against oneself. Faguet remarks that Flaubert writes his letters in an absolutely different style from his novels, and that good style and correct language by no means come to him naturally and as a matter of course.[91] Nothing sheds a more piercing light on the distance between the natural man and the artist in Flaubert than this statement. There are few writers of whose working methods we know so much, but there has certainly never been a writer who wrote his works with such torture, with such convulsions and so much against his own instincts. His constant wrestling with language, his struggle for the 'mot juste', is, however, only a symptom—the sign of the unbridgeable gulf between the 'possession' of life and the 'expression' of it. The 'mot juste', the uniquely correct word, no more exists than does the uniquely correct form; they are both the invention of aesthetes for whom art as a vital function has ceased to have any meaning. 'I prefer to die like a dog rather than hasten by a single moment any sentence of mine before it is mature'—no writer with a spontaneous human relationship to his work would have spoken like that. Matthew Arnold's Shakespeare smiled at such scrupulousness in the Elysian Fields. Complaints about the daily, heart-, brain- and nerve-deadening struggle, about the life of the fettered galley-slave that he leads, are the leitmotif of Flaubert's letters. 'For three days I have been tossing about on all my

75

furniture trying to get ideas', he writes to Louise Colet in 1853.[92] 'I can no longer distinguish the days of the week one from another . . . I am leading a mad, absurd life. . . . This is pure, absolute nothingness', he writes to Ernest Feydeau in 1858.[93] 'You don't know what it means to sit all day long with your head in both hands, trying to squeeze a word out of your brain', he writes to George Sand in 1866.[94] Working regularly for seven hours, he writes one page a day, then twenty pages in a month, then again two pages in a week. It is pitiable. 'La rage des phrases t'a désséché le cœur', his mother tells him, and probably no one ever spoke a more cruel and truer word about him. The worst of all is that, in spite of his aestheticism, Flaubert also despairs of art. Perhaps in the end it is nothing but a kind of playing at skittles, perhaps everything is mere humbug, he remarks on one occasion.[95] His whole uncertainty, the forced, tortured features of his work, his absolute lack of the light-mindedness of the old authors, come from the fact that he always feels his works are endangered and that he never really believes in them. 'What I am doing now', he declares while he is at work on *Madame Bovary*, 'can easily develop into something like Paul de Kock. . . . In a book like this the displacement of a single line can divert one from the goal.'[96] And while he is working at the *Éducation sentimentale*, he writes: 'What drives me to despair is the feeling that I am doing something useless and contrary to art. . . .'[97] It becomes a standing formula in his letters that he is occupying himself with things for which he is not suited, and that he never succeeds in writing what he would really like to write and in the way he would like to write it.[98]

Flaubert's statement, '*Madame Bovary*, c'est moi', is true in a double sense. He must often have had the feeling that not merely the romanticism of his youth, but also his criticism of romanticism, the judicial mantle which he presumed to don in literary matters, was a life-fantasy. *Madame Bovary* owes its artistic veracity and opportuneness to the intensity with which he experienced the problem of this life-fantasy, the crises of self-deception and the falsification of his own personality. When the meaning of romanticism became problematical, the whole questionableness of modern man was revealed—his escape from the

76

present, his constant desire to be somewhere different from where he has to be, his unceasing yearning for foreign lands, because he is afraid of the proximity and responsibility for the present. The analysis of romanticism led to the diagnosis of the disease of the whole century, to the recognition of the neurosis, the victims of which are incapable of giving an account of themselves, and would always prefer to be inside other peoples' skins, who do not, in other words, see themselves as they really are, but as they would like to be. In this self-deception and falsification of life, this 'Bovarysm', as his philosophy has been called,[99] Flaubert seizes hold of the essence of the modern subjectivism that distorts everything with which it comes in contact. The feeling that we possess only a deformed version of reality and that we are imprisoned in the subjective forms of our thinking is first given full artistic expression in *Madame Bovary*. A straight and almost uninterrupted road leads from here to Proust's illusionism.[100] The transformation of reality by the human consciousness, already pointed out by Kant, acquired in the course of the nineteenth century the character of an alternately more or less conscious and unconscious illusion, and called forth attempts to explain and unmask it, such as historical materialism and psycho-analysis. With his interpretation of romanticism, Flaubert is one of the great revealers and unmaskers of the century, and, therefore, one of the founders of the modern, reflexive outlook on life.

Flaubert's two main novels, the story of the romantic and futile provincial woman and of the well-to-do, tolerably gifted young bourgeois who squanders his intellectual powers and talents, are closely connected. Frédéric Moreau has been called the intellectual child of Emma Bovary; but both are the children of that 'tired civilization'[101] in which the life of the successful middle class moves and has its being. Both embody the same emotional confusion and represent the same type of 'ratés' so characteristic of this generation of heirs. Zola called the *Éducation sentimentale* the modern novel par excellence, and, as the story of a generation, it does in fact form the climax of the development which begins with the *Rouge et Noir* and is continued in the *Comédie humaine*. It is an 'historical' novel, that is,

77

NATURALISM AND IMPRESSIONISM

a novel in which the hero is time, in a double sense. In the first place, time appears in it as the element which conditions and gives life to the characters, and then as the principle by which they are worn out, destroyed and devoured. Creative, productive time was discovered by romanticism; corrupting time, which undermines life and hollows man out, was discovered in the fight against romanticism. The realization that it is, as Flaubert says, 'not the great disasters but the small ones of which one has to be afraid',[102] in other words, that we are not destroyed by our greatest and most shattering disappointments, but perish slowly with our faded hopes and ambitions, is the saddest fact of our existence. This gradual, imperceptible, irresistible pining away, this silent undermining of life, which does not even produce the startling bang of the great, imposing catastrophe, is the experience around which the *Éducation sentimentale* and practically the whole modern novel revolves—an experience that, owing to its non-tragic and undramatic character, can only be portrayed in the epic mode. The unrivalled position of the novel in the literature of the nineteenth century is, no doubt, to be explained above all by the fact that the feeling that life is being irresistibly hackneyed and mechanized, and the conception of time as a destructive force, had completely taken hold of men's minds. The novel develops its formal principle from the idea of the corrosive effects of time, just as tragedy derives the basis of its form from the idea of the timeless fate which destroys man with one fell blow. And as fate possesses a superhuman greatness and a metaphysical power in tragedy, so time attains an inordinate, almost mythical dimension in the novel. In the *Éducation senti-mentale*—and this is the very reason for the novel's historical importance—Flaubert discovers the constant presence of passing and past time in our life. He is the first to realize that, with their relation to time, things also change their meaning and value— they can become significant and important for us only because they form a part of our past—and that their value in this function is absolutely independent of their effective content and objective bearings. This revaluation of the past, and the consolation that lies in the fact that time, which buries us and the ruins of our life, 'leaves buds and traces of the lost meaning everywhere',[103]

78

is, however, still an expression of the romantic feeling that the present, that every present, is barren and without significance, and that even the past was lacking all value and importance so long as it was the present. That is, in fact, the meaning of the final pages of the *Éducation sentimentale*, which contain the key to the whole novel and to Flaubert's whole conception of time. That is the reason why the author singles out an episode from his hero's past life at random, and calls it the best he probably ever had from life. The absolute nothingness of this experience, its complete triviality and emptiness, means that there is always one link missing in the chain of our existence, and that every detail of our life is replete with the melancholy of objective purposelessness and a purely subjective significance.

Flaubert marks one of the lowest points in the curve which describes the emotional outlook of the nineteenth century. In spite of its sombre notes, Zola's work already expresses a new hope, a turning towards optimism. And, although he is just as bitter, Maupassant is, nevertheless, more light-hearted and more cynical than Flaubert; ideologically, his stories form the transition to the light fiction of the bourgeoisie. As far as its optimistic and pessimistic elements are concerned, this ideology is just as complicated and contradictory as that of the lower classes; to form a correct judgement here one must differentiate strictly between the emotional attitude of the individual strata of society to the present and the future. The rising classes are confident about the future, however pessimistically they regard the present, whereas the ruling classes, for all their power and glory, are often filled with the choking feeling of their own imminent destruction. In the minds of the ascending classes a pessimistic attitude to the present is connected with optimism about the future, for they have every confidence in themselves and their advancement in society; in the minds of the classes doomed to destruction the conception of present and future is just as conflicting, but the signs are reversed. For this reason Zola, who identifies himself with the oppressed and the exploited and whose attitude to the present is thoroughly pessimistic, is by no means hopeless about the future. This antagonism is also in accordance with his scientific outlook. He is, as he himself declares, a determinist, but not a fatalist, in other words, he is perfectly conscious of the fact that men are dependent on the material conditions of their life in their whole behaviour, but he does not believe that these conditions are unalterable. He accepts Taine's milieu theory unreservedly and presses it even further, but he considers it the real task and the absolutely attainable goal of the social sciences to transform and improve the external conditions of human life —to plan society, as we should say today.[104]

The whole of Zola's scientific thinking is stamped with this utilitarian character and is filled with the reforming and civilizing spirit of the enlightenment. His psychology itself is dependent on practical aims; it stands in the service of a spiritual hygiene and is based on the theory that as soon as their mechanism is understood, even the passions can be influenced. The scientism peculiar to naturalism reaches its summit in Zola and begins to veer into its opposite. Hitherto the representatives of naturalism had regarded science as the handy-man of art; Zola sees art as the servant of science. Flaubert also believes that art has reached a scientific stage in its development and endeavours not merely to describe reality in accordance with the most meticulous observation, but stresses the scientific and especially the medical character of his observation. But he never claims other than artistic merits for himself, whereas Zola desires to be regarded as a research worker and to support his reputation as an artist by his realiability as a scientist. This is an expression of the same apotheosis of science, the same scientific fetish-worship which is characteristic of socialism in general and is peculiar to the social strata which expect the improvement of their position in society to come from science. For Zola, as for the scientific and socialistic ideology in general, man is a being whose qualities are conditioned by the laws of heredity and environment, and, in his enthusiasm for the natural sciences, he goes so far as to define naturalism in the novel as simply the application of the experimental method to literature. But in this context experiment is only a big word with no meaning at all, or at least no more exact meaning than mere observation.[105] Zola's literary theories are not entirely free of charlatanism, but his novels have, nevertheless, a certain theoretical value, for, even if they do not contain

80

any new scientific insights, they are, as has rightly been said, the creations of a considerable sociologist. And they are, and this is extremely remarkable from the point of view of artistic development, the result of a systematic scientific method previously quite unknown in art. The artist's experience of the world is without plan and system; he gathers his empirical material as it were in passing by the features and data of life, which he carries around with him, which he allows to grow and mature, in order one day to draw unknown, undreamt-of treasures from this store. The scholar chooses to take the opposite way. He starts with a problem, that is, with a fact of which he knows nothing or does not know the very thing he would really like to know. The gathering and sifting of the material begins with the setting of the problem, that is, a closer acquaintance with the section of life to be treated begins with the setting of the problem. It is not the experience which leads him to the problem, but the problem which leads him to the experience. That is also Zola's method and procedure. He begins a new novel as the German professor of the anecdote begins a new course of lectures, in order to obtain more exact information about a subject with which he is unfamiliar. What Paul Alexis has related about the origins of *Nana*, about Zola's voyages of discovery into the world of prostitution and the theatre, is, at any rate, reminiscent of this anecdote.

The whole idea on which Zola bases his cycle of novels seems like the plan for a scientific undertaking. The individual works constitute, in accordance with the programme, the parts of a great, encyclopedic system, a kind of Summa of modern society. 'I want to explain how a family, that is, a small group of human beings, behaves in a society', he writes in the preface to the *Fortune des Rougon*. And by society he means the decadent and corrupt France of the Second Empire. No artistic programme could sound more exact, more objective, more scientific. But Zola does not escape the fate of his century; in spite of his scientific attitude he is a romantic, and indeed much more whole-heartedly so than the other less radical naturalists of his day. His one-sided, undialectical rationalization and schematization of reality is already boldly and ruthlessly romantic. And the symbols to which he reduces motley, many-sided, contradictory life—the city, the machine, alcohol, prostitution, the department store, the market-hall, the stock exchange, the theatre, etc.—are all the more the visions of a romantic systematizer, who sees allegories instead of concrete individual phenomena everywhere. To this fondness of Zola's for the allegorical is added the fascination which every-thing big and excessive exerts on him. He is a fanatical devotee of the masses, of numbers, of raw, compact, inexhaustible factual reality. He is enchanted by material abundance, the luxuriance and the great 'tutti' of life. It is not for nothing that he is a con-temporary of the 'grand opera' and Baron Haussmann.

It is, in fact, not naturalism but the idealistic light reading of the bourgeoisie which is sober and unromantic in this age of the upper middle class and high capitalism. In spite and, indeed, often precisely because of its radical materialism, naturalistic literature offers a wildly fantastic picture of reality. Bourgeois rationalism and pragmatism, on the other hand, strive towards a balanced, harmonious, peaceful picture of the world. By 'ideal' subjects the middle class means such as have a calming and sooth-ing influence. The task which it sets literature is to reconcile the unhappy and the discontented to life, to conceal reality from them, and to dangle before them the possibility of attaining an existence in which they actually have and can have no part. The goal that it pursues is the deluding, not the enlightenment of the reader. To the naturalistic novel of Flaubert, Zola and the Gon-courts, which always excites and agitates the reader, the social élite opposes the novel of the *Revue des Deux Mondes*, above all the novels of Octave Feuillet. Works which describe the life of polite society and represent its aims as the supreme ideal of civilized humanity; works in which there are still real heroes, strong, brave and selfless knights, ideal characters who are either members of the higher ranks of society or are embodied in youths whom this society is prepared to adopt. Hitherto, in spite of revolutions and the social upheavals, the life of the aristocracy had always been described with a certain naturalness and ease; in spite of its being behind the times, it still preserved a certain spontaneity and common sense. But now the existence led by the great world of genteel society in novels loses all relation-ship to real life and suddenly appears in the pale, indistinct, elegantly softened drawing-room lighting of our Hollywood films. Feuillet sees no difference between elegance and culture, between good manners and good character; to his mind good education is synonymous with a noble disposition, and a loyal attitude to the higher classes a proof that one is 'something better' oneself. The hero of his *Roman d'un jeune homme pauvre* (1858) is the embodiment of this good breeding and noblesse; he is generous and handsome, sportsmanlike and intelligent, virtuous and sensitive, and only proves by his poverty that the distribution of the material goods of life sets no limits to the realization of aristocratic ideals. Just as the plays of Augier and Dumas propound a thesis, so this is a novel with a thesis. The dictates of Christian morality, of political conservatism and social conformism are proclaimed and extolled; the danger of vast, chaotic passions, wild despair and passive resistance is fought against.

The hypocrisy of the bourgeoisie is accompanied by an unprecedented lowering of the general cultural level. The Second Empire, which produces the art of Flaubert and Baudelaire, is at the same time the period in which the bad taste and inartistic trash of modern times are born. There had, of course, been bad painters and untalented writers, rough-hewn and quickly finished works, diluted and bungled artistic ideas, in earlier times; but the inferior had been unmistakably inferior, vulgar and tasteless, unpretentious and insignificant—the elegant rubbish, inartistic trifle turned out with dexterity and a show of skill had never existed before, or at most as a by-product. Now, however, these trifles become the norm, and the substitution of quality by the mere appearance of quality the general rule. The aim is to make the enjoyment of art as effortless and agreeable as possible, to take from it all difficulty and complication, everything problematical and tormenting, in short, to reduce the artistic to the pleasant and the ingratiating. Art as a form of 'relaxation' in which the public knowingly and deliberately sinks below its own level is the invention of this period; it dominates all forms of production, but above all that which is most resolutely and unscrupulously a public art: the theatre.

In the novel and in painting, naturalism prevails alongside the tendencies which are in accord with bourgeois taste, whereas nothing opposed to the interests and ideas of the bourgeoisie appears in the theatre at all. In warding off the tendencies which may threaten it, the government by no means relies only on the majority of the 'pro-government' forces in the auditorium, but combats such tendencies with all possible regulations and pro- hibitions. The theatre, as the art of the broad masses, is handled more strictly than the other genres, just as today the film is subjected to restrictions which are not applied to the theatre. From the middle of the century the efforts of the playwrights are concentrated, in accordance with the intentions of the govern- ment, on the creation of a propaganda instrument for the ideology of the bourgeoisie, for their economic, social and moral principles. The ruling classes' hunger for amusement, their weakness for public entertainments, their pleasure in seeing and being seen, make the theatre the representative art of the period. No previous society had ever taken such delight in the theatre, for none had a première ever meant so much, as for the public of Augier, Dumas *fils* and Offenbach.[106] The passion of the middle class for the theatre is highly satisfactory to those who shape public opinion; they are encouraged to hold fast to this enthusiasm and they are confirmed in their standards of aesthetic value. The judgement passed on the public by Sarcey, the most influential dramatic critic of the day, is undoubtedly connected with this tendency. For it is not merely in keeping with the general progress of the social sciences and the concentration of interest on collective intellectual phenomena, when he asserts that the public is the essence of the theatre and that one could more easily imagine a play being performed without anything than without the audience.[107] For Sarcey the principle that the public is always right is the criterion of all criticism and he keeps to this touchstone, although he knows perfectly well that the old cultivated public has already disintegrated and that of the old habitués, amongst whom a real consensus of taste prevailed, only a small group of regular theatre-goers exists—the public of the first-nights.[108] Sarcey regards the social changes which have produced the theatre public of the modern metropolis as a com- paratively new process taking place within the framework of the middle class itself. The rapid increase in this public as a result of the development of the railways, which enables people from the provinces and abroad to stream to Paris and replaces the comparatively homogeneous circle of the old habitués with the mixed society of ad-hoc visitors—a phenomenon which other contemporary critics beside Sarcey draw attention to and represent as the most important reason for the change of style in the drama[109]—marks, however, only the last, by no means the most important, stage in a process that had already begun with the French Revolution.

The decisive turning point in the history of the modern French drama is represented by Scribe, who is not only the first to give dramatic expression to the money-based bourgeois ideology of the Restoration, but also creates, with his play of intrigues, the instrument best calculated to serve the bourgeoisie as a weapon in its struggle to enforce its ideology. Dumas and Augier represent merely a more highly developed form of his 'bon sens' and signify for the middle class of 1850 what he had meant for the bourgeoisie of the Restoration and the July monarchy. They both proclaim the same shallow rationalism and utilitarianism, the same superficial optimism and materialism, the only difference being that Scribe was more honest than they are, and spoke without false modesty and affectation about money, careers and marriages de convenance, where they speak about ideals, duties and eternal love. The middle class, which in the days of Scribe was a rising class still fighting for its position, has now attained a recognized status and is already threatened from below, imagines that it must dress up its materialistic aims in a cloak of idealism and thereby shows a timidity which classes still fighting for position never feel.

Nothing was so well calculated to serve as a basis for the idealization of the middle class as the institution of marriage and the family. It was possible to represent it in all good faith as one of those social forms in which the purest, most selfless and most noble feelings are respected, but no doubt, it was the only institution which, since the dissolution of the old feudal ties, still guaranteed permanence and stability to property. However that may have been, the idea of the family, as the bulwark of bourgeois society against dangerous intruders from without and

85

destructive elements from within, became the intellectual foundation of the drama. It was all the more suited for this function as it could be brought into direct relationship with the love motif. This did not happen, however, until the idea of love had been reinterpreted and freed of its romantic features. It could no longer be allowed to be the great wild passion or be accepted and extolled as such. Romanticism had always understood and forgiven unbridled, rebellious, triumphant love—it was justified by its intensity; for the bourgeois drama, on the other hand, the meaning and value of love consists in its permanence, in its standing the test of daily married life. This transformation of the idea of love can be followed step by step from Hugo's *Marion de Lorme* to Dumas's *Dame aux Camélias* and *Demi-Monde*. Already in the *Dame aux Camélias* the hero's love for the fallen girl is incompatible with the moral principles of a bourgeois family, but the author still stands, at any rate with his feelings, if not with his mind, on the side of the victim; in the *Demi-Monde* his attitude to the woman with the doubtful reputation is already entirely negative—she must be removed from the social body as a centre of infection. For she constitutes an even greater danger for the bourgeois family than a poor but respectable girl, who can after all become a good mother, a faithful companion and a trustworthy guardian of the family property. If one has already seduced such a girl, then one should also marry her, not only to make amends for the error committed, but also in order to settle things and—as Zola sums up the moral of Augier's *Fourchambaults*—in order not to finish up a bankrupt. If one has, however, brought an illegitimate child into the world, and there is nothing praiseworthy about that either, then one should, as Dumas pleads in the *Fils naturel* and in *Monsieur Alphonse*, legitimize it, above all, in order not to add to the uprooted elements which are a constant danger to bourgeois society. The only point of view from which adultery is judged is whether it endangers the family as an institution. In certain circumstances a man can be forgiven for it, a woman never. A woman who is morally of any account at all is, incidentally, quite incapable of adultery (*Francillon*). In short, everything is permitted that can be reconciled with the idea of the family, everything taboo that conflicts with it. These are the norms and ideals with which the plays of Augier and Dumas are concerned; they were written to justify them and their success proves that the writers had read the public's inmost thoughts.

The inferior quality of the plays—for they are inferior—is not due to the fact that they serve a special purpose and propound a thesis—even the comedies of Aristophanes and the tragedies of Corneille did that—but to the fact that the purpose is attached to them from outside and does not become flesh and blood in any of the characters. Nothing is more typical of the unorganic combination of thesis and exposition in these plays than the stock figure of the 'raisonneur'. The mere fact that a character has no other function than to be the author's mouthpiece shows that the moral doctrine never gets beyond the stage of the purely abstract and that the ideology in the background does not form a unity with the body of the play. The authors concern themselves with or rather accept the views of the ruling classes on the good and bad habits of the time and have, independently of these ideas, a certain gift for entertainment, a certain ability to arouse interest and create tension by means of the stage. They now combine these data and use their theatrical talents to sell the ·iews and theories which they have to proclaim. But they do it in an all too direct and brutal way and unwittingly contribute much to justify the principle of 'art for art's sake'. For propaganda in art is most disturbing when it does not completely permeate the work and when the idea to be proclaimed does not entirely coincide with the artist's vision.

In contrast to romanticism, the Second Empire is an age of rationalism, reflection and analysis.[110] Everywhere technical problems are in the foreground, in all genres the critical intellect is predominant. In the novel this spirit of criticism is represented by Flaubert, Zola and the Goncourt brothers, in lyric poetry by Baudelaire and the Parnassiens, in the drama by the masters of the 'pièce bien faite'. The formal problems, which counterbalance the emotional romantic trend in most of the genres, are preponderant on the stage. And it is not merely the external conditions of the representation, its narrow temporal and spatial limits, the mass character of the public and the directness of the reaction to the impression it receives, which induce the dramatist to attend to the problems of order and artistic economy, the didactic and propagandist intention itself makes for a formally clarified and closely packed, technically efficient and purposeful treatment of the material from the very outset. Authors and critics become more and more conscious of the fact that the theatre is intrinsically not concerned with literature, that the stage conforms to its own laws and its own logic, and that the poetic element of a drama often runs directly counter to its effectiveness on the stage. What Sarcey understands by theatrical perspective ('optique de théâtre') and theatrical instinct ('génie de théâtre') or simply what he means when he says 'c'est du théâtre', is suitability for the stage quite apart from literary considerations, a drastic use of purely theatrical methods, an all-out effort to win the public at any price, in short, an attitude which identifies the 'stage' with the 'platform'. Voltaire already knew that it is more important in the theatre 'de frapper fort que de frapper juste', but the practitioners and theoreticians of the 'well-made play' are the first to establish the rules of this hard-hitting and well-aimed type of drama. Their most important discovery consists in the recognition that stage effectiveness, indeed the mere possibility of the performance of a play at all, depends on a series of conventions and tricks of the trade, 'tricheries', as Sarcey says, and that the tacit agreement between the productive and receptive elements is even more decisive in the drama than in the other genres. The most important convention of the theatre is the public's readiness to be taken by surprise by the turns of the plot: its conscious self-deception, its unresisting acceptance of the rules of the game. Without this readiness we should not only be unable to see a play operating with purely theatrical means a second time, we could not even enjoy it once. For in such a play everything must seem surprising, although everything is foreseeable. Its 'scènes à faire' are the inevitable discussions of which, as Sarcey points out, the public knows exactly that they must and will come,[111] and its 'dénouement' is the solution which the audience expects and which it hankers after.[112] Consequently, the theatre becomes a party game played according to the strictest conventions and with the greatest possible skill, but with something naïve and primitive about it, all the same. The difficulties result not from the differentiation of the material with which the playwright is concerned, but from the complication of the rules of the game. It is their task to compensate the more fastidious members of the audience for the poverty and dullness of the contents of the play. The precision with which the machine functions is intended to divert attention from the fact that it is running empty. The public, and even the better-educated public, wants light, unexacting entertainment; it does not want obscurities, insoluble problems and unfathomable depths. Hence the strong emphasis now laid on strictness of construction and logical consistency. The development of the plot must be like a mathematical operation; the internal must be replaced by an external inevitability, just as the inner truth of the thesis is replaced by the jugglery of the argumentation.

The 'dénouement' is the final solution of the problem. If the result is wrong, the whole operation is wrong, says Dumas. Therefore one must, as he thinks, begin working on the end, the solution, the last word of the play. Nothing sheds a more piercing light than this crab's walk on the difference between the calculating intelligence with which a 'pièce bien faite' is constructed, and the impulses by which the true poet allows himself to be carried away. To take a step forwards, the playwright has to take two steps back at the same time; he has to compare every idea, every new motif, every new move with the already firmly established motifs and moves and to make them agree. Writing plays means a constant forestalling and referring back, a continual arranging and rearranging, a groping forwards and building upwards with one capacity-test after another and with the gradual consolidation and safeguarding of the several strata of the play. A rationalism of this kind is more or less characteristic of every palatable artistic product and especially of every performable dramatic work—the works of Shakespeare, which are based on the genius of the stage, as much as the plays of Augier and Dumas—but the effectiveness of a 'well-made play' rests solely on the succession of its tricks and trump cards, whereas that of a Shakespearian drama depends on an infinity of components beyond the sphere of purely mathematical relationships. Emerson preferred to read

89

Shakespeare's plays in the reverse order of the scenes and deliberately renounced all interest in their effectiveness as stage plays, in order to concentrate entirely on their poetic contents. Read in this way, a real 'pièce bien faite' would not only be unpalatable, it would also be unintelligible, for the details of that kind of play have no inner value of their own, but merely in relation to the whole of which they are part. In developing them, the playwright's eye is fixed on the final constellation, as in a game of chess; and how mechanically this constellation can be developed is best demonstrated by the method with the aid of which Sardou adopted Scribe's technique. According to his own assertion, he always read only the first act of the master's plays and then tried to derive the 'right' sequel from the premises thus acquired. In the course of time, this 'purely logical exercise', as he calls it, brought him nearer and nearer to the solution chosen by Scribe in the second and third acts of his plays, and at the same time he came to the view, also held by Dumas, that the whole plot follows with a certain inevitability from the situation from which one starts out. Dumas was of the opinion that there is no art at all in inventing a dramatic situation and thinking out a conflict; the art consists rather in the due preparation of the scene in which the plot culminates and in the smooth unravelling of the knot. The plot, which seems at first sight to be the most spontaneous, most unproblematical and most immediate datum of the drama, thus proves to be its most artificial and most laboriously acquired ingredient. It is by no means mere raw material or a pure product of the imagination, but consists of a series of moves which leave no scope at all for the playwright's spontaneous inventions and sovereign discretion.

One can, if one cares to, regard the scaffolding of a well-constructed work as the ladder leading upwards into the region of wonderful heights or merely as the schedule of a routine that has nothing to do with genuine art and humanity. One can extol, with Walter Pater, the artistic intelligence that 'foresees the end in the beginning and never loses sight of it, and in every part is conscious of all the rest, till the last sentence does but, with undiminished vigour, unfold and justify the first', but one can also, like Bernard Shaw, fear the worst for the dramatist from the tyranny of the logic, of which he writes that 'it is almost impossible for its slaves to write tolerable last acts to their plays, so conventionally do their conclusions follow their premises'. But, in order to believe that Shaw really despises and scorns the tricks and dodges of this artistic intelligence, one would have to forget that he is the author of plays like *The Devil's Disciple* and *Candida*, which on closer examination turn out to be regular 'pièces bien faites'. Not only Shaw, however, but Ibsen and Strindberg as well, and with them the whole theatrically effective drama of the present age, are based more or less on the French 'pièce bien faite'. The art of producing entanglements and tension, of tying the knot and delaying its unravelling, of preparing the turns in the plot and, nevertheless, surprising the audience with them, the rules of the proper distribution and timing of the 'coups de théâtre', the casuistry of the big discussions and the curtain-lines, the sudden sensation of the falling curtain and the last-minute solution—all these things they learnt from Scribe, Dumas, Augier, Labiche and Sardou. That does not mean at all that modern stage technique is entirely the creation of these playwrights. On the contrary, the line of development can be traced back through the melodrama and the vaudeville of the post-revolutionary period, the domestic drama and the comedy of the eighteenth century, the 'commedia dell'arte' and Molière, to the Roman comedy and the medieval farce. Nevertheless, the contribution to this tradition of the masters of the 'pièce bien faite' is extraordinary.

The most original and in many respects the most expressive artistic product of the Second Empire is the operetta.[113] It too is, of course, in no sense an absolute innovation—this would be unthinkable in such an advanced stage in the history of the theatre—it represents rather the continuation of two older genres, the *opera buffa* and the vaudeville, and it transmits to this ponderous and humourless age something of the light-hearted, cheerful, unromantic spirit of the eighteenth century. It is the only playful, light and airy form of the period. Alongside the conformist trends in keeping with sober bourgeois taste and the naturalistic art of the opposition, it constitutes a world of its own—a middle kingdom. It is much more attractive than the contemporary drama or the popular novel, sociologically more representative than naturalism and, as such, the only genre in which popular works with both a wide appeal and a certain artistic value are produced.

The most conspicuous and, from the naturalistic point of view, the most peculiar characteristic of the operetta is its absolute improbability, the unreal, entirely imaginative nature of its whirling scenes. It has the same significance for the nineteenth century as the pastoral play had had for earlier centuries; the set formulae of its contents, the conventionality of its entanglements and dénouements, are pure play forms unrelated to reality. Both the marionette-like nature of the characters and the apparently improvised form of the presentation only heighten the impression of fictitiousness. Sarcey already notes the similarity between the operetta and the 'commedia dell'arte',[114] and points out the impression of dreamlike unreality that Offenbach's works make on him; by which he only intends to say, however, that they have a quite peculiar fantastic quality. An admirer of Offenbach in our own time, the Viennese writer Karl Kraus, was the first to give a more definite meaning to this quality by pointing out that in the Offenbach operetta life is just as improbable and nonsensical, just as grotesque and uncanny as reality itself.[115] Such an interpretation would, naturally, have been absolutely foreign to Sarcey and it would have been altogether inconceivable before the expressionism and surrealism of modern art had emphasized the dream- and phantom-like character of life. Only the eye with its vision sharpened by these artistic trends was able to see that the operetta was not only an image of the frivolous and cynical society of the Second Empire but, at the same time, a form of self-mockery, that it not only expressed the reality, but also the unreality of this world, that it arose, in a word, out of the operetta-like nature of life itself[116]—so far as one may speak of the 'operetta-like nature' of such a serious, sober and critical age as this. The peasants at the plough, the workers in the factories, the merchants in their offices, the painters in Barbizon, Flaubert in Croisset, they were what they were, but the ruling class, the court in the Tuileries and the world of carousing bankers, dissolute aristocrats, parvenu journalists and pampered beauties, had something improbable, something phantom-like and unreal, something ephemeral about it—it was a land of operetta, a stage whose wings threatened to collapse at any moment.

The operetta was the product of a world of 'laissez faire, laissez passer', that is, a world of economic, social and moral liberalism, a world in which everyone was able to do what he liked, so long as he abstained from questioning the system itself. This limitation meant, on the one hand, very wide, on the other, very narrow frontiers. The same government that summoned Flaubert and Baudelaire to a court of law tolerated the most insolent social satire, the most disrespectful ridiculing of the authoritarian régime, the court, the army and the bureaucracy, in the works of Offenbach. But it tolerated his frolics only because they were not or did not seem to be dangerous, because he confined himself to a public whose loyalty was beyond doubt and needed no other safety-valve, in order to be quite happy, than this apparently harmless banter. The joke seems mischievous only to us; the contemporary public missed the sinister undertone which we can hear in the frantic rhythm of Offenbach's galops and cancans. The entertainment was, however, not quite so harmless. The operetta demoralized people, not because it scoffed at everything 'venerable', not because its deriding of antiquity, of classical tragedy, of romantic opera was only criticism of society in disguise, but because it shattered the belief in authority without denying it in principle. The immorality of the operetta consisted in the thoughtless tolerance with which it conducted its criticism of the corrupt system of government and the depraved society of the time, in the appearance of harmlessness which it gave to the frivolity of the little prostitutes, the extravagant gallants and the lovable old 'viveurs'. Its lukewarm, hesitant criticism merely encouraged. corruption. One could, however, expect nothing else but an ambiguous attitude from artists who were successful, who loved success more than anything and whose success was bound up with the continuance of this indolent and pleasure-seeking society. Offenbach was a German Jew, a homeless, vagrant musician, an artist whose existence was doubly threatened; he inevitably felt a stranger, a déraciné, an apathetic spectator in a double and manifold sense in the French capital, in the midst of this corrupt and yet so alluring world. He inevitably felt the problematical position of the artist in modern society, the contradiction between his ambitions and his resentment, his beggar's pride and his courting of the public, even more intensely than most of his professional colleagues. He was no rebel, not even a genuine democrat, on the contrary, he welcomed the rule of the 'strong hand', and enjoyed with the greatest peace of mind the advantages which he derived from the political system of the Second Empire; but he regarded all the bustling activity around him with the astonished, cold and piercing eye of an outsider, and involuntarily hastened the fall of the society to which he owed his success in life.

The rise of the operetta marks the penetration of journalism into the world of music. After the novel, the drama and the graphic arts, it is now the turn of the musical stage to comment on the events of the day. But the journalism of the operetta is not restricted to the topical references in the songs and jokes of the comics; the whole genre is rather like a gossip column devoted to the scandals of genteel society. Heine has rightly been called the predecessor of Offenbach. The origins, the temperament and the social position of both are more or less the same; they are both born journalists, critical and practical natures, who do not wish to live outside but in and with society, if not by any means always in agreement with its aims and methods. Heine had intrinsically the same chances of success in the cosmopolitan Paris of the July monarchy and the Second Empire as Meyerbeer and Offenbach, only he did not have at his disposal the international means of communication used by his more fortunate countrymen. His fame remained confined to a comparatively narrow circle, whilst Meyerbeer and Offenbach conquered the French capital and the whole civilized world. They not only created two of the most characteristic genres of French art, but represented the Parisian taste of the time more faithfully and more comprehensively than their French colleagues. Offenbach can be regarded as the very epitome of his age; his work contains its most characteristic and original features. His contemporaries already felt him to be so representative that they identified him

94

with the spirit of Paris and described his art as the continuation of the classical French tradition. His music united Western Europe in a mood of exuberance.[117] *The Grand Duchess of Gerolstein* proved to be the greatest and most lasting attraction of the World Exhibition of 1867; the sovereigns and princes who visited Paris were just as enthusiastic about the play, with the irresistible Hortense Schneider in the title rôle, as the libertines of the French capital and the petty bourgeois from the provinces. Three hours after his arrival in Paris the Russian Czar was already sitting in a box in the 'Variétés', and, although he was apparently better able to control his impatience, Bismarck was just as enchanted as the crowned heads themselves. Rossini called Offenbach the 'Mozart of the Champs Elysées' and Wagner confirmed this judgement—though only after the death of his envied rival.

The heyday of the operetta was the period between the two world exhibitions of 1855 and 1867. After the political unrest at the end of the 'sixties it lacked an appropriately light-hearted public or even one deluding itself with light-heartedness and security. With the Second Empire the best days of the operetta came to an end; the pleasure which later generations took in it was not derived from the genre as the living, spontaneous and direct expression of the present, but from the 'good old times' which were associated with this genre more directly than with any other. Thanks to this association of ideas, the operetta survived the upheavals of the 'fin de siècle' and, in such an intellectually unstable city as Vienna, it remained the most popular vehicle of idealization of the past right up to the Second World War. The experiences of the last ten years were necessary to bring about a revision of the idea of the 'good old times' connected in one part of Europe with Napoleon III and Offenbach, in the other with the Emperor Franz Joseph and Johann Strauss. The class struggle, which was suppressed everywhere between 1848 and 1870, blazed up again at the end of this period and threatened the rule of the bourgeoisie as the beneficiaries of reaction. The operetta now seemed to be the picture of a happy life free from care and danger—of an idyll which had, however, never existed in reality.

The Goncourts were right when they prophesied that the circus, the variety show and the revue would displace the theatre. The film, which, owing to its pictorial quality and display, can be reckoned among these visual forms, entirely confirms their prediction. The operetta came nearest to the revue, but it by no means represented the oldest form in which spectacle had triumphed over the drama. The real turning point occurred with the emergence of 'grand opera' during the July monarchy, even though spectacle had always formed an integral component of the theatre and had repeatedly gained the upper hand over its dramatic and acoustic elements. This was above all the case in the baroque theatre, in which the festive character of the performance, the decorations, costumes, dances and processions, often overran everything else. The bourgeois culture of the July monarchy and the Second Empire, which was a parvenu culture, also looked for the monumental and the imposing in the theatre and exaggerated the appearance of greatness, the more so as it lacked true spiritual greatness itself. There are, in fact, two different impulses which drive society to ceremonial, grandiose and pretentious forms; on the one hand, it may be impelled to seek for grandeur because that is in line with its natural way of life, or the rage for the colossal may be due to a need to compensate for a more or less painfully felt weakness. The baroque of the seventeenth century corresponded to the grand proportions in which the court and the aristocracy of the period naturally breathed and moved, the pseudo-baroque of the nineteenth century corresponded to the ambitions with which the risen bourgeoisie was trying to fill out these proportions. Opera became the favourite genre of the bourgeoisie because no other art offered such great possibilities for ostentation, for display and scenery, for the accumulation and working up of effects. The type of opera realized by Meyerbeer combined all the allurements of the stage, and created a heterogeneous mixture of music, song and dance that demanded to be seen as well as to be heard and in which all the elements were intended to beguile and overwhelm the audience. The Meyerbeer opera was a great variety show, the unity of which consisted more in the rhythm of the moving spectacle on the stage than in the absolute predominance of the musical form.[118] It was intended for a public whose connection with music was purely external.

The idea of the 'universal work of art' (*Gesamtkunstwerk*) made its mark here long before Wagner, and expressed a need before anyone had thought of formulating it in a set programme. Wagner sought to justify the complex nature of opera by means of the analogy of Greek tragedy, which was actually nothing more than an oratorio, but the desire for such a justification arose from the baroque heterogeneity of the genre, which ever since Meyerbeer had been threatening to become more and more 'styleless and formless'. 'Grand opera' owed its authority, which is still perceptible in *The Mastersingers* and *Aïda* and which probably represented a more rigid convention than that of earlier Italian opera,[119] to the fact that the culture of the French bourgeoisie served the whole continent as a model and everywhere met genuine needs rooted in social conditions. Nothing satisfied these needs more perfectly and more readily than the concerted ensemble of this opera, the organization of the means at its disposal—the gigantic orchestra, the enormous stage and the huge choir—into a whole, which was intended only to impress, overwhelm and subjugate the audience. That was above all the aim of the great finales, which often invented new and strong effects, but had nothing in common with the deep humanity of Mozart's and the sprightly grace of Rossini's final scenes. What we usually call 'operatic'—monumental scenery, empty emphases, blustering heroics, artificial emotions and language—is, however, in no sense Meyerbeer's creation and is in no way limited to the opera of the age. Even an artist of such fastidious taste as Flaubert is not wholly free of theatricality. It is part of the romantic legacy inherited by this generation, and Victor Hugo had no less a share in its development than Meyerbeer.

Of all the important representatives of the age, Richard Wagner stands nearest to Meyerbeer's operatic style, not only because he wants to link his work on to a living art, but also because no one is more keen on success than he. He accepts the predominant convention without opposition and, as has been said, only gradually fights his way through to originality, in contrast to the typical development, which starts with an individual

97

experience, a personal discovery and ends with a more or less stereotyped manner.[120] Much more remarkable, however, than Wagner's setting out from 'grand opera' is his continual attachment to a form which combines the expression of the most inward, most intimate and most sublimated feelings with the ostentation of the Second Empire. For it is not only *Rienzi* and *Tannhaeuser* that are still thorough-going spectacular operas in which the scenic apparatus predominates, but *The Mastersingers* and *Parsifal* are also to some extent musical show-pieces, intended to engage all the senses and surpass all expectations. The fondness for the magnificent and the massive is just as strong in Wagner as in Meyerbeer or Zola, and he is, no less than Victor Hugo and Dumas, a born man of the theatre, a 'histrion' and 'mimomaniac', as Nietzsche called him.[121] But his theatricality is by no means simply the result of his writing operas; on the contrary, his operas are themselves the expression of his undiscriminating theatrical taste and his loud ostentatious nature. Like Meyerbeer, Napoleon III, la Païva or Zola, he loves the obtrusive, the precious, the voluptuous, and it is easy to realize what his operas and the *salons* of the period, filled with silk, velvet, gold brocade, upholstered furniture, carpets and door curtains, have in common, even without knowing that he wanted to have stage-scenes painted by Makart.[122] The mania for grandeur and exuberance has more complicated origins in Wagner, however; its strands lead back not merely to Makart but also to Delacroix. The connections between the 'Death of Sardanapal' and the *Twilight of the Gods* are just as close as between the lavish splendour of Parisian 'grand opera' and the celebrations of the Bayreuth festivals. But even that does not complete the story; Wagner's sensualism is not only more elemental than' mere ostentation, but also more genuine and spontaneous than the whole 'blood, death and lust' mysticism of his time. It was not without reason that for many of the most sensitive minds of the century his work signified the very essence of art—the paradigm which first revealed the meaning and underlying principle of music to them. It was certainly the last and perhaps the greatest revelation of romanticism, the only form of it that is still alive today. No other allows us to apprehend so intimately with what intoxication of the senses it impressed itself on the contemporary public, and how much it was felt to be a revolt against all dead conventions and the discovery of a young, blissful and forbidden world. It is comprehensible, although at first surprising, that Baudelaire, who was himself not musical at all, but the only one of Wagner's contemporaries whose accents create in us the same feeling of happiness as the Tristan music, was the first to recognize the significance of Wagner's art.

Apart from his overstrained nerves, his passion for narcosis and narcotizing effects, Wagner shares with Baudelaire the same quasi-religious feelings, the same romantic yearning for redemption. And apart from a weakness for glowing colours and exuberant forms, he is related to Flaubert by a kind of dilettantism and a thoroughly reflexive relationship to his own work. He has just as little natural, spontaneous talent, he forces his works just as violently and desperately from himself and has just as little genuine faith in art as Flaubert. Nietzsche points out that none of the great masters was still such a bad musician as Wagner at twenty-eight, and, with the exception of Flaubert, certainly no great artist doubted his own ability for so long. Both felt that art was the torment of their life, that it stood between them and the enjoyment of life, and both regarded the gulf between reality and art, between 'avoir' and 'dire', as unbridgeable. They were members of the same late romantic generation that fought a fight as unremitting as it was hopeless against their egotism and aestheticism.

3. THE SOCIAL NOVEL IN ENGLAND AND RUSSIA

The Industrial Revolution began in England, had the most fruitful results and called forth the loudest and most passionate protests there. The charges levelled against it did not, however, by any means prevent the ruling classes from opposing the social revolution with all the greater energy and success. The failure of the revolutionary endeavours then brought it about that, whilst in France a section of the intelligentsia and the literary élite began to adopt an anti-democratic attitude after the experiences of the Revolution, by and large the opinions of the English intellectuals remained, if not always revolutionary, at any rate radical. But the most striking difference between the frame of mind of the intellectual élite in the two countries was that the French were and remained unflinching rationalists, whatever their attitude to the Revolution and democracy, whereas the English became desperate irrationalists, in spite of their radical outlook and opposition to industrialism, indeed often precisely because of their opposition to the ruling class, and took refuge in the nebulous idealism of German romanticism. Strange to say, here in England the capitalists and the utilitarians were more closely in touch with the ideas of the enlightenment than their opponents, who denied the principle of free competition and the division of labour. At any rate, from the point of view of the history of ideas, the machine-breaking idealists were the reactionaries and the materialists and capitalists the representatives of rationalism and progress.

Economic freedom had the same historical roots as political liberalism; both were among the achievements of the enlightenment and were logically inseparable. The moment one adopted the standpoint of personal freedom and individualism, one had to allow the validity of free competition as an integral component of human rights. The emancipation of the middle class was a necessary step in the liquidation of feudalism and presupposed in its turn the liberation of economic life from medieval ties and restrictions. The middle class's participation in equality of rights can only be explained as the result of a development in which pre-capitalist forms of economy had become outmoded. Only after economic life had reached the stage of absolute autonomy and the middle class had pierced the rigid frontiers of the feudal class system, was it possible to think of emancipating society from the anarchy of free competition. It was also pointless to attack individual aspects of capitalism without questioning the system itself. So long as capitalist economy remained undisputed there could be no question of anything more than purely philanthropic mitigation of its abuses. And to keep to the principle of rationalism and liberalism was the only way of making an ultimate remedy of the abuses possible; all that was necessary was to understand the concept of freedom as surpassing its bourgeois limitations. The abandonment of reason and the liberal idea led inevitably, however good and honest the original intention, to an uncontrollable intuitionism and a loss of intellectual maturity. One is always conscious of this danger in Carlyle, but it threatens the idealism of most Victorian thinkers, and the proverbial compromise of the age, the middle course which it pursued between tradition and progress, is nowhere expressed so forcibly as in the romantic hankering for the past of its intellectual leaders. None of the representative Victorians is entirely free from the readiness to compromise and the resulting ambiguity impairs the political influence of even such a genuine radical as Dickens. In France, the intelligentsia felt itself compelled to choose between the Revolution and the bourgeois attitude, and even though the choice was often accompanied by divided feelings, it was, nevertheless, clear-cut and final. In England, on the other hand, the section of the intellectual élite that opposed industrialism based itself on just as conservative an ideology as the capitalistic bourgeoisie itself, an ideology that was in fact often even more reactionary.

The utilitarians, who represented the economic principles of industrialism, were the pupils of Adam Smith and proclaimed the doctrine that an economy left to run itself was most in accordance not merely with the spirit of liberalism but also with the interest of the general public. What aroused the strongest opposition to them on the part of the idealists was, however, not so much the indefensibility of this thesis, as the fatalism with which they represented the egoistic instincts as the ultimate principle of human action and the mathematical inevitability with which they imagined they could derive the laws of economic and social life from the fact of human egoism. The protest of the idealists against the reduction of man to 'homo economicus' was the eternal protestation of the romantic 'philosophy of life'—of the belief in the logical inexhaustibility of life and the impossibility of subduing it to man's design—against rationalism and thought abstracted from immediate reality. The reaction against utilitarianism was a second romanticism, in which the fight against

101

social injustice and the opposition to the actual theories of the 'dismal science' played a much smaller part than the urge to escape from the present, whose problems the anti-utilitarians had no ability and no desire to solve, into the irrationalism of Burke, Coleridge and German romanticism. The cry for state intervention was, especially in the case of Carlyle, just as much the sign of anti-liberal, authoritarian tendencies as an expression of humanitarian and altruistic feeling, and his lament about the atomic disintegration of society was both the expression of a desire for real community and of a yearning for the beloved and dreaded leader.

With the end of the heyday of English romanticism, a current of anti-romantic rationalism sets in about 1815 and reaches its climax with the electoral reform of 1832, the new Parliament and the triumph of the middle class. The successful bourgeoisie becomes more and more conservative and starts a reaction to democratic aspirations, which is again essentially romantic in character. Alongside rationalistic England a sentimental England makes itself felt and the hard-boiled, clear- and sober-minded capitalists flirt with ideas of philanthropic reform. The theoretical reaction against economic liberalism therefore proves to be an internal affair, a kind of self-deliverance, of the bourgeoisie. It is supported by the same stratum as in practice represents the principle of economic freedom and it merely serves to counterbalance the materialism and egoism in the Victorian compromise.

The years between 1832 and 1848 are a period of the most acute social crises, full of unrestrained bloody conflicts between capital and labour. After the Reform Bill, the English working class received the same treatment from the bourgeoisie as their brethren received in France after 1830. The aristocracy and the common people thus become, to a certain extent, fellow-sufferers and fellow-victims in a struggle against the common enemy, the capitalistic middle class. To be sure, this ephemeral relationship can never lead to a real community of interests and comradeship in arms, but it is sufficient to hide the real state of affairs from such an emotionally inclined thinker as Carlyle and to turn his fight against capitalism into a romantic and reactionary enthusiasm for history. In contrast to France, where hatred for the bourgeoisie is expressed in a strict and sober naturalism, the above-mentioned second romantic movement arises in England, where there had been no revolution since the seventeenth century and where the political experiences and disappointments of the French were lacking. In France, romanticism as a movement had been overcome by the middle of the century and the tussle with it takes on a more or less private character. In England, the situation develops differently: here the antagonism between the rationalistic and irrationalistic trends is by no means limited to an internal struggle, as it is in Flaubert for example, but divides the country into two camps, which are in reality much more heterogeneous in character than Disraeli's 'two nations'. Here too, as in the whole of Western Europe, the main line of development is positivistic, that is to say, in harmony with the principles of rationalism and naturalism. Not merely the political and economic rulers, not merely the technicians and scientists, but also the common man and the practical man, with his roots in ordinary professional life, think rationalistically and untraditionalistically. But the literature of the period is replete with a romantic nostalgia, a yearning for the Middle Ages and a Utopia in which the laws of capitalistic economy, of commercialism, of mercilessly impersonal competition and all the unpleasant realities of modern society have no place. Disraeli's feudalism is political romanticism, the 'Oxford Movement' religious romanticism, Carlyle's attacks on contemporary culture social romanticism and Ruskin's philosophy of art aesthetic romanticism; all these theories repudiate liberalism and rationalism and take refuge from the complicated problems of the present in a higher, superpersonal and supernatural order, in an enduring state beyond the anarchy of liberal and individualistic society. The loudest and most seductive voice is that of Carlyle, the first and most original of the pied pipers who prepared the way for Mussolini and Hitler. For, however important and fruitful the influence that he exerted in certain respects and however much the last century owed him in its fight for the spiritual immediacy of cultural forms, he was, nevertheless, a muddle-headed fellow, who succeeded for generations in obscuring and hiding facts with the clouds of smoke and vapour which belched forth from his enthusiasm for infinity and eternity, his superman morality and mystical hero-worship.

Ruskin is Carlyle's direct heir; he takes over his arguments against industrialism and liberalism, repeats his jeremiads about the soullessness and godlessness of modern culture and shares his enthusiasm for the Middle Ages and the communal culture of the Christian West. But he transforms the abstract hero-worship of his master into a concrete philosophy of beauty, his vague social romanticism into an aesthetic idealism with definite tasks and exactly definable aims. Nothing proves the timeliness and realism of Ruskin's doctrines better than the fact that he was able to become the spokesman of such an important and historically representative movement as Pre-Raphaelitism. His ideas and ideals, above all his rejection of the art of the Renaissance, of grandiose, dashing, self-satisfied and autocratic forms, and the return to pre-classical, 'Gothic' art, to the timid and inspired way of the 'primitives', were in the air; they were the symptoms of a general cultural crisis affecting the whole of society. Ruskin's doctrine and the art of the Pre-Raphaelites spring from the same spiritual condition and find expression in the same protest against the conventional outlook on art and the world of Victorian England. In the academicism of their age the Pre-Raphaelites recognize and combat what Ruskin interprets as the degeneration of art since the Renaissance. Their attack is aimed at the classicism, the aesthetic canon of the school of Raphael, that is to say, at the empty formalism and smooth routine of an art with which the bourgeoisie wants to provide the proof of its respectability, puritanical morality, high ideals and feeling for poetry. The Victorian middle class is obsessed with the idea of 'high art',[123] and the bad taste which dominates its architecture, its painting, its arts and crafts is partly the result of its self-deception—of the ambitions and pretensions which muffle the spontaneous expression of its nature.

Victorian painting swarms with historical, poetic, anecdotal motifs; it is 'literary' painting par excellence, a hybrid art, in which it is more to be regretted, however, that it contains so little pictorial value than that it contains so much literature. It is, above all, the fear of any kind of sensuality and spontaneity that

104

here stands in the way of that genuine, luxuriant style of painting which is so typical of the French conception of art. Expelled
nature creeps in again, however, by the backstairs.—In the
Chantrey Collection, that unique monument of Victorian bad
taste, there is a picture of a young nun who, in renouncing the
world, has also stripped off all her worldly clothes. She kneels
stark naked before the altar of a chapel dim with nocturnal light
and turns the alluring forms of her delicate body towards the
monks standing behind her. It is difficult to imagine anything
more embarrassing than this picture, for it belongs to the worst,
because most insincere, kind of pornography.

Pre-Raphaelite painting is just as literary, just as 'poetic' as
the whole of Victorian art, but it combines with its intrinsically
non-pictorial subjects, that is, subjects which can never be completely mastered in terms of painting, certain pictorial values,
which are often not only very attractive but also new. With its
Victorian spiritualism, its historical, religious and poetic themes,
its moral allegories and fairy-tale symbolism, it unites a realism
which finds expression in a delight in minute details, in the
playful reproduction of every blade of grass and every pleat in a
skirt. This meticulousness is in accordance not only with the
naturalistic tendency of European art in general, but at the same
time with that bourgeois ethic of good workmanship which
sees a criterion of aesthetic value in flawless technique and
careful execution. In keeping with this Victorian ideal, the Pre-
Raphaelites exaggerate the signs of technical ability, imitative
skill and the finishing touch. Their pictures are turned out just
as neatly as those of the academic painters and we feel any antithesis between the Pre-Raphaelites and the rest of the Victorian
painters much less acutely than, for example, the difference
between the naturalists and the academicians in France. The
Pre-Raphaelites are idealists, moralists and shamefaced erotics,
like most Victorians. They have the same contradictory conception
of art, betray the same embarrassment, the same inhibitions in
giving artistic expression to their experiences, and their puritanical abashment in face of the medium in which they express
themselves goes so far that we always have the feeling of a timid,
though supremely gifted dilettantism when considering their

105

works. This distance between the creator and his work deepens still more the impression of decorative art which adheres to all Pre-Raphaelite painting. This is why this painting seems so affected, so dainty and pretty and always has about it something of the unreal and ornamental quality of mere tapestries. The precious, intellectual and, in spite of its lyrical nature, cold note of modern symbolism, the austere gracefulness and somewhat affected angularity of neo-romanticism, the studied shyness and restraint, the secrecy and secretiveness of the art at the turn of the century, partly have their source in this artificial style.

Pre-Raphaelitism was an aesthetic movement, an extreme cult of beauty, an assessment of life based on art; but it must no more be identified with 'l'art pour l'art' than Ruskin's philosophy itself. The thesis that the highest value of art consists in the expression of a 'good and great soul'[124] accorded with the conviction of all the Pre-Raphaelites. It is true that they were playful formalists, but they lived in the faith that their playing with forms had a higher purpose and an elevating educational effect. There is just as great a contradiction between their aestheticism and their moralism as between their romantic archaism and their naturalistic treatment of details.[125] It is the same Victorian contradiction which also produces a cleft in Ruskin's writings; his epicurean enthusiasm for art is by no means always compatible with the social gospel which he proclaims. According to this gospel, perfect beauty is possible only in a community in which justice and solidarity reign supreme. Great art is the expression of a morally healthy society; in an age of materialism and mechanization the feeling for beauty and the ability to create art of a high quality must wither. Carlyle had already brought the stereotyped charge against modern capitalistic society that it blunts and kills the souls of men with its 'cash nexus' and mechanical methods of production; Ruskin merely repeats his predecessor's fierce words. The lamentations over the decay of art are not new either. Ever since the legend of the Golden Age the art of the present had always been felt to be inferior to the creations of the past, and it was believed that signs of the same decay could be detected in it as were evident in the morals of the time. But artistic decay had never been regarded

106

as the symptom of a disease involving the whole body of society and there has never been such a clear awareness of the organic relationship between art and life as since Ruskin.[126] He was indubitably the first to interpret the decline of art and taste as the sign of a general cultural crisis, and to express the basic, and even today not sufficiently appreciated, principle that the conditions under which men live must first be changed, if their sense of beauty and their comprehension of art are to be awakened. On the strength of this insight Ruskin exchanged the study of the history of art for that of economics and moved away from Carlyle's idealism in so far as he did greater justice to the materialism of this science. Ruskin was also the first person in England to emphasize the fact that art is a public concern and its cultivation one of the most important tasks of the state, in other words, that it represents a social necessity and that no nation can neglect it without endangering its intellectual existence. He was, finally, the first to proclaim the gospel that art is not the privilege of artists, connoisseurs and the educated classes, but is part of every man's inheritance and estate. But for all that, he was by no means a socialist, indeed, he was not even a democrat.[127] Plato's philosophers' state, in which beauty and wisdom reigned supreme, came nearest to his ideal and his 'socialism' was limited to a belief in the educability of human beings and in their right to enjoy the blessings of culture. According to him, real wealth consists not in the possession of material goods, but in the ability to enjoy the beauty of life and art. This aesthetic quietism and the renunciation of all violence mark the limits of his reformism.[128]

William Morris, the third in the series of representative social critics of the Victorian age, thinks much more consistently and advances much further in the practical sphere than Ruskin. In some respect he is, in fact, the greatest,[129] that is to say, the bravest, the most intransigent of the Victorians, although even he is not completely free of their contradictions and compromises. But he drew the ultimate conclusion from Ruskin's doctrine of the involvement of the fate of art in that of society, and became convinced that 'to make socialists' is a more urgent task than to make good art. He pursued to the very end Ruskin's idea that the inferiority of modern art, the decline of artistic culture and the bad taste of the public are only the symptoms of a more deeply rooted and more far-reaching evil, and realized that there is no point in trying to improve art and taste and leaving society unchanged. He knew that directly to influence artistic development is useless and that all one can do is to create social conditions which will facilitate a better appreciation of art. He was quite aware of the class struggle within which the social process and, consequently, the development of art takes place and he regarded it as the most important task to imbue the proletariat with consciousness of this fact.[130] For all their clarity on fundamental issues, his theories and demands still contain, as we have said, numerous contradictions. In spite of his sound conception of social reality and the function of art in the life of society, he is a romantic lover of the Middle Ages and the medieval ideal of beauty. He preaches the need for an art created by and intended for the people, but he is and remains a hedonistic dilettante producing things which only the rich can afford and only the well-educated can enjoy. He points out that art arises from work, from practical craftsmanship, but he fails to recognize the significance of the most important and most practical modern means of production—the machine. The source of the contradictions which exist between his teachings and his artistic activity is to be sought in the petty bourgeois traditionalism behind the judgement passed on the technical age by his teachers, Carlyle and Ruskin, and from whose provincialism he is never able entirely to free himself.

Ruskin attributed the decay of art to the fact that the modern factory, with its mechanical mode of production and division of labour, prevents a genuine relationship between the worker and his work, that is to say, that it crushes out the spiritual element and estranges the producer from the product of his hands. With him the fight against industrialism lost the barb directed against the proletarianization of the masses and became transformed into a romantic enthusiasm for something irretrievable, for handicraft, the home industry, the guild, in short, for the medieval forms of production. But the service rendered by Ruskin was that he drew attention to the ugliness of the Victorian arts and crafts and recalled his contemporaries to the charms of solid, careful craftsmanship as opposed to the spurious materials, senseless forms and crude, cheap execution of Victorian products. His influence was extraordinary, almost beyond description. Production within the framework of a comparatively small workshop, maintaining the personal relationship of the workers with one another and the absolute predominance of handicraft, with individual tasks concentrated on the single, self-contained work, became the ideal in the production of modern art and applied art. The purposefulness and solidity of modern architecture and industrial art are very largely the result of Ruskin's endeavours and doctrines, although his direct influence brought about a rather exaggerated cult of manual labour which failed to recognize the tasks and possibilities of machine industry and led to the awakening of an unrealizable hope. It was mere romanticism to believe that technical achievements, which had arisen from real economic needs and which secured tangible economic advantages, could simply be pushed aside; and it was extremely childish to try and arrest the progress of technical and economic developments with polemical pamphlets and protests. Ruskin and his disciples were right inasmuch as man did in fact lose control over the machine, that technics became autonomous and produced, especially in the field of industrial art, the most insipid and respulsive objects; but they forgot that there was no other way to control the machine than to accept it and to conquer it spiritually.

The logical mistake they made consisted in an all too narrow definition of technics, in failing to recognize the technical nature of every kind of material production, of every manipulation of things, of every contact with objective reality. Art always makes use of a material, technical, tool-like device, of an appliance, a 'machine', and does so so openly that this indirectness and materialism of the means of expression can even be described as one of its most essential characteristics. Art is perhaps altogether the most sensual, the most sensuous 'expression' of the human spirit, and already bound as such to something concrete outside itself, to a technique, to an instrument, no matter whether this instrument is a weaver's loom or a weaving machine, a paint brush or a camera, a violin or—to mention something really frightful—a cinema organ. Even the human voice—and even the vocal apparatus of a Caruso—is a material instrument, not a spiritual reality. It is only in mystical ecstasy, in the happiness of love, in compassion—perhaps only in compassion—that the soul flows directly, without mediation and without instrumentality, to other souls—but it never flows thus in the experience of a work of art.

The whole history of industrial art can be represented as the continuous renewal and improvement of the technical means of expression, and when this is developing normally and smoothly it can be defined as the complete exploitation and control of these means, as the harmonious adjustment of ability and purpose, of the vehicles and the contents of expression. The obstruction which has occurred in this development since the Industrial Revolution, the lead that technical achievements have gained over intellectual, is to be attributed not so much to the fact that more complicated and more diverse machines began to be used, as to the phenomenon that technical development, spurred on by prosperity, became so rapid that the human mind had no time to keep pace with it. In other words, those elements which might have transferred the tradition of craftsmanship to mechanical production, the independent masters and their apprentices, were eliminated from economic life before they had had any chance of adapting themselves and the traditions of their craft to the new methods of production. What produced the disturbance of the balance in the relationship between technical and intellectual developments was, therefore, a crisis of organization, and by no means a basic change in the nature of technics—all of a sudden there were too few experts in the industries rooted in the old traditions of craftsmanship.

Morris shared Ruskin's prejudices on the subject of mechanical production as well as his enthusiasm for handicraft, but he assessed the function of the machine much more progressively and rationally than his master. He upbraided the society of his time with having misused technical inventions, but he already knew that in certain circumstances they might prove a blessing to humanity.[131] His socialistic optimism only enhanced this hope in technical progress. He defines art as 'man's expression of his joy in labour';[132] for him, art is not only a source of happiness but, above all, the result of a feeling of happiness. Its real value lies in the creative process; in his work the artist enjoys his own productivity and it is the joy of work which is artistically productive. This autogenesis of art is rather mysterious and contains a strong dose of Rousseauism, but it is in no way more mystical and more romantic than the idea that mechanical techniques mean the end of art.

The social phenomena which occupy the art critics and the social critics of the Victorian age also form the subject of the English novel of the time. This too revolves around what Carlyle called the 'condition-of-England' problem, and it describes the social conditions which arose with the Industrial Revolution. But it turns to a more mixed public than the art criticism of the period, is more heterogeneous and speaks a more colourful, less fastidious language. It tries to interest the strata of society into which the works of Carlyle and Ruskin never penetrated and to win for itself readers for whom social reforms are no mere problems of conscience but questions of vital consequence. But, as such readers are still in a minority, the novel remains based in the main on the interests of the upper and middle strata of the bourgeoisie, and provides an outlet for the moral conflicts in which the victors in the class struggle are involved. The stimulus may proceed, as with Disraeli, from patriarchal-feudalistic wish-fulfilment dreams, or, as with Kingsley and Mrs. Gaskell, from a Christian-socialist ideal, or, as with Dickens, from concern about the pauperization of the petty bourgeoisie, but the final result is always a fundamental acceptance of the prevailing order. They all begin with the most violent attacks on capitalistic society, but come in the end to accept its presuppositions in either an optimistic or a quietistic frame of mind, as if they had merely wanted to expose and fight against the abuses, in order to prevent deeper revolutionary upheavals. In the case of Kingsley the conciliatory tendency finds expression in an openly confessed change of mind, with Dickens it is merely concealed by the author's radical and increasingly leftish attitude. Some writers sympathize with the upper classes, others with the 'insulted and injured', but there are no revolutionaries among them. At best, they waver between genuine democratic impulses and the reflection that, in spite of everything, class differences are justified and have a beneficent influence. The differences between them are, at any rate, of subordinate importance in comparison with the common features of their philanthropic conservatism.[133]

The modern social novel arises in England, as in France, in the period around 1830, and enjoys its heyday in the turbulent years between 1840 and 1850, when the country stands on the brink of revolution. Here, too, it becomes the most important literary form of the generation which has come to question the aims and standards of bourgeois society and which wants to explain the sudden rise and threatening ruin of it. But in the English novel the problems discussed are more concrete, of more general significance, less intellectualistic and sophisticated than in the French; the authors' standpoint is more humane, more altruistic, but, at the same time, more conciliatory and opportunistic. Disraeli, Kingsley, Mrs. Gaskell and Dickens are Carlyle's first disciples and are among the writers who accept his ideas most readily.[134] They are irrationalists, idealists, interventionists, they scoff at utilitarianism and national economy, condemn liberalism and industrialism, and place their novels at the service of the fight against the principle of 'laissez-faire' and the economic anarchy which they derive from this principle. Before 1830 the novel as a vehicle of this kind of social propaganda was absolutely unknown, although in England the modern novel had been 'social' from the very beginning, that is, from Defoe and Fielding onwards. It was much more directly and deeply connected with the essays of Addison and Steele than with the pastoral and love novel of Sidney and Lyly, and its first masters owed their insight into the contemporary situation and their moral feeling for the social problems of the day to the stimuli which they had received from journalism. It is true that this feeling becomes blunted at the end of the first great period of the English novel, but it was by no means lost. The novel of terror and mystery, which took the place of Fielding's and Richardson's works in the public favour, had no direct connection with the facts of society or with reality in general, and in Jane Austen's novels social reality was the soil in which the characters were rooted, but in no sense a problem which the novelist made any attempt to solve or interpret. The novel does not become 'social' again until Walter Scott, though in quite a different sense from what it had been in Defoe, Fielding, Richardson or Smollett. In Scott the sociological background is stressed much more consciously than in his predecessors; he always shows his characters as the representatives of a social class, but the picture of society that he draws is much more programmatic and abstract than in the novel of the eighteenth century. He founds a new tradition and is only very loosely connected with the Defoe–Fielding–Smollett line of development. But Dickens, the nearest heir of Walter Scott and, above all, his successor as the best story-teller and the most popular author of his age, resumes a direct connection with this line, for even if he is a pupil of Scott—and who of the novelists of the first half of the century is not?—nevertheless, the genre that he creates is much more similar to the picaresque form of the old writers than to Scott's dramatic mode of writing. Dickens is also closely connected with the eighteenth century by reason of the moralistic-didactic tendency of his art; apart from the picaresque tradition of Fielding and Sterne, he revives the philanthropic trend of Defoe and Goldsmith, which had been equally neglected by Scott.[135] He owes his popularity to the resuscitation of both these literary traditions and he meets the taste of the new reading public halfway both by the picaresque colourfulness and the sentimental-moralistic tone of his works.

Between 1816 and 1850 an average of a hundred novels appear in England every year,[136] and the books published in 1853, most of which are narrative literature, are three times as many as the works that had appeared twenty-five years previously.[137] The increase in the reading public in the eighteenth century was connected with the development of the lending libraries; but they merely led to a more lively activity among publishers and did not contribute in any way to the reduction of book prices. With their growing needs, they helped rather to stabilize the prices on a comparatively high level. The price of a novel in the usual three-volume edition amounted to one and a half guineas, a sum which only extremely few people were in a position to pay for a novel. Hence the readership of light fiction was restricted in the main to the subscribers to lending libraries. It was not until novels began to be published in monthly instalments that a fundamental change in the composition and size of the reading public took place. Payment by instalments, even though this reduced the price only by a third, allowed many people, who had hardly ever been able to buy books before, to purchase the works of their favourite authors. The publication of novels in monthly numbers represented a book-selling innovation, which was in fundamental accordance with the introduction of the serial novel and had similar results both sociologically and artistically. The return to the picaresque form of the novel was one of these results.

Dickens, whose successes also mean the triumph of the new method of publication, enjoys all the advantages and suffers from all the disadvantages connected with the democratization of literary consumption. The constant contact with broad masses of the public helps him to find a style which is popular in the best sense of the word; he is one of the none too numerous artists who are not only great and popular, not merely great, although they are popular, but great, because they are popular. To the loyalty of his public and the feeling of security with which the affection of his readers inspires him, he owes his grand epic style, the evenness of his language and that spontaneous, unproblematical, almost entirely artless mode of creation, which is quite unparalleled in the nineteenth century. On the other hand, his popularity only partly explains his greatness as a writer, for Alexandre Dumas and Eugène Sue are just as popular as he, without being great in any sense. And his greatness explains his popularity even less, for Balzac is incomparably greater, just as vulgar and yet much less successful, although he produces his works under quite similar outward conditions. The disadvantages of popularity for Dickens are much easier to explain. Fidelity to his readers, intellectual solidarity with the great masses of simple followers, and the desire to maintain the affection of this relationship produce in him a belief in the absolute artistic value of the methods which go down well with the emotionally inclined masses and, consequently, also a belief in

the infallible instinct and soundness of the great public's uni-
sonously beating heart.[138] He would never have admitted that
the artistic quality of a work often stands in an inverse relationship to the number of people who feel moved by it. There are
certain means by which we can all be moved to tears, even
though we are afterwards ashamed of not having resisted the
'universally human' appeal of these means. But we shed no tears
over the fate of the heroes of Homer, Sophocles, Shakespeare,
Corneille, Racine, Voltaire, Fielding, Jane Austen and Stendhal,
whereas in reading Dickens we feel the same thoughtless, complacent emotions with which we react to the films of today.

Dickens is one of the most successful writers of all time and
perhaps the most popular great writer of the modern age. He is,
at any rate, the only real writer since romanticism whose work
did not spring from opposition to his age, nor from a strained
relationship to his environment, but coincided absolutely with
the demands of his public. He enjoys a popularity for which there
is no parallel since Shakespeare and which approaches nearest to
the idea we have of the popularity of the old mimes and minstrels.
Dickens owes the totality and integrity of his world-view to the
fact that he does not need to make any concessions, when he
speaks to his public, that he has just as narrow a mental horizon,
just as undiscriminating taste and just as artless, though incomparably richer, an imagination as his readers. Chesterton remarks
that, in contrast to Dickens, the popular writers of our day
always feel they must climb down to their public.[139] Between
them and their readers there exists just as painful, though quite
differently constituted and much less deeply founded a breach as
between the great writers and the average public of the period.
There is no question of any such breach in Dickens. He is not
only the creator of the most comprehensive gallery of figures ever
to have penetrated the general consciousness and imaginative
world of the English reading public, his inner relationship to
these figures is the same as that of his public. His readers'
favourites are also his favourites and he talks of little Nell or
little Dombey with the same feelings and in the same tone as the
most harmless little grocer or the simplest old maid.

The series of triumphs began for Dickens with his first full-length work, the *Pickwick Papers*, forty thousand copies of the separate instalments of which were sold from the fifteenth number onwards. This success determined the style of bookselling in which the English fiction of the succeeding quarter of a century was to develop. The power of attraction of the author, who had become famous all of a sudden, never slackened throughout his whole career. The world was always hungry for more and he worked almost as feverishly and breathlessly as Balzac to meet the enormous demand. These two colossi belong together; they are exponents of the same literary boom, they supply the same book-hungry public, which, after the upheavals of an age filled with revolutionary agitation and disillusionments, seeks in the fictitious world of the novel for a substitute for reality, a signpost in the chaos of life and a compensation for lost illusions. But Dickens penetrates into wider circles than Balzac. With the aid of the cheap monthly instalments he wins a completely new class for literature, a class of people who had never read novels before, and beside whom the readers of the older novel literature seem like so many beaux esprits. A charwoman tells how where she lived the people met on the first Monday of every month at the house of a snuff shop proprietor and received tea on payment of a small sum; after tea the master read aloud the latest instalment of *Dombey* and all the occupants of the house were admitted to the reading without charge.[140] Dickens was a purveyor of light fiction for the masses, the continuer of the old 'shilling-shocker' and the inventor of the modern 'thriller',[141] in short, the author of books which, apart from their literary quality, corresponded in all respects to our 'best-sellers'. But it would be wrong to assume that he wrote his novels merely for the uneducated or the half-educated masses; a section of the upper middle class and even a section of the intelligentsia were part of his enthusiastic public. His novels were the up-to-date, topical literature of the time, just as the film is the 'contemporary art' of our age, and has even for people who are perfectly aware of its artistic inadequacies the inestimable value of being a living form, pregnant with the future.

From the very start, Dickens was the representative of the new type of artistically and ideologically progressive literature; he aroused interest even when he did not please, and even when people found his social gospel anything but agreeable, they found his novels entertaining. It was, in any case, possible to separate his artistic from his political philosophy. He raged with flaming words against the sins of society, the heartlessness and the insolence of the rich, the harshness and lack of sympathy of the law, the cruel treatment of children, the inhuman conditions in the prisons, factories and schools, in short, against the lack of consideration for the individual which is the property of all institutional organizations. His accusations rumbled in all ears and filled all hearts with the uneasy feeling of an injustice of which the whole of society was guilty. But the cry of distress and the satisfaction that always follows after a good cry did not lead to anything more tangible. The author's social message was politically fruitless, and even artistically his philanthropy bore very mixed fruits. It deepened his sympathetic insight into the psychology of his characters, but it produced, at the same time, a sentimentalism which was liable to cloud his vision. His uncritical benevolence, his 'Cheeryblism', his confidence in the ability of private charity and the kind-heartedness of the propertied class to repair social defects, sprang, in the final analysis, from his vague social consciousness, from his undecided position between the classes as a petty bourgeois. He was never able to overcome the shock of having been slung out of the middle class in his youth and having reached the brink of the proletariat; he always felt that he had fallen in the social scale, or rather was in danger of falling.[142] He was a radical philanthropist, a liberal-minded friend of the people, a passionate opponent of conservatism, but he was by no means a socialist and a revolutionary—at most a petty bourgeois in revolt, a victim of humiliation who never forgot what had been inflicted on him in his youth.[143] And he remained the life-long petty bourgeois who imagined he was under the necessity of protecting himself not only against a danger from above but also against one from below. He felt and thought like a petty bourgeois, and his ideals were those of the petty bourgeoisie. He regarded work, perseverance, thrift, the ascent to security, lack of worry and respectability as forming the true substance of life. He thought that happiness consisted in a

117

state of modest prosperity, in the idyll of an existence protected from the hostile outside world, in the family circle, in the sheltered comfort of a well-heated room, of a cosy parlour or of the stage-coach taking its passengers to a safe destination.

Dickens is incapable of overcoming the inner contradictions of his social ideology. On the one hand, he hurls the bitterest charges at society, on the other, however, he under-estimates the extent of the social evils, because he refuses to admit it.[144] Actually, he still holds fast to the principle: 'everything for the people —nothing with the people', for he is unable to get away from the prejudice that the people is incompetent to rule.[145] He is afraid of the 'rabble' and identifies the 'people', in the ideal sense of the term, with the middle class. Flaubert, Maupassant and the Goncourts are, despite their conservatism, unbending rebels, whereas, in spite of his political progressiveness and his opposition to existing conditions, Dickens is a peace-loving citizen, who accepts the presuppositions of the prevailing capitalistic system without question. He knows only the burdens and grievances of the petty bourgeoisie, and fights only against evils which can be remedied without shaking the foundations of bourgeois society. Of the situation of the proletariat and life in the great industrial cities, he knows almost nothing and he has a very queer conception of the labour movement. He is only troubled about the fate of the crafts, the small independent masters and tradesmen, the assistants and apprentices. The demands of the working class, that great and constantly growing power of the future, only frighten him. He is not particularly interested in the technical achievements of his age, and the romanticism with which he adheres to antiquated ways of life is much more spontaneous and genuine than Carlyle's and Ruskin's enthusiasm for the Middle Ages with its monasteries and guilds. Compared with Balzac's metropolitan, technicistic outlook, with his delight in inventions and innovations, all this seems to indicate a paltry, sluggish provincialism. In the works of his later period, especially in *Hard Times*, a certain widening of his outlook can no doubt be observed: the problem of the industrial city enters into his range of ideas, and he discusses with growing interest the fate of the industrial proletariat as a class. But how inadequate is his conception of the inner structure of capitalism, how prejudiced and childish his judgement on the aims of the labour movement, how philistine his view that socialistic agitation is nothing but demagogy and the strike parole nothing but blackmail![146] The author's sympathy is with good Stephen Blackpool, who does not take part in the strike and feels an unconquerable, although strongly concealed, sense of solidarity with his master, based on an atavistic, cringing loyalty. The 'dog's morality' plays a great part in Dickens. The further removed an attitude is from the mature, critical, intellectual approach of a serious-minded man, the more understanding and sympathy he has for it. The uneducated, simple folk are always closer to his heart than the educated, and children more so than grown-ups.

Dickens absolutely misunderstands the significance of the conflict between capital and labour; he simply does not grasp that two irreconcilable forces confront each other here, and that the settlement of the quarrel does not depend on the good will of the individual. The gospel truth that man does not live by bread alone does not seem very convincing in a novel describing the struggle of the proletariat for daily bread. But Dickens cannot give up his childish belief in the possibility of reconciling the classes. He indulges in the illusion that patriarchal-philanthropic feelings, on the one, and a patient, self-sacrificing attitude, on the other side, guarantee social peace. He preaches the renunciation of violence, because he regards insurrection and revolution as greater evils than suppression and exploitation. If he never uttered such a harsh phrase as Goethe's 'rather injustice than disorder', it was only because he was not so brave and had not come to anything like such a clear understanding with himself as Goethe. He transformed the healthy, unsentimental egoism of the older bourgeoisie into an adulterated, sugary 'philosophy of Christmas', best summarized as follows by Taine: 'Be good and love one another; the feeling of the heart is the one real joy. . . . Leave science to the scholars, pride to the noble, luxury to the rich. . . .'[147] Dickens did not know how hard the kernel of this gospel of love really was, and what the peace it promised would have cost the weaker classes of society. But he felt it, and the inner contradictions of his philosophy are unmistakably reflected in the serious neurotic disturbances which tormented him. The world of this apostle of peace is by no means a peaceful and harmless world. His sentimentality is often only the mask hiding a terrifying cruelty, his humour smiles in the midst of tears, his good temper fights against a choking fear of life, a grimace is hidden behind the features of his most good-natured characters, his bourgeois decorum is always on the verge of criminality, the scenery of his beloved old-fashioned world is an uncanny lumber-room, his enormous vitality, his joy of life stand in the shadow of death and his fidelity to nature is a feverish hallucination. This apparently so decent, correct, respectable Victorian turns out to be a desperate surrealist tormented by fear-ridden dreams.

Dickens is not merely a representative of truth to life and fidelity to nature in art, not only a consummate master of the 'petits faits vrais', but the artist to whom English literature owes the most important naturalistic achievements. The whole modern English novel derives its art of milieu description, its character drawing and its mastery of dialogue from him. But, in reality, all the characters of this naturalist are caricatures, all the features of real life are exaggerated, pushed to extremes, overstrained, everything becomes a fantastic shadow-play and puppet-show, everything is transformed into the stylized, simplified and stereotyped relationships and situations of the melodrama. His most lovable figures are notorious fools, his most harmless petty bourgeois impossible cranks, monomaniacs and sprites; his carefully drawn milieus seem like romantic opera scenes and his whole naturalism often produces merely the sharpness and the dazzling light of apparitions in a dream. Balzac's worst absurdities are more logical than some of his visions. The Victorian repressions and compromises create an absolutely unbalanced, uncontrolled 'neurotic' style in him. But neuroses are by no means always complicated and there was in fact nothing complicated and sublimated about Dickens. He was not only one of the most uneducated English writers, not only just as ill-informed and unlettered as, for example, Richardson or Jane Austen, but, in contrast above all to the last-named, primitive and in some respects obtuse, a big child with no feeling for the deeper problems of life.

There was nothing intellectual about him and he never thought much of intellectuals. Whenever he had occasion to describe an artist or a thinker, he made fun of them. He maintained the puritan's hostile attitude to art and added to it the unintellectual and anti-artistic convictions of the matter-of-fact bourgeoisie; he regarded art as unnecessary and immoral. His hostility to the things of the mind was worse than bourgeois, it was petty bourgeois and narrow-minded. He refused to have any intercourse with artists, poets and suchlike wind-bags, as if he wanted thereby to bear witness yet again to the sense of solidarity with his public.[148]

In the Victorian age the reading public was already divided into two precisely definable circles and, in spite of his adherents in the upper classes, Dickens was regarded as the author of the uneducated, undiscriminating public. This cleavage had already existed in the eighteenth century, of course, and Richardson can be considered to represent the more elevated middle-class taste, especially in contrast to Defoe and Fielding; but the readers of Richardson, Defoe and Fielding were still on the whole the same people. From 1830 onwards, however, the gulf between the two cultural strata became much more perceptible, and it was fairly easy to mark off Dickens's public from that of Thackeray and Trollope, even though many readers were still on the borderline. It is quite clear that there had already been people in the eighteenth century who found it easier to identify themselves with Richardson's heroes and heroines than with those of Fielding, but there are now readers who can simply not endure Dickens and others who can hardly understand Thackeray or George Eliot. The phenomenon, so characteristic of the present-day situation, that alongside the educated, critical reading public there exists a circle of equally regular readers, who seek for nothing more in literature than easy, ephemeral entertainment, was unknown before the Victorian age. The public interested only in literary entertainment was still made up very largely of casual readers, whereas the regular reading public was restricted to the cultured class. But in Dickens's day, as in our own, there are two groups of people interested in belles-lettres. The only difference between that age and our own is that the popular light literature of that time still embraced the works of a writer like Dickens and that there were still many people who were able to enjoy both kinds of literature,[149] whereas today good literature is fundamentally unpopular and popular literature is unbearable to people of taste.

The World Exhibition of 1851 marks a turning point in the history of England; the mid-Victorian age is, in contrast to the early Victorian period, an age of prosperity and pacification. England becomes the 'workshop of the world', prices rise, the living conditions of the working class are improved, socialism is rendered harmless, the political ascendency of the bourgeoisie is consolidated. It is true that the social problems are not solved, but their sharp edge is removed. The catastrophe of 1848 produces a fatigue and passivity in the progressive strata of society and the novel thereby loses its intolerant and aggressive character. Thackeray, Trollope, and George Eliot no longer write 'social novels' as understood by Kingsley, Mrs. Gaskell and Dickens. Certainly, they draft great pictures of society, but they seldom discuss the social problems of the day, and renounce the propagation of a social-political thesis. With George Eliot, whose outlook on the world is particularly characteristic of the intellectual atmosphere of this period,[150] society is no longer in the foreground of the exposition, although it is, as in the novels of Jane Austen, the vital element in which the characters move and determine each other's fate. George Eliot always describes the mutual dependence of human beings, the magnetic field that they create around themselves, the influence of which they increase with every action and every word;[151] she shows that no one can lead an isolated, autonomous life within modern society,[152] and in this sense her works are social novels. The accent has shifted however: society appears as a positive, all-embracing reality, but as a fact that has to be endured.

The turning towards introversion in the history of the English novel is accomplished in the works of George Eliot. The most important events in her novels are of an intellectual and moral nature, and the soul, the inner citadel, the moral consciousness of man is the scene of the great conflicts of destiny. In this sense her works are psychological novels.[153] Instead of external happenings and adventures, instead of social questions and conflicts, moral problems and crises are central in her plots. Her heroes are thoughtful people for whom intellectual and moral experiences are as immediate as physical facts. Her works are to some extent psychological-philosophical essays which more or less conform to the ideal of the novel that the German romantics had in mind. In spite of that, her art signifies a break with romanticism and, in addition, the first successful attempt to replace the spiritual values created by the romantics with different, fundamentally unromantic values. With George Eliot, the novel acquires a new intellectual-emotional content—that intellectual content, the emotional value of which had been lost since the days of classicism; it hinges not on sentimental experiences of an irrational nature, but on an attitude which George Eliot herself calls 'intellectual passion'.[154] The real subject of her novels is the analysis and interpretation of life, the knowledge and appreciation of intellectual values. Understanding is a word that constantly recurs in her works;[155] to be alert, to be responsible, to deal uncompromisingly with oneself, is the demands he is always repeating. 'The highest calling and election is to do without opium, and live through all our pain with conscious, clear-eyed endurance,' she writes in a letter of 1860.[156]

The destiny of thoughtful people, with its problems and contradictions, its tragedies and defeats, could only attain the immediacy and force that it has in *Middlemarch*, in the work of a writer who was so deeply involved in the intellectual life of her time as George Eliot. The best and most progressive thinkers of the England of that period, including J. S. Mill, Spencer and Huxley, are among George Eliot's friends; she translates Feuerbach and D. F. Strauss and stands at the centre of the rationalistic and positivistic movement of her age. The serious, critical purpose, free from all frivolity and credulity, which informs her moral outlook, is typical of her whole thinking. She is the first to be able adequately to describe an intellectual in the English novel. Apart from her, none of the contemporary novelists can speak of an artist or a scholar without ridiculing him or making himself ridiculous. Even Balzac really regards them as strange, exotic creatures, who fill him with naïve amazement and force a more or less good-natured smile out of him. Compared with George Eliot, he seems a half-educated autodidact, even though, as in the *Chef-d'oeuvre inconnu*, he opens up perspectives the depth and breadth of which lie far beyond George Eliot's artistic powers. Balzac's strength is description, George Eliot's the analysis of experience. She knows from her own experience the torment of wrestling with intellectual problems, she knows or has some idea of the tragedies connected with spiritual defeats, otherwise she would never have been able to create a character like Dr. Casaubon.[157] Thanks to her intellectuality, she attains a new ideal and a new conception of the 'abortive life', and she adds a new type to that series of 'manqués' to which, almost without exception, the heroes of the modern novel belong.

George Eliot's intellectualism is, however, not the real and final reason for the psychologizing of the social novel, but itself only a symptom of the recession of social in favour of psychological problems. The psychological novel is the literary genre of the intelligentsia as the cultural stratum in process of emancipating itself from the bourgeoisie, just as the social novel was the literary form of the cultural stratum which was still fundamentally one with the bourgeoisie. It is not until the beginning of the mid-Victorian period that the intelligentsia comes forward in England as a group without ties, 'socially unattached',[158] 'beyond all class distinctions',[159] 'mediating' between the various classes.[160] Until this time there had never been an intelligentsia here with any feeling of being an independent social group in revolt against the bourgeoisie. The cultured stratum maintains its connection with the bourgeoisie so long as this class allows it to have its own way. The estrangement which set in with romanticism between the progressive literary élite and the conservative middle class was smoothed over again with the conversion of the romantics to the idea of conservatism. The writers of the early Victorian period fought for reforms within bourgeois society, but never thought of destroying this society. The bourgeoisie had also never regarded them in any way as traitors or even as foreigners; on the contrary, it followed their activities in the field of social and cultural criticism with sympathy and goodwill. The cultural stratum fulfilled a function in bourgeois society of the importance of which the ruling classes were on the whole quite aware. It formed the safety-valve that prevented an explosion and, by giving expression to conflicts of conscience which were in danger of being repressed, it provided an outlet for tensions within the bourgeoisie itself.

It was only after its victory over the Revolution and the defeat of Chartism that the bourgeoisie felt so safely entrenched that it no longer had any qualms and twinges of conscience and imagined that it was no longer in any need of criticism. But the cultural élite, and especially its literarily productive section, thereby lost the feeling of having a mission to fulfil in society. It saw itself cut off from the social class of which it had hitherto been the mouthpiece and it felt completely isolated between the uneducated classes and the bourgeoisie. It was this feeling that first gave rise to the replacement of the earlier cultural stratum with its roots in the middle class by the social group that we call the 'intelligentsia'. But this development really formed only the final stage in a process of emancipation in the course of which the representatives of culture had gradually detached themselves from the representatives of power. Humanism and the enlightenment are the first stations in this development; they complete the emancipation of culture, on the one hand, from the dogma of the Church, on the other, from the aesthetic dictatorship of the aristocracy. The French Revolution marks the end of the cultural monopoly that had been exercised until then by the two higher estates and it paves the way for the cultural monopoly of the bourgeoisie, which appears to be absolutely assured with the advent of the July monarchy. The conclusion of the revolutionary era around the middle of the century marks the final step towards the emancipation of the cultural stratum from the ruling classes and the first step towards the creation of the 'intelligentsia' in the narrower meaning of the word.

The intelligentsia arose out of the bourgeoisie and its predecessor was that vanguard of the middle class which paved the way for the French Revolution. Its cultural ideal is enlightened and liberal, its human ideal is based on the concept of the free, progressive personality unrestrained by convention and tradition. When the bourgeoisie spurns the intelligentsia and the intelligentsia deserts the class from which it had arisen and to which it is bound by innumerable ties of common interest, what takes place is really an unnatural and absurd proceeding. The emancipation of the intelligentsia can be regarded as a phase of the universal process of specialization, that is to say, as part of that process of abstraction which, since the Industrial Revolution, has been abolishing the 'organic' relationship between the various strata of society, between the different professions and provinces of culture, but it can also be interpreted as a direct reaction against this very specialization, as an attempt to realize the ideal of the total, all-round human being in whom the values of culture are combined in an integrated whole. The intelligentsia's apparent independence of the middle class, and consequently, of all social ties, is in accordance with the illusion, cherished by both the bourgeoisie and the intelligentsia, that the things of the mind live in a realm beyond the distinctions of class. The intellectuals try to believe in the absoluteness of truth and beauty, because that makes them seem the representatives of a 'higher' reality and because it compensates for their lack of influence in society; the bourgeoisie again allows this claim of the intelligentsia to a position between and above the classes to stand, because it fancies it can see therein a proof of the existence of universally human values and the possibility of class differences being forgotten. But like 'art for art's sake', science for science's sake or truth for truth's sake is merely a product of the estrangement of the intellectuals from practical affairs. The idealism which it contains costs the bourgeoisie the overcoming of its hatred for the things of the mind; the intelligentsia, on the other hand, thereby gives expression to its jealousy of the mighty middle class. The resentment of the cultured strata towards their masters is nothing new; the humanists had already suffered from it and had produced all the neurotic symptoms of an inferiority complex. But how could a class that imagined it was in possession of the truth help feeling jealousy, envy and hatred for the class that was in possession of all economic and political power? In the Middle Ages, the clergy had all the sanctions of 'truth' at their disposal, but partly the instruments of economic and political power as well. Thanks to this coincidence, the pathological phenomena which resulted from the later division of these spheres of authority were still unknown.

In contrast to the medieval clergy, the modern intelligentsia is recruited from various financial and professional classes and represents the interests and views of various and often antagonistic strata of society. This heterogeneity strengthens its feeling of standing above class differences and of representing the living conscience of society. As a result of its mixed descent, it feels the boundaries dividing the various ideologies and cultures more strongly than the earlier cultured strata and it gives a sharper edge to the social criticism, which it already felt called upon to make as the ally of the middle class. From the very beginning its task consisted in making clear the presuppositions of cultural values; it formulated the ideas which were at the root of the bourgeois outlook, it worked out the ideological content of the bourgeois attitude to life, in a world of practical business it fulfilled the function of contemplative thinking, of introversion and sublimation—it was, in short, the mouthpiece of the bourgeois ideology. But now that the bonds between the intelligentsia and the middle class have slackened, the self-imposed censorship of the ruling class turns into destructive criticism, and the principle of dynamics and renewal into that of anarchy. The cultural stratum still at one with the bourgeoisie was the pioneer of reforms; the intelligentsia which had deserted the bourgeoisie becomes an element of revolt and decomposition. Until about 1848 the intelligentsia is still the intellectual vanguard of the bourgeoisie, after 1848 it becomes, consciously or unconsciously, the champion of the working class. As a result of the insecurity of its own existence, it feels that it is to a certain extent in the same boat as the proletariat, and this feeling of solidarity increases its readiness to conspire, when occasion offers, against the bourgeoisie and to take part in preparing the anti-capitalistic revolution.

With the bohème the points of contact between the intelligentsia and the proletariat go far beyond this general feeling of sympathy. The bohemians are in fact themselves only a part of the proletariat. In certain respects they represent the consummation, but at the same time also a caricature of the intelligentsia. They complete the emancipation of the intelligentsia from the middle class, but at the same time they transform the fight against bourgeois conventions into an obsession, often into a kind of persecution mania. They realize, on the one hand, the ideal of absolute concentration on spiritual aims, but, on the other hand, they neglect the remaining values of life and deprive the mind, victorious over life, of the very purpose of its victory. Their independence of the bourgeois world turns out to be only a semblance of freedom, for they feel their estrangement from society as a heavy burden of guilt, unconfessed though it may be; their arrogance proves an overcompensation for an excess of weakness; their exaggerated self-assertion as a doubt in their own creative powers. In France this development takes place earlier than in England where, around the middle of the century, with Ruskin, J. S. Mill, Huxley, George Eliot and their adherents, the first representatives of an 'unattached', 'independently thinking' intelligentsia appear, but where, for the time being, there is no question either of a turning to proletarian revolution, or of the formation of a bohème. The connection with the middle class here continues to be so close that the intelligentsia prefers to take refuge in an 'aristocratic moralism',[161] than to make common cause with the broad masses. Even George Eliot regards as an essentially psychological and moral problem what is in reality a sociological problem, and looks in psychology for the answer to questions which can only be answered sociologically. She thereby leaves the path which is now trodden by the Russian novel and on which it achieves its consummation.

The modern Russian novel is in essentials the creation of the Russian intelligentsia, that is to say, of that intellectual élite which renounces official Russia and interprets literature as meaning above all social criticism and the novel as the 'social' novel. In Russia the novel as mere entertainment or pure analysis of character, with no claim to social significance and usefulness, is unknown until the beginning of the 'eighties. The nation is in such a violent ferment and political and social consciousness is so strongly developed in the reading public that it is quite impossible for a principle like 'art for art's sake' to arise here at all. In Russia the concept of the intelligentsia is always related to that of activism, and its connection with the democratic opposition is much more intimate than in the West. The conservative nationalists can in no sense be reckoned as belonging to this intransigent intelligentsia with its sectarian exclusiveness,[162] and even the greatest masters of the Russian novel, Dostoevsky and Tolstoy, only belong to it to a limited extent; in their critical attitude to society they are, however, very largely influenced by the way of thinking of the intelligentsia, and with their art they contribute to its destructive work, although they refuse personally to have anything to do with it.[163]

The whole of modern Russian literature arises from the spirit of opposition. It owes its first golden age to the literary activities of the progressive, cosmopolitan gentry who strive to obtain recognition for the ideas of the enlightenment and of democracy as against the despotism of the czars. In the age of Pushkin the liberal nobility, with its tendency to Western ideas, is the only cultured stratum of society in Russia. It is true that with the rise of commercial and industrial capitalism the class of intellectual workers, which had previously been made up mainly of officials and doctors, received a considerable influx of technicians, lawyers and journalists,[164] but literary production remained in the hands of the aristocratic officers who, finding no satisfaction in their profession, promised themselves more from the free bourgeois world than from the tottering feudalism of their time.[165] The reaction, which sets in with renewed strength after the defeat of the Decembrist Revolt, succeeds in scattering the rebels, but it does not succeed in preventing the formation of a new political and literary vanguard—that of the intelligentsia. With the rise of this cultured class the predominance of the nobility in Russian literature, which was all-powerful until the end of the 'eighties, comes to an end. The death of Pushkin marks the close of an age: intellectual leadership passes into the hands of the intelligentsia and remains there right up to the Bolshevist revolution.[166]

The new cultural élite is a mixed group, consisting of noble and plebeian elements, recruited from déclassés from above and below. Its members are, on the one hand, so-called 'conscious-stricken noblemen' whose outlook is still fairly close to that of the Decembrists and, on the other, the sons of small shopkeepers, subordinate civil servants, urban clergymen and emancipated

129

serfs who are usually described as 'people of mixed descent' and most of whom lead the uncertain life of 'free artists', students, private tutors and journalists. Until the middle of the century these plebeians are in a minority compared with the gentry, but they gradually increase in numbers and they end by absorbing all the other élements of the intelligentsia. The most important part in the new pattern is played by clergymen's sons who, owing to the natural antagonism between father and son, give most pointed expression to the anti-religious and anti-traditionalist convictions of the intelligentsia. They fulfil the same function as the pastors' sons in eighteenth-century Europe, where during the enlightenment the situation was similar to that prevailing in pre-revolutionary Russia. It is therefore no accident that two of the most important pioneers of Russian rationalism, Chernyshevsky and Dobrolyubov, are the sons of priests and emerge from the middle-class population of the great commercial cities.

Moscow University, with its student associations and cultural societies, is the centre of the new 'classless' intelligentsia. The contrast between the old, pleasure-seeking and blasé residence with its high officials and generals, and the modern university city with its youth capable of enthusiasm and eager for knowledge, denotes the origin of the cultural change that now takes place.[167] The poor student, dependent on himself, is the prototype of the new intelligentsia, just as the noble officer in the Guards was the representative of the old intellectual élite. The cultured society of Moscow continues to preserve its semi-aristocratic stamp for a time, however, and philosophical discussions still take place very largely in the *salons* until about the end of the 'forties,[168] but the latter no longer have an exclusive character and gradually lose their former importance. In the 'sixties, the democratization of literature and the formation of the new intelligentsia is complete. After the emancipation of the peasants it is considerably extended by the masses that crowd in from the ranks of the impoverished lower nobility, but the new elements do not alter the inner structure of the group. The ruined landowners are to some extent forced to do intellectual work and to adapt themselves to the way of life of the bourgeois intelligentsia, in order to support themselves. It is to be noted, however, that they not only add to the number of the progressive, cosmopolitan Westernizers, but to an equal, if not to a higher degree that of the Slavophils as well, thereby creating a certain balance between the two groups.

The intellectual reaction which the rationalism of the Westernized intelligentsia calls forth corresponds to the romantic historicism and traditionalism with which Western Europe had reacted to the Revolution half a century earlier. The Slavophils are the indirect and mostly unconscious intellectual heirs of Burke, de Bonald, de Maistre, Herder, Hamann, Moeser and Adam Mueller, just as the Westernizers are the disciples of Voltaire, the Encyclopaedists, German idealism and later, on the one hand, of the socialists Saint-Simon, Fourier and Comte, and on the other, of the materialists Feuerbach, Buechner, Vogt and Moleschott. They stress, in opposition to the cosmopolitan and atheistic free thought of the Westernizers, the value of national and religious traditions, and proclaim their mystical belief in the Russian peasant and their fidelity to the orthodox Church. As opposed to rationalism and positivism, they declare themselves believers in the irrational idea of 'organic' historical growth, and they represent the old Russia, with its 'genuine Christianity' and its freedom from Western individualism, as the ideal and the salvation of Europe, just as the Westernizers, for their part, see the ideal and salvation for Russia in Europe. Slavophilism itself is very old, indeed even older than the resistance to Peter the Great's reforms, but it begins its official existence only with the struggle against Belinsky. At any rate, the movement owes its fervour and its definite programme to the opposition to the 'men of the 'forties'. The leaders of this theoretically clarified and pro-grammatically conscious Slavophilism are, to begin with, mainly aristocratic landowners, still living under the old feudal condi-tions, who clothe their political and social conservatism in the ideology of 'holy Russia' and the 'messianic task of the Slav peoples'. Their cult of national traditions is mostly no more than a means of fighting the progressive ideas of the Westernizers, and their Rousseauist and romantic enthusiasm for the Russian peasant only the ideological form of their endeavour to hold fast to patriarchal-feudal conditions.

131

The Slavophil movement is not, however, wholly identical with conservatism and reaction. There are many real friends of the people among the Slavophils, just as there are many enemies of democracy among the Westernizers. Herzen himself is well known to have had certain reservations against the democratic institutions of the West. The first Slavophils, however, are opponents of czarist autocracy and attack the government of Nicholas I. It is true that the later Slavophils adopt a more positive attitude to czardom, the idea of which forms an integral component of their political theory and philosophy of history, but they continue to count democrats among their supporters. The Slavophil movement as a whole has to be divided into two stages, just as there are two different generations of Westernizers. For, just as the reformism and rationalism of the 'forties develops into the socialism and materialism of the 'sixties and 'seventies, so the Slavophilism of the feudal landowners changes into the panslavism and populism of Danilevsky, Grigoriev and Dostoevsky. The modern democratic trend is sharply opposed to the former aristocratic tendency.[169] After the liberation of the peasants many of the older writers turn away from the Westernized intellectuals and join the nationalists; so that it is hardly any longer possible to assert that 'conservative literature is notably weaker than progressive literature, both quantitatively and qualitatively'.[170]

The Slavophils and the Westernizers now differ more in their fighting methods than in their aims. The whole of intellectual Russia adopts the 'Slav idea'; all the intellectuals are patriots and prophets of the 'Russian mission'. They 'kneel in mystic adoration before the Russian sheepskin',[171] they study the Russian soul and develop an enthusiasm for 'ethnographical poetry'. Peter the Great's dictum, 'We need Europe for a few decades, then we shall be able to turn our backs on it', still accords with the opinion of most of the reformers. The very word 'narod', which means both 'people' and 'nation', makes it possible for the difference between democrats and nationalists to become blurred.[172] The Slavophil inclinations of the radicals are to be explained above all by the fact that the Russians, still in the very earliest stages of capitalism, are much more homogeneous as a nation, that is to say, much less divided by class differences, than the peoples of the West. The whole intellectual élite in Russia is Rousseauist in its outlook and is more or less hostile to art and sophisticated culture; it feels that the cultural traditions of the West, classical antiquity, the Roman Church, medieval scholasticism, the Renaissance and the Reformation, and partly even modern individualism, scienticism and aestheticism are an obstacle to the realization of its own aims.[173] The aesthetic utilitarianism of Belinsky, Chernyshevsky and Pisarev is just as anti-traditionalistic as Tolstoy's hostility to art. The rôles are not even exactly divided between Westernizers and Slavophils in the great controversy between subjectivism and objectivism, individualism and collectivism, freedom and authority, although the Westernizers naturally incline more to the liberal and the Slavophils more to the authoritarian ideal. But Belinsky and Herzen wrestle just as desperately and often just as helplessly with the problem of individual liberty as Dostoevsky or Tolstoy. The entire philosophical speculation of the Russians hinges on this problem and the danger of moral relativism, the spectre of anarchy, the chaos of crime, occupy and frighten all the Russian thinkers. The Russians see the great and crucial European question of the estrangement of the individual from society, the loneliness and isolation of modern man, as the problem of freedom. Nowhere has this problem been lived through more deeply, more intensively and more disturbingly than in Russia, and no one felt the responsibility involved in the attempt to solve it with greater anguish than Tolstoy and Dostoevsky. The hero of the *Memoirs from Underground*, Raskolnikov, Kirilov, Ivan Karamazov—they all wrestle with this problem, they all fight against the danger of being swallowed up in the abyss of unrestricted freedom, individual discretion and egoism. Dostoevsky's rejection of individualism, his criticism of rationalistic and materialistic Europe, his apotheosis of human solidarity and love, have no other purpose than to impede a development which must lead inevitably to Flaubert's nihilism. The Western novel ends with the description of the individual estranged from society and collapsing under the burden of his loneliness; the Russian novel depicts, from beginning to end, the fight against the demons which induce the individual to revolt against the world and the community of his fellow-men. This difference explains not only the problematic nature of characters such as Dostoevsky's Raskolnikov and Ivan Karamazov or Tolstoy's Pierre Bezukhov and Levin, not only these writers' gospel of love and faith, but the messianism of the whole of Russian literature.

The Russian novel is much more strictly tendentious than the novel of Western Europe. Social problems not only occupy much more space and a more central position, they maintain their predominance for a longer time and more undisputedly than in Western literature. The connection with the political and social questions of the day is closer here from the very outset than in the works of the French and English writers of the same period. In Russia despotism offers intellectual energies no other possibility of making themselves felt than through the medium of literature and the censorship forces social criticism into literary forms as the only possible outlet.[174] The novel, as the form of social criticism par excellence, here acquires an activisit, pedagogical and, indeed, prophetic character, such as it never possessed in the West, and the Russian writers still remain the teachers and prophets of their people, when the literati in Western Europe are already declining into absolute passivity and isolation. For the Russians, the nineteenth century is the age of enlightenment; they preserve the enthusiasm and optimism of the pre-revolutionary years a century longer than the peoples of the West. Russia did not experience the disillusionment of the treacherously defeated and adulterated European revolutions; there is no trace of the fatigue by which France and England are overcome after 1848. It is due to the youthful inexperience of the nation and its undefeated social idealism that, at a time when in France and England naturalism begins to develop into a passive impressionism, the naturalistic novel remains fresh and full of promise in Russia. Russian literature, which passes out of the hands of the tired and ill-fated gentry into those of a rising class, when the bourgeois cultured élite is already exhausted in the West and feels threatened by forces from below, not only overcomes the weariness of life which was beginning to make itself felt in the writings of the romantically inclined nobility, but also the mood of resignation and scepticism that dominates modern Western literature. In spite of its darker streaks, the Russian novel is the expression of an invincible optimism, evidence of a belief in the future of Russia and the human race; it is and remains inspired with a hopeful spirit of attack, an evangelical yearning for and certainty of redemption. This optimism is not by any means expressed in mere wish-fulfilment dreams and cheap 'happy endings', but in the certain faith that human sufferings and sacrifices have a meaning and are never in vain. The works of the great Russian novelists nearly always end in a conciliatory mood, though often very sadly; they are more serious than the novels of the French writers, but they are never so bitter, never so hopeless.

The miracle of the Russian novel consists in the fact that, in spite of its youth, it not only reaches the heights of the French and English novel, but takes over the lead from them and represents the most progressive and most vigorous literary form of the age. Compared with the works of Dostoevsky and Tolstoy, the whole of Western literature in the second half of the century seems weary and stagnant. *Anna Karenina* and *The Brothers Karamazov* mark the summit of European naturalism; they sum up and surpass the psychological achievements of the French and English novel without ever losing their feeling for the great superindividual relationships of life. Just as the social novel attains its perfection with Balzac, the 'Bildungsroman' with Flaubert, the picaresque novel with Dickens, so the psychological novel enters the phase of its full maturity with Dostoevsky and Tolstoy. These two novelists represent the close of the development which starts, on the one hand, with the sentimental novel of Rousseau, Richardson and Goethe, on the other, with the analytical novel of Marivaux, Benjamin Constant and Stendhal. Modern psychology begins with the description of the inner strife of the soul—of a dissension which cannot simply be reduced to a definite inner conflict. Antigone already wavers between duty and inclination, and Corneille's heroes can almost be said to know nothing but this struggle. Shakespeare makes the hero's indecision the main subject of the drama. The inhibitions are here not derived merely from a moral impulse, as in Sophocles and Corneille, but also from the nerves, that is, from an unconscious and uncontrolled region of the soul. But the antagonistic psychological inclinations still appear separated from one another and the characters' moral judgement on their own impulses is absolutely clear-cut and consistent. At most, they waver in their moral identification with one or the other part of their impulses. The disintegration of the personality, in which the emotional conflict goes so far that the individual is no longer clear about his own motives and becomes a problem to himself, does not take place until the beginning of the last century. The concomitants of modern capitalism, romanticism and the estrangement of the individual from society, first create the consciousness of spiritual dissension and hence the modern problematical character. The psychological contradictions in Shakespeare and the Elizabethans are mostly mere absurdities; they represent a stage of development *prior to* the synthesis of classicism. In other words: the dramatists have not yet learnt by experience how to draw characters who act uniformly and consistently, and they also attach no special importance to the uniformity of the total picture. The inconsistent characters of romantic literature, on the other hand, are the expression of a conscious and programmatically stressed reaction against the rationalism of classicistic psychology. Wild and fantastic figures are favoured, because chaotic feelings are considered more genuine and original than consistent and methodical reason. The most obvious, although still somewhat crude expression of the mind at variance with itself and no longer capable of being reduced to any rational unity is the idea of the 'double', which Dostoevsky takes over from the romantics as a standing requisite of character drawing and which he preserves to the end. It is, however, only the fight against romanticism and the constant wavering between the romantic and anti-romantic attitudes which brings about the absolute dissolution of the unity of the character, that is, the disintegration which consists not only in the incoherence of the constituents of the human soul, but also in their constant displacement and transformation, revaluation and reinterpretation. With Stendhal, who introduces this phase, we see the different components of the soul changing their nature before our very eyes. The provisional character of any description

136

of a spiritual condition and the indefinable quality of spiritual attitudes now becomes the criterion of any feasible psychology and only an iridescent and kaleidoscopic picture of the human soul is now regarded as artistically interesting. The final stage in this development is reached with the absolute incalculability and irrationality of Dostoevsky's characters. The aspect of 'You are not what you seem to be' now becomes the psychological norm, and the strange and uncanny, the demonic and inscrutable, in man is regarded from now onwards as the presupposition of his psychological significance. Compared with Dostoevsky's characters, the figures of older literature always seem more or less idyllic and non-committal. Today, of course, we realize that even Dostoevsky's psychology is still full of conventional traits, and that it makes the most abundant use of the remains of romantic gruesomeness and Byronism. We see that Dostoevsky is not a beginning but an end and that, for all his originality and productivity, he is quite willing to take over the achievements of the West European psychological novel and develop them consistently.

Dostoevsky discovers the most important principle of modern psychology: the ambivalence of the feelings and the divided nature of all the spiritual attitudes which express themselves in exaggerated and over-demonstrative forms. Not only love and hate, but also pride and humility, conceit and self-humiliation, cruelty and masochism, the yearning for the sublime and the 'nostalgia for filth', are interconnected in his characters; not only figures like Raskolnikov and Svidrigailov, but also Myshkin and Rogozhin, Ivan Karamazov and Smerdyakov, belong together as variations of one and the same principle; every impulse, every feeling, every thought, produces its opposite, as soon as it emerges from the consciousness of these people. Dostoevsky's heroes are always confronted with alternatives, between which they ought to but cannot choose; hence their thinking, their self-analysis and self-criticism is a constant raving and raging against themselves. The parable of the swine possessed by evil refers not only to the characters of *The Possessed*, but more or less to the whole collection of people he describes in his novels. His novels take place on the eve of the Last Judgement; everything is in a state of the most fearful tension, of the most mortal fear, and the wildest chaos; everything is waiting to be purified, reassured and saved by a miracle—waiting for a solution based not on the power and acuteness of the mind and the dialectic of the reason, but on renunciation of this power and the sacrifice of reason. In the idea of intellectual suicide for which Dostoevsky pleads, is expressed the whole questionableness of his philosophy, in which he attempts to solve real problems and correctly posed questions in an absolutely unreal and irrational way.

Dostoevsky owes the depth and refinement of his psychology to the intensity with which he experiences the problematical nature of the modern intellectual, whereas the naïvety of his moral philosophy comes from his anti-rationalistic escapades, from his betrayal of the reason and his inability to resist the temptations of romanticism and abstract idealism. His mystical nationalism, his religious orthodoxy and his intuitive ethics form an intellectual unity, and obviously originate in the same experience, the same spiritual shock. In his youth, Dostoevsky belonged to the radicals and was a member of the socialistically-minded circle around Petrashevsky. He was condemned to death for the part he played here, and after all the preparations for his execution, he was pardoned and sent to Siberia. This experience and the years of imprisonment seem to have broken his rebelliousness. When he returns to St. Petersburg, after an absence of ten years, he is no longer a socialist and a radical, even though he is still far removed from his later political and religious mysticism. Only the terrible privations of the following period, his worsening illness and his vagabondage in Europe succeed in breaking his resistance completely. The author of *Crime and Punishment* and *The Idiot* already seeks for protection and peace in religion, but it is only the creator of *The Possessed* and *The Brothers Karamazov* who becomes an enthusiastic apologist of the ecclesiastical and secular authorities and a preacher of positive dogma. It is only in his later years that Dostoevsky becomes the moralist, the mystic and the reactionary that he is often summarily described to be.[175] But even with this qualification, it is not easy to classify him politically. His criticism of socialism is pure nonsense; the world he describes cries out for socialism, however, and for the deliverance of mankind from poverty and humiliation. In his case, too, one must speak of the 'triumph of realism', of the victory of the clear-sighted, realistically-minded artist over the bewildered, romantic politician. But with Dostoevsky the situation is much more complicated than with Balzac. In his art there is a deep sympathy and solidarity with the 'insulted and injured', which is completely lacking in Balzac, and in his work there is something in the nature of a nobility of poverty, even though there is much in his novels about the poor that is based only on literary convention and a stereotyped romantic pattern. Dostoevsky is at least one of the few genuine writers on poverty, for he writes not merely out of sympathy with the poor, like George Sand or Eugène Sue, or as a result of vague memories, like Dickens, but as one who has spent most of his life in need and has literarily starved from time to time. That is why, even when he is speaking of his religious and moral problems, the impression Dostoevsky makes is more rousing and revolutionizing than when George Sand and Dickens speak of the economic distress and social injustice of their time. But he is in no sense a spokesman of the revolutionary masses. In spite of his idealization of the 'people' and his Slavophil convictions, he has no intimate contact with the industrial proletariat and the peasantry.[176] It is only to the intellectual proletariat that he really feels drawn. He calls himself a 'literary proletarian' and a 'post-horse', who always works under the pressure of a contract, who has never in his life sold a work other than for payment in advance and often has no idea of the end of a chapter, when the beginning of it is already with the printers. He complains that work has stifled and consumed him; he has worked until his brain has become dull and broken. If only he could write a single novel as Turgenev and Tolstoy write their works! But proudly and challengingly he calls himself a 'man of letters', and considers himself the representative of a new generation and a new social class, which have never before had a chance to speak their mind in literature. And despite his opposition to the political aspirations of the intelligentsia, he is the first valid representative of this class in the history of the Russian novel. Gogol, Goncharov and Turgenev still express the outlook of the gentry, although they stand to some extent for very progressive ideas and, in contrast to their class-conditioned interests, are among the pioneers of the transformation of Russia into a bourgeois society. Dostoevsky rightly considers Tolstoy one of the representatives of this 'landowners' literature' and calls him the 'historian of the aristocracy', who keeps the form of the Aksakovian family chronicle in his great novels, above all in *War and Peace*.[177]

Most of Dostoevsky's heroes, especially Raskolnikov, Ivan Karamazov, Shatov, Kirilov, Stepan Verhovensky, are bourgeois intellectuals and Dostoevsky bases his analysis of society on their point of view, even though he never expressly identifies himself with them. But what decides the world-view of a writer is not so much whose side he supports, as through whose eyes he looks at the world. Dostoevsky envisages the social problems of his time, first of all the atomization of society and the deepening gulf between the classes, from the standpoint of the intelligentsia, and sees the solution in the reunion of the educated with the simple, faithful people, from whom they have become estranged. Tolstoy reviews the same problems from the standpoint of the nobility and bases his hopes for the recovery of society on an understanding between the landowners and the peasants. His thinking is still associated with patriarchal-feudal concepts, and even those characters who come nearest to the realization of his ideas, Levin and Pierre Bezukhov, are at best benefactors of the people, not really democrats. In Dostoevsky's world, on the other hand, a perfect intellectual democracy predominates. All his characters, both the rich and the poor, the aristocrats and the plebeians, wrestle with the same moral problems. The rich Prince Myshkin and the poor student Raskolnikov are both homeless vagabonds, déclassés and outlaws with no place in modern bourgeois society. All his heroes stand to some extent outside this society and form a classless world, in which only spiritual relationships prevail. They are present in all their activities with their whole nature, their whole soul, and in the midst of the routine of the modern world they represent a purely intellectual, spiritual, Utopian reality. 'We have no class interests, because strictly speaking we have no classes and because the Russian soul is wider than class differences, class interests and class law,' Dostoevsky writes in

An Author's Diary, and nothing is more characteristic of his way of thinking than the contradiction between this assertion and the consciousness of his class-determined divergence from his aristocratic colleagues. The same Dostoevsky who draws such a sharp dividing line between himself and the representatives of the 'landowners' literature' and bases his *raison d'être* as a writer on his plebeian intellectualism, denies .the very existence of classes and believes in the primacy of a-social spiritual relationships.

Attention has repeatedly been drawn to the similarity between the social position of Dostoevsky and Dickens. It has been noticed that both were the sons of fathers with no very firm roots in society, and that they both knew the feeling of social insecurity and uprootedness from their youth upwards.[178] Dostoevsky was the son of a staff-doctor and of a merchant's daughter. His father acquired a small property and had his sons educated in a school otherwise attended only by the children of nobles. The mother died early and the father, who gave himself up to drink, was killed by his own peasants, whom he is said to have treated very badly. Dostoevsky now sank from a relatively respectable social level to that of the intellectual proletariat by which he felt alternately repelled and attracted. Nothing is more probable than that there was, in fact, a connection between the contradictory and often unclarified social outlook of both Dostoevsky and Dickens and the wavering social position of their fathers and their own early acquaintance with the feeling of having fallen in the social scale.

Dostoevsky's position in the history of the social novel is marked above all by the fact that the first naturalistic representation of the modern metropolis with its petty bourgeois and proletarian population, its small shop-keepers and officials, its students and prostitutes, idlers and down and outs, is his creation. Balzac's Paris was still a romantic wilderness, the scene of fantastic adventures and miraculous encounters, a theatrical setting painted in a chiaroscuro of contrasts, a fairyland in which dazzling riches and picturesque poverty live next door to each other. Dostoevsky, on the other hand, paints the picture of the big city in altogether sombre colours, as a place of utterly dark, colourless misery. He shows its drab official buildings, its gloomy gin-shops, its furnished rooms, these 'coffins' of rooms, as he calls them, in which the saddest victims of the life of a big city pass their days. All this has an unmistakable social significance and a political point; but Dostoevsky attempts to take away the class-determined co-efficients from his characters. He demolishes the economic and social barriers between them and mixes them all up one with another, as if something in the nature of a common human destiny really did exist. His spiritualism and nationalism fulfil the same function: they create the legend of a moral being that leads a life ordered in accordance with higher laws and beyond the limitations of birth, class and education. With Goncharov, Turgenev and Tolstoy the class-determined features of the characters are not effaced; the fact that they belong to the nobility, the middle class or the common people is not overlooked or forgotten for a moment. Dostoevsky, on the other hand, often neglects these differences, and he sometimes seems to pass them over deliberately. The fact that the class character of his figures makes itself felt all the same, and that we feel, above all, his intellectuals as an exactly defined social group, is part of that triumph of realism which makes Dostoevsky a materialist in spite of himself.

This 'materialism' is, however, only one of the invisible and often unconscious presuppositions of his intellectuality—an intellectuality which is a real passion, a demoniac compulsion to reduce experience to its ultimate threads, to probe feelings to their last impulse, to think deeper and deeper, to experiment with all the consequences of thought and to descend into its deepest subconscious sources. Dostoevsky's heroes are impassioned, fearless, maniacal thinkers wrestling with their ideas and visions just as desperately as the heroes of the novels of chivalry wrestled with giants and monsters. They suffer, murder, and die for ideas; for them life is a philosophical task, and thought is the one and only constant occupation in their life, its sole content. They struggle with real monsters—with still unborn, indefinable ideas to which as yet no shape can be given, with problems which cannot be solved, cannot even be formulated. Dostoevsky is not only the first modern novelist to know how to give as concrete and evident form to an intellectual experience as to a sensual experience, but he also advances into regions of the mind into which no one before him had ever ventured. He discovers a new dimension, a new depth, a new intensity of thought. To be sure, the discovery owes its effect of novelty above all to the fact that romanticism has accustomed us to keep thoughts and feelings, ideas and passions in strictly water-tight compartments, and only regard feelings and passions as fit subjects for artistic treatment.[179] The real innovation in Dostoevsky's intellectual constitution is the fact that he is a romantic in the world of thought, and that the movement of thought has the same motive power and the same emotional, not to say pathological, impetus in him as the flood and stress of the feelings had in the romantics. The synthesis of intellectualism and romanticism is the epoch-making innovation in the art of Dostoevsky; it gives rise to the most progressive literary form of the second half of the last century, the form which best met the needs of this age with its indissoluble ties with romanticism and its impetuous striving after intellectualism.

Dostoevsky did not, however, move only on the heights, but also in the lowlands of romanticism. His work represented not merely the continuation of the romantic literature of confession, but also that of the romantic thriller.[180] In this respect, too, he was a genuine contemporary of Dickens—a writer who showed himself as indiscriminate in his choice of methods as the other purveyors of the serial novel. Perhaps he would actually have avoided certain lapses of taste and inaccuracies, if he had been able to work like Tolstoy and Turgenev. The melodramatic quality of his style was, nevertheless, inseparably bound up with his conception of the psychological novel and the drastic methods he employed were not merely a vehicle of thrilling exposition, but were intended to contribute to the creation of that over-heated spiritual atmosphere without which the dramatic situations of his novels would be quite unthinkable. One can, if one likes, think of *The Brothers Karamazov* as a shilling-shocker, of *Crime and Punishment* as a detective novel, of *The Possessed* as a penny-dreadful, and *The Idiot* as a thriller; murder and crime, mysteries and surprises, melodrama and atrocities, morbid and macabre moods, play a leading part in them: but it would be a mistake to assume that all this is only to compensate the reader for the abstractness of the intellectual content, the author wants rather to induce the feeling that the spiritual processes on which the story hinges are just as elemental as the most primitive impulses. In Dostoevsky we find again the whole gallery of heroes from the romantic adventure novel: the handsome, strong, mysterious and lonely Byronic hero (Stavrogin), the wild, unbridled, dangerous but good-natured man of instinct (Rogozhin and Dimitri Karamazov), the angelic figures of light (Myshkin and Alyosha), the inwardly pure prostitute (Sonya and Nastasya Philippovna), the old debauchee (Fedor Karamazov), the escaped convict (Fedka), the dissolute drunkard (Lebyadkin), etc., etc. We find all the requisites of the thriller and the adventure novel: the seduced and forsaken girl, the secret marriage, the anonymous letters, the mysterious murder, the madness, the fainting fits, the sensational slap on the face and, above all and repeatedly, the explosive scenes of social scandals.[181] These scenes best show what Dostoevsky is capable of developing from the methods of the thriller. They not only serve, as one might think, to produce effective endings and brilliant 'coups de théâtre', but are present, as it were, from the very beginning as a threatening danger and produce the feeling that the great passions and elemental spiritual relationships always approach the limits of the conventional and the socially permissible. The Utopian isle of spiritual beings, on which Dostoevsky's heroes lead their moral life, turns out to be a narrow cage; wherever the immanence of their existence is broken through, a social scandal results. It is a characteristic feature of these scandal scenes that they take place in the presence of the most mixed society conceivable, with the participation of the socially most incompatible elements. Both in the great scandal scene in the house of Nastasya Philippovna, in *The Idiot*, and in that which takes place in the house of Varvara Petrovna, in *The Possessed*, all the participants in the drama are gathered together, as if the author were trying to prove that social differentiation is least capable of withstanding the universal dissolution. Each of these scenes seems like a fear-ridden dream, in which a crowd of human beings are squeezed together in an incredibly narrow room, and the nightmarish character which is peculiar to them shows what an uncanny power society, with its differences of class and rank, its taboos and vetos, had for Dostoevsky.

Most critics emphasize the dramatic structure of Dostoevsky's great novels; but they usually interpret this formal peculiarity merely as a means of achieving theatrical effects, and they contrast it with the broad-surging, epic flow of Tolstoy's novels. Dostoevsky does not, however, use a dramatic technique merely to create climaxes, in which the threads of the plot converge and the threatening conflict breaks out, he uses it rather to fill the whole plot with dramatic life and to express a world-view completely different from the epic outlook on life. According to Dostoevsky, the meaning of existence is not contained in its temporality, in the rise and fall of its aims, in memories and illusions, not in the years, days and hours which descend on one another and bury us, but in those high moments in which human souls are stripped bare and seem to be reduced to simple, unequivocal formulae, in which they feel they are their real unquestionable selves and in which they declare themselves one with themselves and one with their destiny. That there are such moments is the basis of Dostoevsky's tragic optimism, of that reconciliation with fate, which the Greeks called the catharsis in their tragedies. This is also the basis of his philosophy and its opposition to the pessimism and nihilism of Flaubert. Dostoevsky always described the feeling of greatest happiness and the most perfect harmony as an experience of timelessness; thus, above all, Myshkin's condition before his epileptic fits and Kirilov's 'five seconds', the ecstasy of which would, as he says, have been intolerable for any greater length of time. In order to describe the kind of existence that culminates in such moments, the Flaubertian conception of the novel, based entirely on the feeling of time, had to be changed so fundamentally that the result often seemed to have hardly anything in common with the usual idea of the novel. It is true that Dostoevsky's form represents the direct continuation of the social and psychological novel, but it also signifies the beginning of a new development. What is usually described as its dramatic structure depends on a formal principle quite different from that of the unity of the romantic novel which superseded the old picaresque form. It represents rather a return to the picaresque novel, inasmuch as its dramatic scenes are scattered and form several independent focal points. With this abolition of continuity in favour of a series of substantial, expressive, but mosaic-fashion combined episodes, it anticipates the formal principles of the modern expressionistic novel. The narrative recedes in favour of the explication, the psychological analysis and the philosophical discussion, and the novel develops into a collection of dialogue scenes and internal monologues to which the author adds an accompaniment of commentaries and digressions.

This method is often as remote from the style of naturalism as from the novel as an epic genre. Dostoevsky represents, as far as sharpness of psychological observation is concerned, the most highly developed form of the naturalistic novel, but if one understands by naturalism the representation of the normal, the average and the everyday, then one is bound to see in his fondness for situations with a quality of dreamlike exaggeration and fantastically overdone characters a reaction against naturalism. Dostoevsky himself defines his position in the history of literature with perfect exactness: 'I am called', he says, 'a psychologist, that is wrong, I am only a realist on a higher level, in other words, I describe all the depths of the human soul.' These depths are, for him, the irrational, the demonic, the dreamlike and ghostlike in man; they call for a naturalism that is not the truth of the surface; they point to phenomena, in which the elements of real life intermingle, displace and outbid each other in a fantastic way. 'I love realism in art beyond all measure,' he declares, 'the realism which approaches the fantastic. . . . What can be more fantastic and unexpected for me than reality? In fact, what can be more improbable than reality?' There could be no more exact definition of expressionism and surrealism. That which in Dickens is still a merely occasional and usually unconscious contact with the no man's land between reality and dream, experience and vision, is here developed into a permanent openness of the spirit to the 'mysteries of life'. The break with scientism, which was expressed in nineteenth-century naturalism, is here being made ready. A new spiritualism is in process of arising from the reaction against the scientific outlook, from the revolt against naturalism, from the distrust in the rationalistic mastery of the problems of life. Life itself is felt to be something essentially irrational, mysterious voices are supposed to be audible from all directions, and art becomes the echo of these voices.

In spite of the deepest conceivable antithesis, there is a basic unity between Dostoevsky and Tolstoy in their attitude to the problem of individualism and freedom. Both regard the emancipation of the individual from society, his loneliness and isolation, as the greatest possible evil. Both desire to ward off the chaos that threatens to invade the individual estranged from society by all the means at their disposal. Above all in Dostoevsky, everything hinges on the problem of freedom, and his great novels are fundamentally nothing but analyses and interpretations of this idea. The problem itself was by no means new; it had always occupied the romantics, and from 1830 onwards it had held a central place in political and philosophical thought. For romanticism, freedom meant the victory of the individual over convention; it regarded a personality as free and creative only if it had the intellectual force and courage to disregard the moral and aesthetic prejudices of its own age. Stendhal formulated the problem as that of the genius, especially that of Napoleon, for whom success, as he thought, was a question of the ruthless enforcement of his will, of his great personality and impetuous nature. The arbitrariness of the genius, and the victims which it demands, seemed to him the price the world has to pay for the sight of its spiritual heroes. Dostoevsky's Raskolnikov represents the next stage in the development. He stands for an abstract, virtuoso-like form, as it were a play form, of the individual genius. The personality requires its victims no longer in the interest of a higher idea, of an objective goal, or a materially valuable achievement, but merely in order to prove that it is capable of free and sovereign action. The deed itself becomes absolutely immaterial; the question that is to be settled is a purely formal one: is personal freedom a value in itself? Dostoevsky's answer is by no means so clear-cut as it might appear to be at first sight. Individualism certainly leads to anarchy and chaos—but where then do coercion and order lead to? The problem is given its final and deepest setting in the story of *The Grand Inquisitor*, and the solution to which Dostoevsky comes can be regarded as the sum-total of his whole philosophy

147

of morals and religion. The abolition of freedom produces rigid institutions and replaces religion by the Church, the individual by the state, the restlessness of questioning and seeking by the reassurances of dogma. Christ signifies inward freedom but, therefore, an endless struggle; the Church implies an inner compulsion, but also peace and security. One can see how dialectically Dostoevsky thinks, and how difficult it is to give a clear definition of his moral and socio-political views. The reactionary and dogmatist of ill-repute ends his work with an open question.

It is true that the problem of freedom does not play anything like so important a part in Tolstoy's work as in that of Dostoevsky, but even with him it forms the key to an understanding of his psychologically most interesting and morally most revealing characters. Levin, above all, is wholly conceived as the exponent of this problem and the violence of his inner struggles shows how seriously Tolstoy wrestled with the idea of the estrangement and the spectre of the individual left to his own devices. Dostoevsky was right: *Anna Karenina* is not an innocuous book at all. It is full of doubts, scruples and apprehensions. Here too the basic idea, and the motif which connects the story of Anna Karenina with that of Levin, is the problem of the detachment of the individual from society and the danger of homelessness. The same fate to which Anna falls victim as a result of her adultery, threatens Levin as a result of his individualism, his unconventional outlook on life and his strange problems and doubts. Both are threatened by the danger of being expelled from the society of normal, respectable people. Only whereas Anna forgoes the consent of society from the very outset, Levin does everything in order not to lose the hold which he has on society. He bears the yoke of his marriage, manages his estate, like his neighbours, submits to the conventions and prejudices of his environment, in short, he is prepared to do anything, merely not to become an uprooted outlaw, an eccentric and a crank.[182]

But the anti-individualism of Dostoevsky and Tolstoy reveals the whole difference in their way of thought. Dostoevsky's objections are of a more irrational and mystic nature; he interprets the 'principium individuationis' as a defection from the world-spirit, from the prime original, from the divine idea, which make themselves known in a concrete historical form in the common people, the nation and the social community. Tolstoy, on the other hand, rejects individualism on purely rational and eudemonist grounds; personal detachment from society can bring man no happiness and no satisfaction; he can find comfort and contentment only in self-denial and in devotion to others.

In the relationship between Tolstoy and Dostoevsky the significant, paradigmatic, fundamentally typical spiritual relationship is repeated which existed between Voltaire and Rousseau and which has an analogy in that which existed between Goethe and Schiller.[183] In all these cases rationalism and irrationalism, sensuality and intellectuality, or as Schiller himself puts it, the naïve and the sentimental, confront each other. In all three cases the conflict of outlook can be traced back to the social gap between the protagonists; in each an aristocrat or a patrician confronts a plebeian and a rebel. Tolstoy's aristocratic nature is, above all, responsible for the fact that his whole art and thought are rooted in the idea of the physical, the organic and the natural. Dostoevsky's spiritualism, his speculative mind, his dynamic, dialectical mode of thinking, can be traced back just as definitely to his bourgeois descent and plebeian uprootedness. The aristocrat owes his position to his mere existence, his birth, his race, whereas the plebeian owes it to his talent, his personal ability and achievements. The relationship between the feudal lord and the scribe has not changed much in the course of the centuries— even though some of the lords have become 'scribes' themselves.

The contrast between Tolstoy's discretion and Dostoevsky's exhibitionism, between the restraint of the one and the 'dancing about naked in public' of the other—as someone says in *The Possessed*—is attributable to the same social gap as separated Voltaire from Rousseau. It is more difficult to ascribe to definite sociological causes such qualities of style and taste as moderation, discipline and order, on the one side, and shapelessness, chaos and anarchy, on the other. In certain circumstances extravagance is just as characteristic of the aristocratic as of the plebeian attitude, and the bourgeois philosophy of art often shows, as we know, just as rigoristic tendencies as that of the courtly class. As far as the composition of his works is concerned, Tolstoy is often just as extravagant and arbitrary as Dostoevsky; in this respect they are both anarchists. Tolstoy is only more restrained in his exposure of the 'depths' of the soul and more discriminating in the means he uses to obtain emotional effects. His art is much more elegant, much more settled and much more graceful than that of Dostoevsky; he has been rightly called a child of the eighteenth century, in contrast to this typical representative of the nervous nineteenth century. Compared with the romantic, mystical 'dionysianly' ecstatic Dostoevsky, he always seems more or less classical, or, to keep to Nietzsche's terminology, 'apollonian', plastic, statuesque. In contrast to Dostoevsky's problematical nature, his whole character has a positive quality in the sense understood by Goethe when he said he wanted to hear other people's opinions expressed in a 'positive' form, since he had enough 'problems' in himself already. This might well have been said by Tolstoy, if not in the same words, for he did, in fact, once say something very similar in connection with Dostoevsky. He compared Dostoevsky with a horse that makes a quite magnificent impression at first sight and seems to be worth a thousand roubles; but suddenly one notices that it has something wrong with its legs and limps, and one concludes with regret that it is not worth twopence. There was indeed 'something wrong' with Dostoevsky's legs and, compared with the robust and healthy Tolstoy, there always seems something pathological about him, just as there does about Rousseau when compared with Voltaire, the well-balanced man of reason. But the categories cannot be divided so sharply as in the case of Voltaire and Rousseau. Tolstoy himself manifests a whole series of Rousseauist characteristics and in some respects stands closer to Rousseauism than Dostoevsky. His striving for simplicity, naturalness and truthfulness is merely a variant of Rousseau's discomfort with culture, and his yearning for the idyllic life of the patriarchal village no more than the renewal of the old romantic antagonism to modern civilization. It is not for nothing that he quotes Lichtenberg's remark that humanity will be finished when there are no more savages.

But this Rousseauism is again merely an expression of Tolstoy's fear of loneliness, uprootedness and social homelessness. He

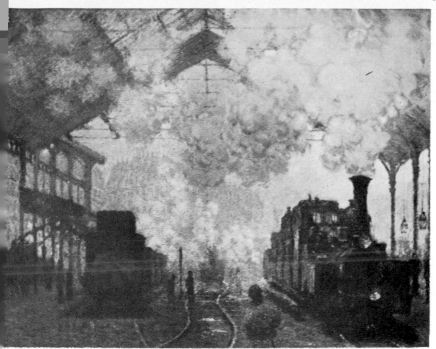

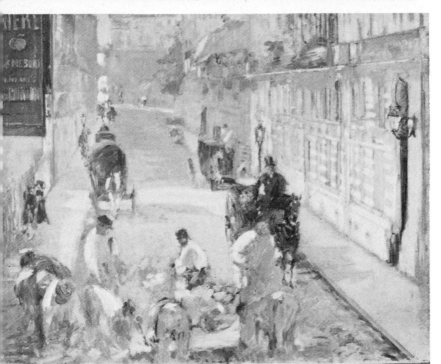

ATMOSPHERICAL EFFECTS

1. MONET: GARE SAINT-LAZARE IN PARIS. *1877. New York, Maurice Wertheim Collection.*

2. MANET: THE ROAD-MENDERS OF THE RUE DE BERNE. *1878. London, formerly Courtauld Collection.*

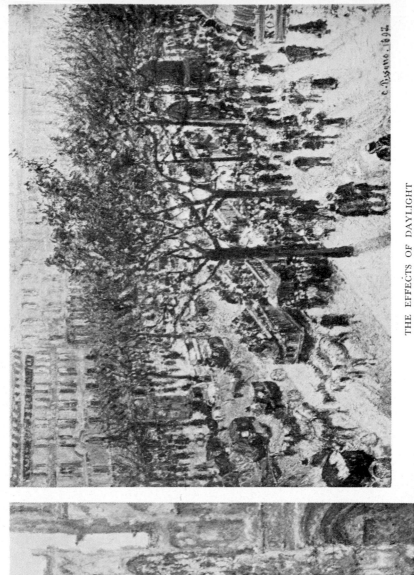

THE EFFECTS OF DAYLIGHT

1. MONET: ROUEN CATHEDRAL.
FORENOON. 1894. Paris, Louvre.

2. PISSARRO: BOULEVARD DES
ITALIENS, AFTERNOON. 1897.

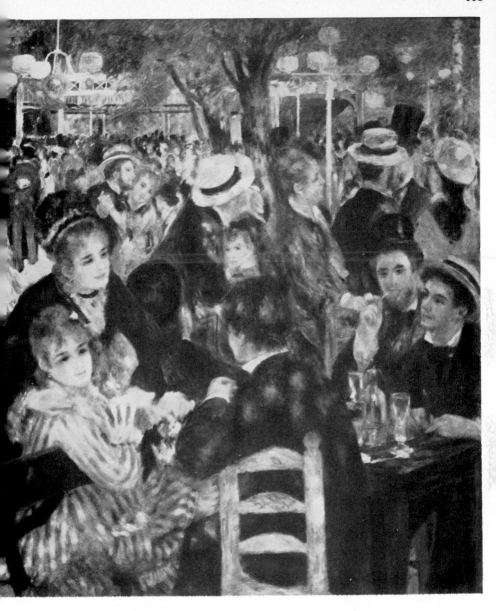

SUNSHINE AND SHADE

RENOIR: DANCING IN THE MOULIN DE LA GALETTE (*Detail*). *1876. Paris, Louvre.*

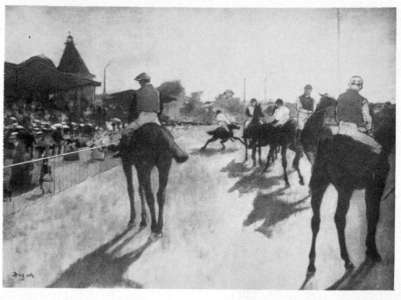

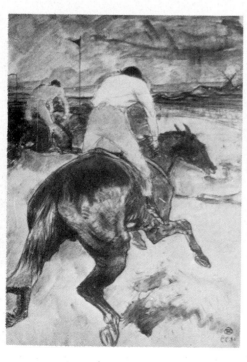

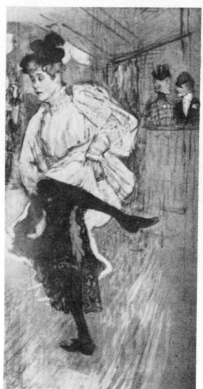

IMPRESSIONISM OF MOVEMENT

1. DEGAS: BEFORE THE TRIBUNES. *About 1871. Paris, Louvre.*
2. TOULOUSE-LAUTREC: THE JOCKEY. *1899.*
3. TOULOUSE-LAUTREC: JANE AVRIL DANCING. *1892. Paris, Louvre.*

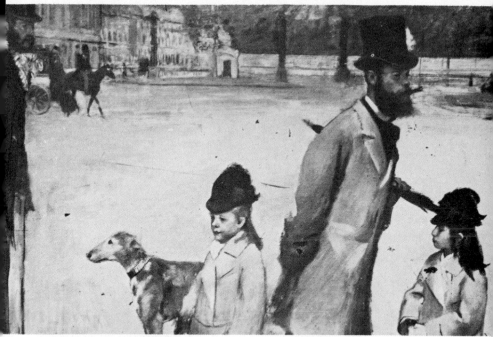

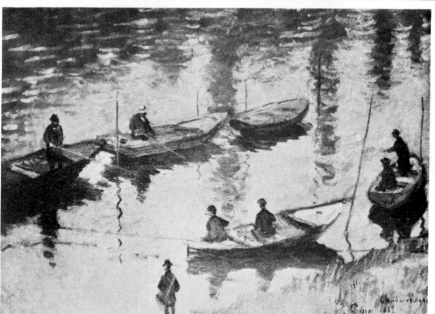

THE ACCIDENTAL CHARACTER OF THE IMPRESSIONISTIC REPRESENTATION
OF REALITY

1. DEGAS: PLACE DE LA CONCORDE. *About 1873. Berlin, Gerstenberg Collection.*

2. MONET: ANGLERS NEAR POISSY. *1882.*

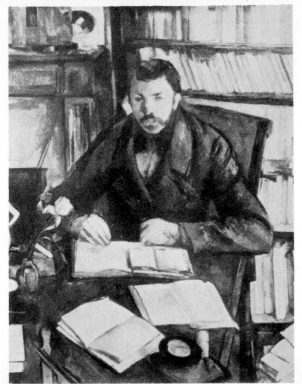

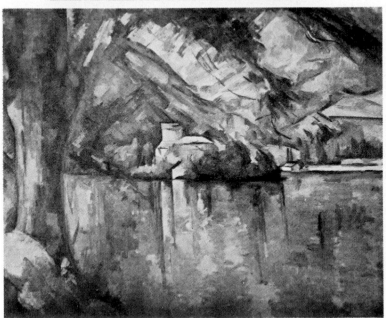

THE SYNTHESIS OF CÉZANNE AS TRANSITION FROM IMPRESSIONISM TO CUBISM

1. CÉZANNE: GUSTAVE GEFFROY. *1895. Paris, Lecomte-Pellerin Collection.*

2. CÉZANNE: LAC D'ANNECY. *1897. London, Courtauld Collection.*

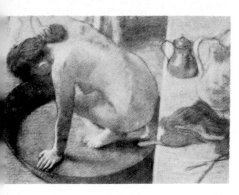
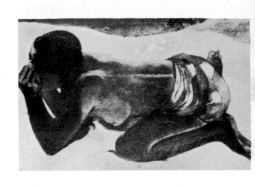
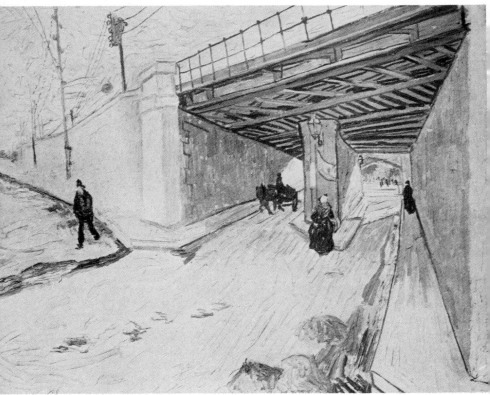

THE STYLIZATION OF GAUGUIN AND VAN GOGH AS TRANSITION FROM
IMPRESSIONISM TO EXPRESSIONISM

1. DEGAS: THE TUB. *About 1895. Paris, Louvre.*

2. GAUGUIN: OTAHI.

3. VAN GOGH: THE RAILWAY BRIDGE OF ARLES. *1888. Porto Ronco, E. M.
Remarque Collection.*

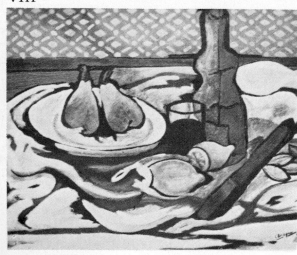

1. GEORGES BRAQUE: STILL LIFE. *Paris, Musée National d'Art moderne.*

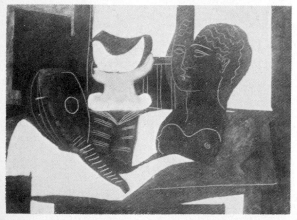

2. PICASSO: TÊTE ANTIQUE. *1925. Paris, Musée National d'Art moderne.*

3. PICASSO: AUBADE. *1942. Paris, Musée National d'Art moderne.*

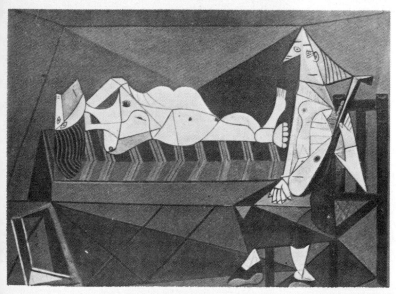

condemns modern culture on account of the differentiation and segregation which it produces, and the art of Shakespeare, Beethoven and Pushkin, because it splits men up into different strata instead of uniting them. That which might be spoken of as collectivism and the fight against class distinctions in Tolstoy's theories, has hardly anything to do, however, with democracy and socialism; it is more the nostalgia of a lonely intellectual for a community from which he awaits above all his own redemption. —When Christ called upon the rich young man to distribute all his possessions among the poor, he wanted, according to Henry George's interpretation, to help the rich young man, not the poor. Tolstoy also thought that it was the 'rich young man' who needed helping. Self-perfection and spiritual salvation are his own goal. This spiritualism and self-centredness explain the unreal, Utopian character of his social gospel and the inner contradictions of his political doctrine. It is this private moral ideal that determines his quietism, his rejection of violent resistance to evil and his endeavour to reform souls, instead of social realities. 'Nothing does more harm to men', he writes in his appeal 'To the Working Class' after the Revolution of 1905, 'than the idea that the causes of their distress lie not in themselves but in external conditions.' Tolstoy's passive attitude to external reality is in accordance with the pacifism of the saturated ruling class and, with its brooding, self-accusing, self-torturing moralism, it expresses an approach completely alien to the thinking and feeling of the common people.

But Tolstoy can no more be forced into a narrow political category than Dostoevsky. He is an incorruptible observer of social reality, a sincere friend of truth and justice and an unsparing critic of capitalism, although he judges the inadequacies and sins of modern society purely and simply from the point of view of the peasantry and agriculture in general. He fails, on the other hand, to recognize the real causes of the grievances and he preaches a morality which implies an *a priori* renunciation of all political activity.[184] Tolstoy is not only no revolutionary, but he is a decided enemy of all revolutionary attitudes; what distinguishes him, however, from the advocates of 'order' and appeasement in the West, the Balzacs, Flauberts and Goncourts, is the fact that he shows even less understanding for the terrorism of the government than for that of the revolutionaries. The murder of Alexander II leaves him quite unmoved, but he protests against the execution of the assassins.[185] In spite of his prejudices and errors, Tolstoy represents an enormous revolutionary force. His fight against the lies of the police state and the Church, his enthusiasm for the community of the peasantry and the example of his own life are, whatever may have been the inner motives of his 'conversion' and his ultimate flight, among the ferments which undermined the old society and promoted not merely the Russian revolution but also the anti-capitalistic revolutionary movement in the whole of Europe. In the case of Tolstoy one can, in fact, speak not only of a 'triumph of realism', but also of a 'triumph of socialism', not only of the unprejudiced description of society by an aristocrat, but of the revolutionary influence of a reactionary.

Its uncompromising rationalism preserves Tolstoy's art and philosophical doctrine from the fate of sterility and ineffectiveness. His sharp and sober eye for physical and psychical facts, and his aversion to lying to himself and others, keep his religiosity free from all mysticism and dogmatism and allows his belief in Christian morality to develop into a political factor of great influence. Dostoevsky's enthusiasm for Russian orthodoxy is just as foreign to him as the ecclesiastical bias of the Slavophils in general. He reaches his faith by a rational, pragmatic and thoroughly unspontaneous way.[186] His so-called conversion is an entirely rational process, which takes place without any direct religious experience. It was, as he says in his *Confession*, 'a feeling of fear, of being orphaned and lonely' that made him a Christian. Not a mystical experience of God and the supernatural, but dissatisfaction with himself, the attempt to find a purpose and an aim in life, despair at his own nothingness and instability, and, above all, his boundless fear of death turn him into a believer. He becomes the apostle of love, because he himself is lacking in love, he glorifies human solidarity, to make up for his mistrust of and contempt for man, and he proclaims the immortality of the human soul, because he cannot bear the thought of death. But his flight from the world has more the character of aristocratic lordliness than of Christian humility; he renounces the world because it cannot be completely mastered and possessed.

The concept of grace is the only irrational element in Tolstoy's religious philosophy.—He admits into his 'folk tales' an old legend based on medieval sources: Long ago there lived a pious hermit on a lonely island. One day fishermen landed near his hut, amongst them an old man who was so simple-minded that he could barely express himself, indeed he could not even pray. The hermit was profoundly upset by such ignorance and with great trouble and pains taught him the Lord's prayer. The old man thanked him kindly and left the island with the other fishermen. After some time, when the boat had already vanished in the distance, the holy man suddenly saw a human figure on the horizon walking towards the island on the surface of the water. Soon he recognized the old man, his pupil, and went towards him, speechless and perplexed, to meet him as he set foot on the island. Stammering, the old man gave him to understand that he had forgotten the prayer. '*You* do not need to pray,' replied the hermit, and left the old man hurrying back over the water to his fishing boat.—The meaning of this story lies in the idea of a certainty of salvation which is tied to no moral criteria. In another story of his later years, *Father Sergius*, Tolstoy represents the theme from the opposite angle; the grace which is bestowed on one man without effort, and apparently without merit, is denied to another, in spite of all manner of torment and agony, in spite of the most superhuman sacrifices and the most heroic self-conquest. This conception of grace, which places election above merit and equates predestination with gift and chance, is obviously more deeply related to Tolstoy's aristocratic background than to his Christianity.

The optimism of the healthy, self-confident aristocrat, who turns *War and Peace* into an apotheosis of organic, vegetative, endlessly creative life, into a great idyll, a 'naïve heroic epic', on whose highest point, as Merezhkovsky remarks with such relish, the novelist plants the napkins of Nastasya's babies 'as the guiding banner of mankind'[187]—this pantheistic optimism is obscured in *Anna Karenina* and approaches the pessimistic mood of Western literature, but the disillusionment with the conven-

153

tionalism and obtuseness of modern culture expressed here is utterly different from that of Flaubert or Maupassant. The triumph of real life over the romanticism of the emotions was already intermingled with some melancholy in *War and Peace*, and Tolstoy had already struck a Flaubertian note in his earlier work, thus for example in *Family Happiness*, by describing the degeneration of the great passions, especially the transformation of love into friendship. The discrepancy between the ideal and the reality, between poetry and prose, youth and old age, never seems so bleak, however, in Tolstoy as in the French writers. His disillusionment never leads to nihilism, never leads to an impeachment of life in general. The novel of Western Europe is always full of a querulous self-pity and self-dramatization of the hero in conflict with reality; here external conditions, society, the state, the social environment, always bear the blame for the antagonism. With Tolstoy, on the other hand, the subjective personality is just as much to blame as objective reality, if it comes to a clash.[188] For, if the life which disillusions is too soulless, the disillusioned hero is too soulful, too poetic, too Utopian; if the one is lacking in tolerance for dreamers, the other lacks a sense of reality.

The fact that the form of Tolstoy's novels is so different from the West European is bound up in the main with this concept of the self and the world and its deviation from the Flaubertian conception. The distance from the naturalistic norm is here, in fact, just as great as in Dostoevsky, only Tolstoy's remoteness from it lies in the opposite direction. If Dostoevsky's novels have a dramatic structure, then Tolstoy's have an epic—epopee-like—character. No attentive reader can ever have failed to feel the surging Homeric flow of these novels, or ever have failed to experience the panoramic, all-embracing picture of the world which they unfold. Tolstoy himself compared his novels to Homer, and the comparison has become a stock formula of Tolstoy criticism. The unromantic, undramatic and unemphatic quality of the form, the forgoing of all theatrical climaxes and intensity, have always been regarded as Homeric. The dramatic concentration of the novel, which first took place with the transformation from the picaresque form of the eighteenth century to the biographical form of pre-romanticism, was not yet adopted by Tolstoy in *War and Peace*. He considers the conflict between the individual and society not as an unavoidable tragedy, but as a calamity which he attributes, following the eighteenth-century view, to a lack of insight, understanding and moral seriousness. He still lives in the age of the Russian enlightenment, in an intellectual atmosphere of faith in the world and faith in the future. But while he is working at *Anna Karenina*, he loses this optimism, and above all his belief in art, which he declares to be absolutely useless, indeed harmful, unless it renounces the refinements and subtleties of modern naturalism and impressionism and turns a luxury article into the universal possession of mankind. In the estrangement of art from the broad masses and the restriction of its public to an ever smaller circle Tolstoy had recognized a real danger. There is no doubt but that the extension of this circle and contact with culturally less exclusive strata of society might well have had fruitful results for art. But how was such a change to be brought about methodically and according to plan, unless the artists who had grown up and were firmly rooted in the tradition of modern art were not prevented from producing works of art and unless it was not made as easy as possible for the dilettanti, who were foreign to this tradition, to engage in artistic activities—to the disadvantage of the others? Tolstoy's rejection of the highly developed and refined art of the present, and his fondness for the primitive, 'universally human' forms of artistic expression, is a symptom of the same Rousseauism with which he plays off the village against the town and identifies the social question with that of the peasantry. It is quite easy to understand why Tolstoy had not much use for Shakespeare, for example. How could a puritan, who hated all exuberance and virtuosity, have found any pleasure in the mannerism of a poet, even though he were the greatest poet of all time? But it is inconceivable that a man who created such artistically exacting works as *Anna Karenina* and *The Death of Ivan Ilych* accepted without reservations out of the whole of modern literature, apart from *Uncle Tom's Cabin*, only Schiller's *Robbers*, Hugo's *Misérables*, Dickens' *Christmas Carol*, Dostoevsky's *Memoirs from Underground* and George Eliot's *Adam Bede*.[189]

Tolstoy's relationship to art can only be understood as the symptom of a historic change, as the sign of a development which brings the aesthetic culture of the nineteenth century to an end and a generation to the fore that judges art once again as the mediator of ideas.[190]

What this generation revered in the author of *War and Peace* was by no means merely the great novelist, the creator of the greatest novel in the literature of the world, but above all the social reformer and the founder of a religion. Tolstoy enjoyed the fame of Voltaire, the popularity of Rousseau, the authority of Goethe and, more than that—he became a legendary figure, whose prestige was reminiscent of that of the old seers and prophets. Yasnaya Polyana became a place to which the members of all nations, social classes and cultural strata went on pilgrimage, and admired the old count in the peasant's smock as if he were a saint. Gorky will not have been the only one to have seen him and thought 'This man is like to God!', a confession with which the unbeliever ends his memories of Tolstoy.[191] Many will certainly have had the feeling, as did Thomas Mann, that Europe became 'without a master' after his death.[192] But these were only feelings and moods, words of gratitude and loyalty. Tolstoy was doubtless something very much like the living conscience of Europe, the great teacher and educator, who expressed, as did no other, the moral unrest and desire for spiritual renewal of his generation, but, with his naïve Rousseauism and quietism, he would never have been able to remain—if he ever really was —the 'master' of Europe. For, it may well be sufficient for an artist, as Chekhov thought, to put the right questions, but a man who was to rule over his century would also have to answer them aright.

4. IMPRESSIONISM

The frontiers between naturalism and impressionism are fluid; it is impossible to make a clear-cut historical or conceptual distinction between them. The smoothness of the stylistic change corresponds to the continuity of the simultaneous economic development and the stability of social conditions. 1871 is of merely passing significance in the history of France. The predominance of the upper middle class remains essentially unchanged and the conservative Republic takes the place of the 'liberal' Empire—that 'republic without republicans',[193] which is acquiesced in only because it seems to guarantee the smoothest possible solution of the political problems. But a friendly relationship is established with it only after the supporters of the Commune have been rooted out and comfort has been found in the theory of the necessity and the healing power of bleeding.[194] The intelligentsia confronts events in a state of absolute helplessness. Flaubert, Gautier, the Goncourts, and with them most of the intellectual leaders of the age, indulge in wild insults and imprecations against the disturbers of the peace. From the Republic they hope at the most for protection against clericalism, and they see in democracy merely the lesser of the two evils.[195] Financial and industrial capitalism develops consistently along the lines long since laid down; but, under the surface, important, though for the time being still unobtrusive changes are taking place. Economic life is entering the stage of high capitalism and developing from a 'free play of forces' into a rigidly organized and rationalized system, into a close-meshed net of spheres of interest, customs territories, fields of monopoly, cartels, trusts and syndicates. And just as it was feasible for this standardization and concentration of economic life to be called a sign of senility,[196] so the marks of insecurity and the omens of dissolution can be recognized throughout middle-class society. It is true that the Commune ends with a more complete defeat for the rebels than any previous revolution, but it is the first to be sustained by an international labour movement and to be followed by a victory for the bourgeoisie associated with a feeling of acute danger.[197] This mood of crisis leads to a renewal of the idealistic and mystical trends and produces, as a reaction against the prevailing pessimism, a strong tide of faith. It is only in the course of this development that impressionism loses its connection with naturalism and becomes transformed, especially in literature, into a new form of romanticism.

The enormous technical developments that take place must

not induce us to overlook the feeling of crisis that was in the air. The crisis itself must rather be seen as an incentive to new technical achievements and improvements of methods of production.[198] Certain signs of the atmosphere of crisis make themselves felt in all the manifestations of technical activity. It is above all the furious speed of the development and the way the pace is forced that seems pathological, particularly when compared with the rate of progress in earlier periods in the history of art and culture. For the rapid development of technology not only accelerates the change of fashion, but also the shifting emphases in the criteria of aesthetic taste; it often brings about a senseless and fruitless mania for innovation, a restless striving for the new for the mere sake of novelty. Industrialists are compelled to intensify the demand for improved products by artificial means and must not allow the feeling that the new is always better to cool down, if they really want to profit from the achievements of technology.[199] The continual and increasingly rapid replacement of old articles in everyday use by new ones leads, however, to a diminished affection for material and soon also for intellectual possessions, too, and readjusts the speed at which philosophical and artistic revaluations occur to that of changing fashion. Modern technology thus introduces an unprecedented dynamism in the whole attitude to life and it is above all this new feeling of speed and change that finds expression in impressionism.

The most striking phenomenon connected with the progress of technology is the development of cultural centres into large cities in the modern sense; these form the soil in which the new art is rooted. Impressionism is an urban art, and not only because it discovers the landscape quality of the city and brings painting back from the country into the town, but because it sees the world through the eyes of the townsman and reacts to external impressions with the overstrained nerves of modern technical man. It is an urban style, because it describes the changeability, the nervous rhythm, the sudden, sharp but always ephemeral impressions of city life. And precisely as such, it implies an enormous expansion of sensual perception, a new sharpening of sensibility, a new irritability, and, with the Gothic and romanticism, it signifies one of the most important turning points in

158

the history of Western art. In the dialectical process represented by the history of painting, the alternation of the static and the dynamic, of design and colour, abstract order and organic life, impressionism forms the climax of the development in which recognition is given to the dynamic and organic elements of experience and which completely dissolves the static world-view of the Middle Ages. A continuous line can be traced from the Gothic to impressionism comparable to the line leading from late medieval economy to high capitalism, and modern man, who regards his whole existence as a struggle and a competition, who translates all being into motion and change, for whom experience of the world increasingly becomes experience of time, is the product of this bilateral, but fundamentally uniform development.

The dominion of the moment over permanence and continuity, the feeling that every phenomenon is a fleeting and never-to-be-repeated constellation, a wave gliding away on the river of time, the river into which 'one cannot step twice', is the simplest formula to which impressionism can be reduced. The whole method of impressionism, with all its artistic expedients and tricks, is bent, above all, on giving expression to this Heraclitean outlook and on stressing that reality is not a being but a becoming, not a condition but a process. Every impressionistic picture is the deposit of a moment in the perpetuum mobile of existence, the representation of a precarious, unstable balance in the play of contending forces. The impressionistic vision transforms nature into a process of growth and decay. Everything stable and coherent is dissolved into metamorphoses and assumes the character of the unfinished and fragmentary. The reproduction of the subjective act instead of the objective substratum of seeing, with which the history of modern perspective painting begins, here achieves its culmination. The representation of light, air and atmosphere, the dissolution of the evenly coloured surface into spots and dabs of colour, the decomposition of the local colour into *valeurs*, into values of perspective and aspect, the play of reflected light and illuminated shadows, the quivering, trembling dots and the hasty, loose and abrupt strokes of the brush, the whole improvised technique with its rapid and rough sketching, the fleeting, seemingly careless perception of
159

the object and the brilliant casualness of the execution merely express, in the final analysis, that feeling of a stirring, dynamic, constantly changing reality, which began with the re-orientation of painting by the use of perspective.

A world, the phenomena of which are in a state of constant flux and transition, produces the impression of a continuum in which everything coalesces, and in which there are no other differences but the various approaches and points of view of the beholder. An art in accordance with such a world will stress not merely the momentary and transitory nature of phenomena, will not see in man simply the measure of all things, but will seek the criterion of truth in the 'hic et nunc' of the individual. It will consider chance the principle of all being, and the truth of the moment as invalidating all other truth. The primacy of the moment, of change and chance implies, in terms of aesthetics, the dominion of the passing mood over the permanent qualities of life, that is to say, the prevalence of a relation to things the property of which is to be non-committal as well as changeable. This reduction of the artistic representation to the mood of the moment is, at the same time, the expression of a fundamentally passive outlook on life, an acquiescence in the rôle of the spectator, of the receptive and contemplative subject, a standpoint of aloofness, waiting, non-involvement—in short, the aesthetic attitude purely and simply. Impressionism is the climax of self-centred aesthetic culture and signifies the ultimate consequence of the romantic renunciation of practical, active life.

Stylistically, impressionism is an extremely complex phenomenon. In some respects it represents merely the logical development of naturalism. For, if one interprets naturalism as meaning progress from the general to the particular, from the typical to the individual, from the abstract idea to the concrete, temporally and spatially conditioned experience, then the impressionistic reproduction of reality, with its emphasis on the instantaneous and the unique, is an important achievement of naturalism. The representations of impressionism are closer to sensual experience than those of naturalism in the narrower sense, and replace the object of theoretical knowledge by that of direct optical experience more completely than any earlier art. But by detaching the

160

optical elements of experience from the conceptual and elaborating the autonomy of the visual, impressionism departs from all art as practised hitherto, and thereby from naturalism as well. Its method is peculiar in that, whilst pre-impressionist art bases its representations on a seemingly uniform but, in fact, heterogeneously composed world-view, made up of conceptual and sensual elements alike, impressionism aspires to the homogeneity of the purely visual. All earlier art is the result of a synthesis, impressionism that of an analysis. It constructs its particular subject from the bare data of the senses, it, therefore, goes back to the unconscious psychic mechanism and gives us to some extent the raw material of experience, which is further removed from our usual conception of reality than the logically organized impressions of the senses. Impressionism is less illusionistic than naturalism; instead of the illusion, it gives elements of the subject, instead of a picture of the whole, the bricks of which experience is composed. Before impressionism, art reproduced objects by *signs*, now it represents them through their components, through *parts* of the material of which they are made up.[200]

In comparison with the older art, naturalism marked an increase in the elements of the composition, in other words, an extension of the motifs and an enrichment of the technical means. The impressionistic method, on the other hand, involves a series of reductions, a system of restrictions and simplifications.[201] Nothing is more typical of an impressionist painting than that it must be looked at from a certain distance and that it describes things with the omissions inevitable in them when seen from a distance. The series of reductions which it carries out begins with the restriction of the elements of the representation to the purely visual and the elimination of everything of a non-optical nature or that cannot be translated into optical terms. The waiving of the so-called literary elements of the subject, the story or the anecdote, is the most striking expression of this 'recollection by painting of its own particular means'. The reduction of all motifs to landscape, still life and the portrait, or the treatment of every kind of subject as a 'landscape' and 'still life', is nothing more than a symptom of the predominance of the specifically 'painterly' principle in painting. 'It is the treatment of a subject for the sake of the tones, and not for the sake of the subject itself, that distinguishes the impressionists from other painters,' as one of the earliest historians and theorists of the movement points out.[202] This neutralization and reduction of the motif to its bare material essentials can be considered an expression of the anti-romantic outlook of the time and seen as the trivialization and stripping bare of all the heroic and stately qualities of the subject-matter of art, but it can also be regarded as a departure from reality, and the restriction of painting to subjects of 'its own' can be looked upon as a loss from the naturalistic point of view. The 'smile' that the Greeks discovered in the plastic arts and that, as has been observed, is being lost in modern art[203] is sacrificed to the purely pictorial aspect; but it means that all psychology and all humanism disappears from painting altogether.

The replacement of tactile by visual values, in other words, the transfer of physical volume and plastic form to the surface, is a further step, bound up with the new 'painterly' trend, in the series of reductions to which impressionism subjects the naturalistic picture of reality. This reduction is, however, in no sense the aim, but only a by-product of the method. The emphasis on colour and the desire to turn the whole picture into a harmony of colour and light effects is the aim, the absorbing of the space and the dissolving of the solid structure of the bodies nothing more than a concomitant. Impressionism not only reduces reality to a two-dimensional surface but, within this two-dimensionality, to a system of shapeless spots; in other words, it forgoes not only plasticity but also design, not only spatial but also linear form. That the picture makes up in energy and sensual charm for what it loses in clarity and evidence is obvious, and this gain was also the main concern of the impressionists themselves. But the public felt the loss more strongly than the gain and now that the impressionistic way of looking at things has become one of the most important components of our optical experience, we are unable even to imagine how helplessly the public confronted this medley of spots and blots. Impressionism formed merely the last step in a process of increasing obscurity that had been going on for centuries. Since the baroque, pictorial representations had confronted the beholder with an increasingly difficult problem; they had become more and more opaque and their relation to reality more and more complex. But impressionism represented a more daring leap than any single phase of the earlier development, and the shock produced by the first impressionist exhibitions was comparable to nothing ever experienced before in the whole history of artistic innovation. People considered the rapid execution and the shapelessness of the pictures as an insolent provocation; they thought that they were being made fun of and the revenge they took was as cruel as they were able to contrive.

With these innovations, however, the succession of reductions employed by the impressionist method is by no means exhausted. The very colours which impressionism uses alter and distort those of our everyday experience. We think, for example, of a piece of 'white' paper as white in every lighting, despite the coloured reflexes which it shows in ordinary daylight. In other words: the 'remembered colour' which we associate with an object, and which is the result of long experience and habit, displaces the concrete impression gained from immediate perception;[204] impressionism now goes back behind the remembered, theoretically established colour to the real sensation, which is, incidentally, in no sense a spontaneous act, but represents a supremely artificial and extremely complicated psychological process.

Impressionistic perception, finally, brings about one further and very severe reduction in the usual picture of reality, inasmuch as it shows colours not as concrete qualities bound to a particular object, but as abstract, incorporeal, immaterial phenomena—as it were colours-in-themselves. If we hold a screen with a small opening in front of an object that is big enough to reveal the colour, but not big enough to enlighten us as to the form of the object and the relationship of the colour in question to the object, it is a well-known fact that we get an indefinite, hovering impression, which is very different from the character of the colours adherent to plastic form we habitually see. In this way the colour of fire loses its radiance, the colour of silk its lustre, the colour of water its transparency, etc.[205] Impressionism always represents objects in these incorporeal surface colours, which make a very direct and lively impression, owing to their freshness and intensity, but considerably reduce the illusionistic effect of the picture and most strikingly reveal the conventionality of the impression-istic method.

In the second half of the nineteenth century painting becomes the leading art. Impressionism here develops into an autonomous style at a time when in the literary world a conflict is still raging around naturalism. The first collective exhibition of the im-pressionists takes place in 1874, but the history of impressionism begins some twenty years earlier, and already comes to an end with the eighth group exhibition in the year 1886. About this time impressionism as a uniform group movement breaks up and a new, post-impressionist period begins which lasts until about 1906, the year of Cézanne's death.[206] After the predominance of literature in the seventeenth and eighteenth centuries and the leading part played by music in the age of romanticism, a change in favour of painting occurs about the middle of the nineteenth century. The art critic Asselineau places the dethronement of poetry by painting as early as 1840,[207] and, a generation later, the Goncourt brothers already exclaim with enthusiasm in their voices: 'What a happy profession that of the painter is compared with that of the writer!'[208] Painting dominates all the other arts not only as the most progressive art of the age, but its productions also surpass the literary and musical achievements of the same period qualitatively, especially in France, where it was perfectly correct to maintain that the great poets of this period were the impressionist painters.[209] It is true that nineteenth-century art remains romantic to some extent and the poets of the century profess a belief in music as the highest artistic ideal, but what they understand thereby is more a symbol of sovereign, un-fettered creation, independent of objective reality, than the con-crete example of music. Impressionist painting discovers, on the other hand, sensations which poetry and music also attempt to express and in which they adapt their means of expression to painterly forms. Atmospherical impressions, especially the experi-ence of light, air and colour, are perceptions native to painting, and when the attempt is made to reproduce moods of this kind in the other arts, we are quite within our rights to speak of a 'painterly' style of poetry and music. But the style of these arts is also painterly, when they express themselves, forgoing distinct 'contours', with the aid of colour and shade effects, and attach more importance to the vivacity of the details than the uniformity of the total impression. When Paul Bourget points out that, in the style of his time, the impression made by the single page is always stronger than that of the whole book, that made by a sentence deeper than that of a page and that of the single words more striking than that of a sentence,[210] what he is describing is the method of impressionism—the style of an atomized, dynamically-charged world-view.

Impressionism is not, however, merely the style of a particular period dominating all the arts, it is also the last universally valid 'European' style—the latest trend based on a general consensus of taste. Since its dissolution it has been impossible to classify stylistically either the various arts or the various nations and cultures. But impressionism neither ends nor begins abruptly. Delacroix, who discovered the law of complementary colours and the coloration of shadows, and Constable, who established the complex composition of colour effects in nature, already anticipate much of the impressionistic method. The energizing of vision, which is the essence of impressionism, at any rate begins with them. The rudiments of plein-airism in the painters of Barbizon represent a further step in this development. But what contributes to the rise of impressionism as a collective movement is above all, on the one hand, the artistic experience of the city, the beginnings of which are to be found in Manet, and, on the other hand, the amalgamation of the young painters which is brought about by the opposition of the public. At first sight, it may seem surprising that the metropolis, with its herding together and intermingling of people, should produce this intimate art rooted in the feeling of individual singularity and solitude. But it is a familiar fact that nothing seems so isolating as the close proximity of too many people, and nowhere does one feel so lonely and forsaken as in a great crowd of strangers. The two basic feelings which life in such an environment produces, the feeling of being alone and unobserved, on the one hand, and the impression of roaring traffic, incessant movement and constant variety, on the other, breed the impressionistic outlook on life in which the most subtle moods are combined with the most rapid alternation of sensations. The negative attitude of the public as a motive for the rise of impressionism as a movement seems just as surprising at first sight. The impressionists never behaved aggressively towards the public; they had every desire to remain within the framework of tradition, and often made desperate efforts to be recognized in official quarters, above all in the Salon, which they considered the normal road to success. At any rate, the spirit of contradiction and the desire to attract attention by flabbergasting the public play a much smaller part with them than with most romantics and many naturalists. All the same, there may never have existed such a deep divergence between official circles and the younger generation of artists, and the feeling of being jeered at may never have been so strong as now. The impressionists certainly did not make it easy for people to understand their artistic ideas—but in what a bad way the art appreciation of the public must have been to allow such great, honest and peaceable artists as Monet, Renoir and Pissarro almost to starve.

Impressionism also had nothing of the plebeian about it, to make an unfavourable impression on the bourgeois public; it was rather an 'aristocrats' style', elegant and fastidious, nervous and sensitive, sensual and epicurean, keen on rare and exquisite subjects, bent on strictly personal experiences, experiences of solitude and seclusion and the sensations of over-refined senses and nerves. It is, however, the creation of artists who not only come very largely from the lower and middle sections of the bourgeoisie, but who are much less concerned with intellectual and aesthetic problems than the artists of earlier generations; they are less versatile and sophisticated, more exclusively craftsmen and 'technicians' than their predecessors. But there are also members of the well-to-do bourgeoisie and even of the aristocracy amongst them. Manet, Bazille, Berthe Morisot and Cézanne are the children of rich parents, Degas is of aristocratic and Toulouse-Lautrec of high aristocratic descent. The refined intellectual style and cultivated well-bred manners of Manet and Degas, the elegance and delicate artistry of Constantin Guys and Toulouse-Lautrec, show the genteel bourgeois society of the Second Empire, the world of the crinoline and the décolleté, the equipages and the riding horses in the Bois, from its most attractive side.

166

The history of literature reveals a much more complicated picture than that of painting. As a literary style, impressionism is, intrinsically, not a very sharply defined phenomenon; its beginnings are hardly recognizable within the total complex of naturalism and its later forms of development are completely merged with the phenomena of symbolism. Chronologically, too, a certain discrepancy is to be observed between impressionism in literature and painting; in painting, the most productive period of impressionism is already past, when its stylistic characteristics are first beginning to emerge in literature. The most fundamental difference, however, is that in literature impressionism loses the connection with naturalism, positivism and materialism comparatively early and becomes almost from the outset the champion of that idealistic reaction which finds expression in painting only after the dissolution of impressionism. The main reason for this is that the conservative élite plays a much more important rôle in literature than in painting, which, as a result of its stronger roots in craft traditions, puts up greater resistance to the spiritualistic aspirations of the age.

The crisis of naturalism, which is only a symptom of the crisis of positivism, does not become evident until about 1885, but the omens are already apparent around 1870. The enemies of the Republic are mostly also enemies of rationalism, materialism and naturalism; they attack scientific progress and expect that a religious revival will also bring about an intellectual rebirth. They talk about the 'bankruptcy of science', the 'end of naturalism', the 'soulless mechanization of culture', but they always mean the Revolution, the Republic and liberalism when they storm against the intellectual poverty of the age. The conservatives have lost their influence on the government, it is true, but they have kept their strong position in public life. They still continue to occupy the most important posts in the administration, diplomacy and the army and they dominate public education, especially in its higher branches.[211] The *lycées* and the University belong as much as ever to the domain of the clergy and high finance, and the cultural ideals which they spread abroad have a stronger currency in literature than ever. We come across academically educated writers in much greater numbers

167

than hitherto and, under their influence, intellectual life acquires a predominantly reactionary character. Flaubert, Maupassant and Zola were not writers of learning, whereas Bourget and Barrès represent the spirit of the Academy and the University; they feel themselves to some extent responsible for the cultural inheritance of the nation and come forward as the competent intellectual leaders of youth.[212] This intellectualization of literature is perhaps the most striking and most universally valid characteristic of the period; it finds expression in both the progressive and the conservative writers.[213] In this respect there is not the slightest difference between Anatole France and his clerical and nationalistic colleagues. And although there is only one Anatole France alongside Bourget, Barrès, Brunetière, Bergson and Claudel, the esteem in which this Voltairian is held proves that the spirit of the enlightenment is by no means dead in France. On the other hand, incidents like the Dreyfus affair and the Panama scandal are needed to awaken it from its trance.

Around 1870 France goes through one of its most serious intellectual and moral crises, but its 'intellectual Sedan' is in no way connected with its military defeat, as Barrès maintains,[214] and its 'fatal weariness of life' is not derived from its materialism and relativism, as Bourget thinks. Bourget and Barrès are no less affected by this weariness of life than are Baudelaire and Flaubert. It is part of the romantic sickness of the whole century, and Zola's naturalism, which the generation of 1885 treats as a scapegoat, actually represents the only serious, though inadequate, attempt to overcome the nihilism which had seized men's minds. From the later 'eighties onwards the literary situation is dominated by the attacks on Zola and the disbandment of naturalism as the leading movement. That is the strongest impression that emerges from the answers to the inquiry organized by Jules Huret, a contributor to the *Écho de Paris*, which also appeared in book form in 1891 under the title *Enquête sur l'évolution littéraire* and which represent one of the most important sources for the intellectual and cultural history of the period. Huret asked the sixty-four most prominent French writers of the day what they thought of naturalism, whether, in their opinion, it

168

was already dead, or whether it could still be saved, and if not, what literary trend would take its place. The overwhelming majority of those questioned, with most of Zola's former disciples at the head, thought the case hopeless. Only the ever-faithful Paul Alexis hastened to wire, 'Naturalisme pas mort. Lettre suit', as if he were anxious to prevent the spread of a dangerous rumour. But his haste was of no avail. The rumour did spread and naturalism was denied even by those who owed it their whole artistic existence. And this meant most of the creative writers of the age. For what was the most influential literature up to the turn of the century, and what is it partly still today, if not naturalistic, form-demolishing literature bent on the expansion of the content of experience? What, above all, was the 'psychological novel' of Bourget, Barrès, Huysmans and even Proust, if not the result of naturalistic observation interested in the 'document humain'? And what is the whole modern novel, in the last analysis, but the exact, minute and increasingly precise description of concrete spiritual reality? It is quite true that certain anti-naturalistic characteristics are as inseparably connected with impressionism in literature as they are in painting, but these, too, grow out of the soil of naturalism. At first sight, therefore, the violence of the public reaction seems inexplicable. The arguments against naturalism were by no means new, the curious thing was simply that, at a time when naturalism already seemed to have won the day, it was attacked with such bitterness. What was it that people could not forgive in naturalism or pretended not to be able to forgive? Naturalism, it was asserted, was an indelicate, indecent and obscene art, the expression of an insipid, materialistic philosophy, the instrument of clumsy, heavy-handed democratic propaganda, a collection of boring, trivial and vulgar banalities, a representation of reality which, in its portrayal of society, described only the wild, ravenous, undisciplined animal in man and only the works of disintegration, the dissolution of human relationships, the undermining of the family, the nation and religion, in short, it was destructive, unnatural, hostile to life. The generation of 1850 merely defended the interests of the upper classes against the inroads of naturalism, that of 1885 defends humanity, creative life, God himself. In the interim

169

NATURALISM AND IMPRESSIONISM

there has been an increase of religion, perhaps, but not of sincerity.

People drivel about the mysteries of being and the depth of the human soul; they call the rational flat and want to explore and divine the unknown and the unknowable. They profess a belief in world-renouncing, 'ascetic ideals', but they omit to ask, with Nietzsche, why they really seem to be necessary. Symbolism is the most celebrated literary trend of the day; Verlaine and Mallarmé stand in the centre of public interest. The greatest names of the romantic movement, Chateaubriand, Lamartine, Vigny, Musset, Mérimée, Gautier, George Sand, are not mentioned at all in the answers which Huret receives.[215] Instead, Stendhal and Baudelaire are discovered, there is enthusiasm for Villiers de l'Isle-Adam and Rimbaud, the vogue of the Russian novel, of English Pre-Raphaelism and German philosophy is predominant. But the deepest and most fruitful influence emanates from Baudelaire; he is regarded as the most important predecessor of symbolist poetry and the creator of the modern lyric in general. It is he who leads the generation of Bourget and Barrès, Huysmans and Mallarmé back to the path of romantic aestheticism and teaches it how to reconcile the new mysticism with the old fanatical devotion to art.

Aestheticism reaches the pinnacle of its development in the age of impressionism. Its characteristic criteria, the passive, purely contemplative attitude to life, the transitoriness and non-committing quality of experience and hedonistic sensualism, are now the standards by which art in general is judged. The work of art is not only considered an end in itself, not only a self-sufficient game, whose charm is apt to be destroyed by any extraneous, extra-aesthetic purpose, not only the most beautiful gift which life has to offer, for the enjoyment of which it is one's duty devotedly to prepare oneself, it becomes, in its autonomy, its lack of consideration for everything outside its sphere, a pattern for life, for the life of the dilettante, who now begins to displace the intellectual heroes of the past in the estimation of poets and writers and represents the ideal of the *fin de siècle*. What distinguishes him above all is the fact that he strives to 'turn his life into a work of art', in other words, into something costly and useless, something flowing along freely and extravagantly, something offered up to the beauty, the pure form, the harmony of tones and lines. Aesthetic culture implies a way of life marked by uselessness and superfluousness, that is to say, the embodiment of romantic resignation and passivity. But it outdoes romanticism; it not only renounces life for the sake of art, it seeks for the justification of life in art itself. It regards the world of art as the only real compensation for the disappointments of life, as the genuine realization and consummation of an existence that is intrinsically incomplete and inarticulate. But this not only means that life seems more beautiful and more conciliatory when clothed in art, but that, as Proust, the last great impressionist and aesthetic hedonist, thought, it only grows into significant reality in memory, vision and the aesthetic experience. We live our experiences with the greatest intensity not when we encounter men and things in reality—the 'time' and the present of these experiences are always 'lost'—but when we 'recover time', when we are no longer the actors but the spectators of our life, when we create or enjoy works of art, in other words, when we remember. Here, in Proust, art takes possession of what Plato had denied it: ideas—the true remembrance of the essential forms of being.

The theoretical foundations of modern aestheticism as the philosophy of the absolutely passive, contemplative attitude to life can be traced back to Schopenhauer, who defines art as the deliverance from the will, as the sedative which brings the appetites and passions to silence. The philosophy of aestheticism judges and evaluates the whole of life from the point of view of this art free from will and passion. Its ideal is a public entirely made up of real or potential artists, of artistic natures for whom reality is merely the substratum of aesthetic experience. It regards the civilized world as a great artist's studio and the artist himself as the best connoisseur. D'Alembert had still said: 'Woe betide the art whose beauty only exists for artists.' The fact that he felt induced to utter such a warning proves, however, that the danger of aestheticism had already existed in the eighteenth century; in the seventeenth that kind of idea would not yet have occurred to anyone. For the nineteenth century D'Alembert's

171

fear again ceased to have any meaning. The Goncourts describe his words as the greatest stupidity imaginable,[216] and are convinced of nothing more deeply than that the precondition of an adequate appreciation of art is a life dedicated to art, in other words, the practice of art.

The aesthetic philosophy of impressionism marks the beginning of a process of complete inbreeding in art. Artists produce their works for artists, and art, that is, the formal experience of the world *sub specie artis*, becomes the real subject of art. Raw, unformed nature untouched by culture loses its aesthetic attraction and the ideal of naturalness is thrust aside by an ideal of artificiality. The city, urban culture, urban amusements, the 'vie factice' and the 'paradis artificiels', seem not only incomparably more attractive, but also much more spiritual and soulful than the so-called charms of nature. Nature itself is ugly, ordinary, shapeless; art alone makes it enjoyable. Baudelaire hates the country, the Goncourts regard nature as an enemy and the later aesthetes, especially Whistler and Wilde, speak of it in a tone of contemptuous irony. This is the end of the pastoral, of the romantic enthusiasm for the natural and the belief in the identity of reason and nature. The reaction against Rousseau and the cult of the state of nature initiated by him now comes to its definite conclusion. Everything simple and clear, instinctive and unsophisticated, loses its value; the consciousness, the intellectualism and the unnaturalness of culture are now sought after. Intelligence and the functions of the critical faculty are again stressed in the process of artistic creation. The imagination of the artist continually produces good, middling and bad things—says Nietzsche —it is his discernment that first rejects, selects and organizes the material to be used.[217] This idea, like the whole philosophy of the 'vie factice', comes fundamentally from Baudelaire, who desires to 'transform his delight into knowledge' and to let the critic in the poet always have his say,[218] in whom the enthusiasm for everything artificial goes, in fact, so far that he even considers nature morally inferior. He maintains that evil takes place without effort, that is to say, naturally, whereas goodness is always the product of design and purpose, and is, therefore, artificial and unnatural.[219]

The enthusiasm for the artificiality of culture is in some respects again only a new form of romantic escapism. Artificial, fictitious life is chosen, because reality can never be so beautiful as illusion and because all contact with reality, all attempts to realize dreams and wishes must lead to their corruption. But people now take refuge from social reality not in nature, as the romantics had done, but in a higher, more sublimated and more artificial world. In Villiers de l'Isle-Adam's *Axel* (1890, post-humous), one of the classical portrayals of the new attitude to life, the intellectual and imaginary forms of being always stand above the natural and practical, and unrealized desires always seem more perfect and more satisfying than their translation into ordinary, trivial reality. Axel wants to commit suicide with Sara whom he loves. She is quite willing to die with him, but she would like, before they die, to know the happiness of one night of love. Axel fears, however, that, afterwards, he would no longer have the courage to die and that their love, like all realized dreams, would not stand the test of time. He prefers the perfect illusion to the imperfect reality. The whole thought of neo-romanticism more or less depends on this feeling; everywhere we come across Lohengrins who, as Nietzsche says, leave their Elsas in the lurch on the wedding night. 'Life?' asks Axel. 'Our servants see to that for us.' In Huysmans' *À rebours* (1884), the principal document of this anti-natural and anti-practical aestheticism, the replacement of practical life by the life of the spirit is carried through even more completely. Des Esseintes, the famous hero of the novel, the prototype of all the Dorian Grays, seals himself off from the world so hermetically that he does not even dare to go on a journey since he is afraid of being disappointed by reality. It is the same crippling, life-destroying subjectivism that finds expression in the aesthete's boredom with nature. 'The age of nature', says Des Esseintes, 'is past; it has finally exhausted the patience of all sensitive minds by the loathsome monotony of its landscapes and skies.' For such minds there is but one way: to make themselves absolutely independent and replace nature by the mind, reality by fiction. They have to make everything straight crooked and to bend all natural instincts and inclinations into their opposite. Des Esseintes lives in his house as in a monas-

173

tery, he visits no one and receives no one, he neither writes nor receives letters, he sleeps by day and reads, indulges in fancies and speculates by night; he creates his own 'artificial paradises' and gives up everything in which ordinary mortals delight. He invents symphonies in colours, scents, drinks, artificial flowers and rare jewels; for the instruments of his spiritual acrobatics must be rare and costly. Natural, cheap, insipid and plebeian are synonyms in his vocabulary.

Perhaps the mysticism of this whole philosophy is, however, expressed nowhere so strongly as in Villiers de l'Isle-Adam's short story *Véra*.[220] Véra is the idolized, early departed wife of the hero, who refuses to acknowledge the fact of her death, because he could not endure the consciousness of it. He throws the key of the vault in which she lies buried back through the grating, goes home and begins a new, artificial life, that is, he continues his former life, as if nothing had happened. He goes in and out, talks and acts, as if she were still alive and beside him. His behaviour is such a consistent and unbroken chain of attitudes and actions that nothing but the physical presence of Véra is needed to make his conduct absolutely reasonable. But she is so completely present spiritually and the radiation of her personality so immediate, so overwhelming that her fictitious life has a much deeper, truer and more genuine reality than her actual death. She does not die until, all at once, these words escape the sleep-walker's lips: 'I remember . . . You are really dead after all!' No intelligent reader will overlook the analogy between this obstinate refusal to admit the relevance of reality and the Christian denial of the world, but none will also fail to recognize the difference between the stubbornness of an obsession and the imperturbability of a religious faith. It is impossible to imagine anything more unchristian, more foreign to the spirit of the Middle Ages than *ennui*, this new, impressionistic form of romantic *Weltschmerz*. This is the expression of a feeling of disgust at the monotony of life,[221] therefore, the precise opposite of the dissatisfaction which, as has been pointed out, earlier ages, in which faith in the divine order was still alive, had felt with the unpleasant aspects of things here on earth.[222] In former ages the fickleness of Fortuna, the inconstancy and incalculability of fate, had been viewed with alarm, there was a general yearning for peace and security, for the monotony and boredom of peace; for the modern aesthete, on the other hand, it is the ordered security of bourgeois life that he finds most intolerable of all. The impressionists' attempt to arrest the fleeting hour, their surrender to the passing mood, as the highest and least replaceable value, their aim of living in the moment, of being absorbed by it, is only the result of this unbourgeois view of life, of this revolt against the routine and discipline of bourgeois practice. Impressionism, too, is the art of an opposition, like all progressive tendencies since the romantics, and the rebelliousness which is latent in the impressionistic approach to life, although the impressionists are not always aware of it, is part of the reason why the bourgeois public rejected the new art.

In the 'eighties people are fond of describing the aesthetic hedonism of the time as 'decadence'. Des Esseintes, the refined epicurean, is at the same time the prototype of the pampered 'décadent'. The concept of decadence, however, contains traits which are not necessarily contained in that of aestheticism, thus above all the feeling of doom and crisis, that is, the consciousness of standing at the end of a vital process and in the presence of the dissolution of a civilization. The sympathy with the old, exhausted, over-refined cultures, with Hellenism, the later years of the Roman Empire, the rococo and the mature, 'impressionistic' style of the great masters, is part of the essence of the feeling of decadence. The awareness of being witnesses of a turning point in the history of civilization was nothing new, but whereas people in former times had deeply lamented the fate of belonging to an ageing culture, as Musset had done for instance, the idea of intellectual nobility is now connected with the concept of old age and fatigue, of over-cultivation and degeneration. Men are seized by a real frenzy of change and decay—by a feeling that is again not entirely new, but much stronger than ever before. The analogies with Rousseauism, the Byronic weariness of life and the romantic passion for death are obvious. It is the same abyss that attracts both the romantic and the decadent, the same delight in destruction, self-destruction, that intoxicates them. But for the decadent 'everything is an abyss', everything replete with the fear of life, with insecurity: 'Tout plein de vague horreur, menant on ne sait où,' as Baudelaire says.

'Who knows whether truth is not sad,' writes Renan—words of the deepest scepticism, to which none of the great Russians would have subscribed. For them it was possible for everything, except truth, to be sad. But how much more sinister are the words of Rimbaud: 'Ce qu'on ne sait pas, c'est peut-être terrible' (*Le Forgeron*). One has but an inkling of the kind of unfathomable and inexhaustible riddles he feels himself surrounded by, even though he immediately adds: 'Nous saurons.' The abyss which, for the Christian, was sin, for the knight, dishonesty, for the bourgeois, illegality, is, for the decadent, everything for which he lacks concepts, words and formulae. Hence his desperate struggle to achieve form and his unconquerable abhorrence for everything unformed, untamed and natural. Hence his fondness for the ages which had the most, if not always the deepest, formulae, which had at their disposal a word, albeit often only a feeble word, for everything.

Verlaine's 'Je suis l'empire à la fin de la décadence' becomes the signature of the age, and although, as the apologist of the period of Roman decline, he has his forerunners in Gérard de Nerval,[223] Baudelaire and Gautier,[224] nevertheless, he utters the catchword at the right moment and lends to what had hitherto been the expression of a mere mood the character of a cultural programme. There have been periods of culture which did not know or refused to know anything of a Golden Age, but, before the decadents of the nineteenth century, there had never been a generation which had decided against the Golden in favour of the Silver Age. This choice implied not only the awareness of being the mere descendants of great ancestors, not only the modesty of belated heirs, but also a kind of consciousness of guilt and a feeling of inferiority. The 'decadents' were hedonists with a bad conscience, sinners who threw themselves, like Barbey d'Aurevilly, Huysmans, Verlaine, Wilde and Beardsley, into the arms of the Catholic Church. This feeling of guilt was expressed more directly than anywhere else in their conception of love, which was completely dominated by the psychological puberty of the romantics. For Baudelaire, love is the essence of the forbidden, the fall of man, the irreparable loss of innocence; 'faire l'amour, c'est faire le mal', he says. But his romantic satanism transforms this sinfulness itself into a source of lust: love is not only the intrinsically evil, its highest pleasure consists precisely in the consciousness of doing evil.[225] The sympathy for the prostitute, which the decadents share with the romantics, and in which Baudelaire is again the intermediary, is the expression of the same inhibited, guilt-laden relationship to love. It is, of course, above all the expression of the revolt against bourgeois society and the morality based on the bourgeois family. The prostitute is the déracinée and the outlaw, the rebel who revolts not only against the institutional bourgeois form of love, but also against its 'natural' spiritual form. She destroys not only the moral and social organization of the feeling, she destroys the bases of the feeling itself. She is cold in the midst of the storms of passion, she is and remains the superior spectator of the lust that she awakens, she feels lonely and apathetic when others are enraptured and intoxicated—she is, in brief, the artist's female double. From this community of feeling and destiny arises the understanding which the artists of decadence show for her. They know how they prostitute themselves, how they surrender their most sacred feelings, and how cheaply they sell their secrets.

This declaration of solidarity with the prostitute completes the estrangement of the artists from bourgeois society. The bad schoolboy sits in the 'back row', as Thomas Mann said of one of his heroes, and feels the relief which one feels on leaving the scene of public strife, and stays in the 'back row', despised but unmolested. It would be curious if, in a thinker such as Thomas Mann, whose whole outlook on life hinges on a single central problem, namely the position of the artist in the bourgeois world, even this apparently innocuous remark were not connected in a way with his interpretation of the artist's way of life. The particular existence the artist leads, which must strike the bourgeois mind as lacking all ambition, is in fact very much like a 'back row' which relieves him of all responsibility and all need to account for his actions. In any case, Thomas Mann's emphatically 'bourgeois' outlook, as also, for example, the 'correct' social philosophy of Henry James, can only be understood as a reaction

177

against the way of life of the type of artist who has taken his seat ostentatiously in the 'back row' and with whom people refuse to have anything to do. Thomas Mann and Henry James know, however, only too well that the artist is forced to lead an extra-human and inhuman existence, that the ways of normal life are not open to him and that spontaneous, unself-conscious, warm human feelings have no relevance to his purpose. The paradox of his lot is that it is his task to describe life from which he himself is excluded. This situation is followed by serious, often insoluble complications. Paul Overt, the younger of the two writers who confront each other in Henry James's *The Lesson of the Master*, revolts in vain against the cruel monastic discipline to which a life devoted to art is subjected and struggles to no avail against the forgoing of all personal and private happiness which Henry St. George, the master, demands of him. He is full of impatience and bitterness against the merciless tyranny of the power to which he has sold himself. 'You don't imagine, by any chance, that I'm defending art?' the master replies to him. 'Happy the societies in which it hasn't made its appearance.' And Thomas Mann's reproach to art is just as stern and implacable. For when he shows that all problematical, ambiguous and disreputable lives, all the feeble, the diseased and degenerate, all the adventurers, swindlers and criminals and, finally, even Hitler are spiritual relations of the artist,[226] he formulates the most dreadful charge ever brought against art.

The age of impressionism produces two extreme types of the modern artist estranged from society: the new bohemians and those who take refuge from Western civilization in distant, exotic lands. Both are the product of the same feeling, the same 'discomfort with culture', the only difference being that the first choose 'internal emigration', the others real flight. But both lead the same abstract life severed from immediate reality and practical activity; both express themselves in forms which must inevitably appear increasingly strange and unintelligible to the majority of the public. The voyage into remote lands, as an escape from modern civilization, is as old as the bohemian protest against the bourgeois way of life. Both have their source in romantic unreality and individualism, but they have become

178

transformed meanwhile and the form in which they now enter the artist's experience is attributable once again above all to Baudelaire. The romantics were still searching for the 'blue flower', for the land of dreams and ideals, 'Mais les vrais voyageurs', says Baudelaire, 'sont ceux-là seuls qui partent Pour partir. . . .' That is the real escape, the voyage into the unknown, which is undertaken not because one is enticed, but because one is disgusted by something.

> O Mort, vieux capitaine, il est temps! levons l'ancre!
> Ce pays nous ennuie, o Mort! Appareillons!
> Si le ciel et la mer sont noirs comme l'encre,
> Nos coeurs que tu connais sont remplis de rayons!

Rimbaud intensifies the pain of departing—'La vie est absente, nous ne sommes pas au monde'—but he scarcely intensifies the beauty of Baudelaire's words of farewell, which are unparalleled in the whole of modern poetry. Nevertheless, he is Baudelaire's only real heir, the only one who realizes the master's imaginary voyages, and turns into a way of life what before him had been mere escapades into the world of bohemianism.

In France the bohème is not a uniform and clear-cut phenomenon. There is no need of special evidence to prove that the frivolous and lovable young people in Puccini's opera have nothing in common with Rimbaud and his possession by the spirit of evil, or with Verlaine and his wavering between criminality and mysticism. But Rimbaud's and Verlaine's genealogy has many ramifications, and to describe it, it is necessary to distinguish between three different phases and forms of artist life: the bohème of the romantic, of the naturalistic and of the impressionistic age.[227] The bohème was originally no more than a demonstration against the bourgeois way of life. It consisted of young artists and students, who were mostly the sons of well-to-do people, and in whom the opposition to the prevailing society was usually a product of mere youthful exuberance and contrariness. Théophile Gautier, Gérard de Nerval, Arsène Houssaye, Nestor Roqueplan and all the rest of them, parted from bourgeois society, not because they were forced, but because they wanted to live differently from their bourgeois fathers. They

179

were genuine romantics, who wanted to be original and extravagant. They undertook their excursion into the world of the outlaws and the outcasts, just as one undertakes a journey into an exotic land; they knew nothing of the misery of the later bohème, and they were free to return to bourgeois society at any time. The bohème of the following generation, that of the militant naturalism with its headquarters in the beer-cellar, the generation to which Champfleury, Courbet, Nadar and Murger belonged, was, on the other hand, a real bohème, that is, an artistic proletariat, made up of people whose existence was absolutely insecure, people who stood outside the frontiers of bourgeois society, and whose struggle against the bourgeoisie was no high-spirited game but a bitter necessity. Their unbourgeois way of life was the form which best suited the questionable existence that they led and was in no sense any longer a mere masquerade. But just as Baudelaire, who belongs to this generation chronologically, marks, intellectually, a reversion to the romantic bohème, on the one hand, and an advance to the impressionistic, on the other, Murger also represents, albeit in a different sense, a transitional phenomenon. Now that the bohème ceases to be 'romantic', the bourgeoisie begins to romanticize and idealize it. In this process Murger plays the part of the *maître de plaisir*, and represents the Quartier Latin tamed and cleansed. For this service he himself is promoted, as he deserves, into the ranks of the authors acknowledged by the middle class. The philistine regards the bohème on the whole as an underworld. It attracts him and it repels him. He flirts with the freedom and irresponsibility which reign supreme in it, but shrinks from the disorder and anarchy which the realization of this freedom implies. Murger's idealization is intended to make the danger which threatens bourgeois society from this side seem more harmless than it is and to allow the unsuspecting bourgeois to continue luxuriating in his equivocal wish-fulfilment dreams. Murger's figures are usually gay, somewhat frivolous, but thoroughly good-natured young people, who will remember their bohemian life when they grow old, as the bourgeois reader remembers the riotous years when he was a student. In the eyes of the bourgeois this impression of the provisional took the final sting out of the bohème. And Murger was by no means alone in his views. Balzac also described the bohemian life of the young artists as a transitional stage. 'The bohème consists', he writes in *Un Prince de la Bohême*, 'of young people, who are still unknown, but who will be well known and famous one day.'

In the age of naturalism, however, not only Murger's conception but also the actual life of the bohemians is still an idyll, compared to the life of the poets and artists of the next generation who shut themselves off from bourgeois society—Rimbaud, Verlaine, Tristan Corbière and Lautréamont. The bohème had become a company of vagabonds and outlaws, a class in which demoralization, anarchy and misery dwell, a group of desperados, who not only break with bourgeois society, but with the whole of European civilization. Baudelaire, Verlaine and Toulouse-Lautrec are heavy drinkers, Rimbaud, Gauguin and Van Gogh tramps and homeless globe-trotters, Verlaine and Rimbaud die in hospital, Van Gogh and Toulouse-Lautrec live for some time in a lunatic asylum, and most of them spend their lives in cafés, music-halls, brothels, hospitals or on the street. They destroy everything in themselves that might be of use to society, they rage against everything that gives permanence and continuity to life and they rage against themselves, as if they were anxious to exterminate everything in their own nature which they have in common with others. 'I am killing myself', Baudelaire writes in a letter of 1845, 'because I am useless to others and a danger to myself.' But it is not merely the consciousness of his own unhappiness that fills him, but also the feeling that the happiness of others is something banal and vulgar. 'You are a happy man,' he writes in a later letter. 'I feel sorry for you, sir, for being happy so easily. A man must have sunk low to consider himself happy.'[228] We find the same contempt for the cheap feeling of happiness in Chekhov's short story *Gooseberries*. And that is no accident in the case of a writer who feels so much sympathy for bohemianism. 'Tell me why you lead such a monotonous life?' the hero of one of his short stories about artists asks his host. 'My life is tedious, dull, monotonous, because I am a painter, a queer fish, and have been worried all my life with envy, discontent, disbelief in my work: I am always poor, I am a vaga-

181

bond, but you are a wealthy, normal man, a landowner, a gentle-man—why do you live so tamely and take so little from life?'[229] The life of the older generation of bohemians was, at least, full of colour; they put up with their misery, in order to live colour-fully and interestingly. But the new bohemians live under the pressure of a dull, fusty and stifling boredom; art no longer intoxicates, it only narcotizes.

Yet neither Baudelaire nor Chekhov nor the others had any idea what a hell life could develop into for a man like Rimbaud. Western culture had to reach the stage of its present crisis before such a life could become conceivable at all. A neurasthenic, a ne'er-do-well, an idler, a thoroughly malignant and dangerous man who, wandering from country to country, manages to scrape a living for himself as language teacher, street hawker, circus employee, docker, agricultural day-labourer, sailor, volunteer in the Dutch army, mechanic, explorer, colonial trader and heaven knows what else, catches an infection somewhere in Africa, has to have a leg amputated in a hospital in Marseilles, in order, at the age of thirty-seven, to die piecemeal in the most terrible agony; a genius who writes immortal poems at the age of seven-teen, gives up writing poetry completely at the age of nineteen, and in whose letters there is never a mention of literature during the rest of his life; a criminal towards himself and others, who throws away his most precious possessions and completely forgets, completely denies that he has ever possessed them; one of the pioneers and, as many people maintain, the real founder of modern poetry, who, when the news of his fame reaches him in Africa, refuses to listen and dismisses it with a 'merde pour la poésie': can one imagine anything more appalling, anything more in conflict with the idea of a poet? Is it not, as Tristan Corbière says: 'His poems were by another; he had not read them'? Is it not the most terrible nihilism conceivable, the extremity of self-denial? And that is the real fruit of the seed sown by the respectable, decent-minded and fastidious bour-geois Flaubert and his sophisticated, cultivated and art-minded friends.

After 1890 the word 'decadence' loses its suggestive note and people begin to speak of 'symbolism' as the leading artistic trend.

Moréas introduces the term and defines it as the attempt to replace reality in poetry by the 'idea'.[230] The new terminology is in accordance with Mallarmé's victory over Verlaine and the shift of emphasis from sensualistic impressionism to spiritualism. It is often very difficult to distinguish symbolism from impressionism; the two concepts are partly antithetical, partly synonymous. There is a fairly sharp distinction between Verlaine's impressionism and Mallarmé's symbolism, but to find the proper stylistic category for a writer like Maeterlinck is by no means so simple. Symbolism, with its optical and acoustic effects, as well as the mixing and combining of the different sense data and the reciprocal action between the various art forms, above all what Mallarmé understood by the reconquest from music of the property of poetry, is 'impressionistic'. But, with its irrationalistic and spiritualistic approach, it also implies a sharp reaction against naturalistic and materialistic impressionism. For the latter, sense experience is something final and irreducible, whereas for symbolism, the whole of empirical reality is only the image of a world of ideas.

Symbolism represents, on the one hand, the final result of the development which began with romanticism, that is, with the discovery of metaphor as the germ-cell of poetry, and which led to the richness of impressionistic imagery, but it not only disowns impressionism on account of its materialistic world-view and the Parnasse on account of its formalism and rationalism, it also disowns romanticism on account of its emotionalism and the conventionality of its metaphorical language. In certain respects symbolism can be considered the reaction against the whole of earlier poetry;[231] it discovers something that had either never been known or never been emphasized before: 'poésie pure'[232]— the poetry that arises from the irrational, non-conceptual spirit of language, which is opposed to all logical interpretation. For symbolism, poetry is nothing but the expression of those relationships and correspondences, which language, left to itself, creates between the concrete and the abstract, the material and the ideal, and between the different spheres of the senses. Mallarmé thinks that poetry is the intimation of hovering and ever evaporating images; he asserts that to *name* an object is to destroy three-quarters of the pleasure which consists in the gradual divining of its true nature.[233] The symbol implies, however, not merely the deliberate avoidance of direct naming, but the indirect expression of a meaning, which it is impossible to describe directly, which is essentially indefinable and inexhaustible.

Mallarmé's generation by no means invented the symbol as a means of expression; symbolic art had also existed in previous ages. It merely discovered the difference between symbol and allegory, and made symbolism as a poetic style the conscious aim of its endeavours. It recognized, even though it was not always able to give expression to its insight, that allegory is nothing but the translation of an abstract idea into the form of a concrete image, whereby the idea continues to a certain extent to be independent of its metaphorical expression and could also be expressed in another form, whereas the symbol brings the idea and the image into an indivisible unity, so that the transformation of the image also implies the metamorphosis of the idea. In short, the content of a symbol cannot be translated into any other form, but a symbol can, on the other hand, be interpreted in various ways, and this variability of the interpretation, this apparent inexhaustibility of the meaning of the symbol, is its most essential characteristic. Compared with the symbol, the allegory always seems like the simple, plain and to some extent superfluous transcription of an idea which gains nothing by being translated from one sphere to another. The allegory is a kind of riddle, the solution to which is obvious; whereas the symbol can only be interpreted, it cannot be solved. The allegory is the expression of a static, the symbol that of a dynamic process of thought; the former sets a limit and a boundary to the association of ideas, the latter sets ideas in motion and keeps them in motion. High medieval art is expressed chiefly in symbols, late medieval art in allegories; the adventures of Don Quixote are symbolical, those of the heroes of the novels of chivalry which Cervantes takes as his model are allegorical. But in almost every age allegorical and symbolical art co-exist, and one often finds them intermingled in the works of one and the same artist. Lear's 'wheel of fire' is a symbol, Romeo's 'night's candles' an allegory; but the very next line in Romeo—'the jocund day

Stands tiptoe on the misty mountain tops'—has again a symbolic ring about it.

Symbolism is based on the assumption that poetry's task is to express something that cannot be moulded into a definite form and cannot be approached by a direct route. Since it is impossible to utter anything relevant about things through the clear media of the consciousness, whereas language discloses as it were automatically the secret relationships existing between them, the poet must, as Mallarmé intimates, 'give way to the initiative of the words';· he must allow himself to be borne along by the current of language, by the spontaneous succession of images and visions, which implies that language is not only more poetic but also more philosophical than reason. Rousseau's concept of a state of nature, which is allegedly better than civilization, and Burke's idea of an organic historical development, which supposedly produces more valuable things than reformism, are the real sources of this mystical poetic theory, and they are still discernible in the Tolstoyan and Nietzschean notion of the body that is wiser than the mind, and in the Bergsonian theory of the intuition that is deeper than the intellect. But this new mysticism of language, this 'alchimie du verbe', comes, like the whole hallucinatory interpretation of poetry, immediately from Rimbaud. He it was who made the statement that has had a decisive influence on the whole of modern literature, namely that the poet must become a *seer* and that it is his task to prepare himself for this by systematically weaning his senses from their normal functions, by denaturalizing and dehumanizing them. The practice which Rimbaud recommended was not only in accordance with the ideal of artificiality, that all the decadents had in mind as their ultimate ideal, but already contained the new element, namely that of deformity and grimace as a means of expression, that was to become so important for modern expressionistic art. It was based in essentials on the feeling that the normal, spontaneous spiritual attitudes are artistically sterile and that the poet must overcome the natural man within himself, in order to discover the hidden meaning of things.

Mallarmé was a Platonist, who regarded ordinary empirical reality as the corrupted form of an ideal, timeless, absolute being,

185

but who wanted to realize the world of ideas, at least partly, in the life of this world. He lived in the vacuum of his intellectualism, completely cut off from ordinary practical life, and had almost no relationships at all with the world outside literature. He destroyed all spontaneity inside himself and became as it were the anonymous author of his works. No one ever followed Flaubert's example more faithfully. 'Tout au monde existe pour aboutir à un livre'—the master himself could not have put it more Flaubertishly. 'À un livre', Mallarmé says; but what results is, in fact, hardly a book. He spends his whole life writing, re-writing and correcting a dozen sonnets, two dozen shorter and about six larger poems, a dramatic scene and some theoretical fragments.[234] He knew that his art was a blind alley leading nowhere,[235] and that is why the theme of sterility takes up so much space in his poetry.[236] The life of the refined, cultured and clever Mallarmé ended in just as dreadful a fiasco as Rimbaud's vagabond existence. They both despaired of the meaning of art, culture and human society, and it is difficult to say which of the two acted more consistently.[237] Balzac proved himself a good prophet in his *Chef-d'œuvre inconnu*; in estranging himself from life, the artist has become the destroyer of his own work.

Flaubert had already thought of writing a book without a subject, which would be pure form, pure style, mere ornament, and it was he on whom the idea of 'poésie pure' first dawned. Perhaps Mallarmé would not have literally made his own the dictum that 'a beautiful line without meaning is more valuable than a less beautiful with meaning'; he did not actually believe in the renunciation of all intellectual content in poetry, but he demanded that the poet should renounce the rousing of emotions and passions and the use of extra-aesthetic, practical and rational motifs. The conception of 'pure poetry' can be considered, at least, the best summing-up of his views on the nature of art and the embodiment of the ideal he had in mind as a poet. Mallarmé began writing a poem without knowing exactly where the first line would lead; the poem arose as the crystallization of words and lines which combined almost of their own accord.[238] The doctrine of 'poésie pure' transposes the principle of this creative method into a theory of the receptive act, and lays down that for a poetic experience to take place it is not absolutely necessary to know the whole poem, however short; often one or two lines are sufficient, sometimes only a few verbal scraps, to produce in us the mood corresponding to the poem. In other words: to enjoy a poem, it is not necessary or it is, at any rate, not sufficient to grasp its rational meaning, indeed, it is, as folk poetry shows, not at all necessary that the poem itself should have an exact 'meaning'.[239] The similarity of the mode of reception described here to the contemplation of an impressionistic painting from a suitable distance is obvious, but the conception of 'pure poetry' contains features which are not necessarily contained in that of impressionism. It represents the purest and most uncompromising form of aestheticism, and expresses the basic idea that a poetic world wholly independent of ordinary, practical, rational reality, an autonomous, self-contained aesthetic microcosm revolving around its own axis, is thoroughly possible.

The aristocratic aloofness expressed in this estrangement and isolation of the poet from reality is still further intensified by the deliberate vagueness of expression and the intentional difficulty of the poetic thought. Mallarmé is the heir of the 'dark rhyming' of the troubadours and the erudition of the humanist poets. He looks for the indefinite, the enigmatical, the obscure not only because he knows that the expression seems to be the more richly allusive the vaguer it is, but also because a poem must, in his opinion, 'be something mysterious to which the reader has to search for the key'.[240] Catulle Mendès expressly refers to this aristocratism of the poetic practice of Mallarmé and his followers. To the question of Jules Huret as to whether he reproaches the symbolists for their obscurity, he replies: 'By no means. Pure art is becoming more and more the possession of an élite in this age of democracy, the possession of a bizarre, morbid and charming aristocracy. It is right that its level should be upheld and that it should be surrounded by a secret.'[241] From the discovery that rational understanding is not the characteristic mental approach to poetry Mallarmé derives the conclusion that the basic feature of all great poetry is the incomprehensible and the incommensurable. The artistic advantages of the elliptic mode of expression, of which he is thinking, are obvious; by omitting certain links in the chain of association a speed and intensity is achieved which is lost when the effects are developed slowly.[242] Mallarmé makes full use of these advantages and his poetry owes its attraction above all to the compression of the ideas and the leaps and bounds of the images. The reasons why he is difficult to understand are not, however, by any means always implicit in the artistic idea itself, but are often connected with quite arbitrary and playful linguistic manipulations.[243] And this ambition to be difficult for the sake of difficulty reveals the poet's very intention to isolate himself from the masses and restrict himself to as small a circle as possible. In spite of their apparent indifference to political affairs, the symbolists were essentially reactionary-minded; they were, as Barrès remarks, the Boulangists of literature.[244] The poetry of the present day, partly for the same reason as that of Mallarmé, seems esoteric and undemocratic and as if it were deliberately shutting itself off from the wider public, different as the political convictions of the individual poets are and much as we know that this difficulty is the result of a development that has been in preparation for a long time and which it is impossible for modern culture to circumvent.

Since the Restoration, England had never been so strongly under French influence as in the last quarter of the nineteenth century. After a long period of prosperity, the British Empire now passes through an economic crisis, which develops into a crisis of the Victorian spirit itself. The 'great depression' begins around the middle of the 'seventies and scarcely lasts longer than a decade, but during this time the English middle class loses its former self-confidence. It begins to feel the economic competition of foreign, mostly younger nations, such as the Germans and the Americans, and finds itself involved in a fierce contest for the possession of the colonies. The direct effect of the new situation is the retrogression of the economic liberalism which the English middle class had hitherto regarded, in spite of all criticism, in the light of an irrefutable dogma.[245] The decline in exports reduces production and depresses the standard of living of the working class. Unemployment increases, strikes multiply and the socialist movement, which had come to a standstill after the revolutionary years in the middle of the century, now not only acquires new strength, but becomes conscious for the first time in England of its real aims and power. This change has far-reaching consequences for the intellectual development of the country. The consciousness of confronting foreign countries capable of competing in the world market brings about the end of British isolationism[246] and prepares the ground for foreign intellectual influences. Amongst these that of French literature is of prime importance; the influence of the Russian novel, of Wagner, Ibsen and Nietzsche, supplements the stimuli coming from France. Much more important than the external influences, indeed, their real precondition, is the fact that, with the shaking of middle-class self-confidence and the belief in England's divine mission in the world, but above all with the new socialistic movement of the 'eighties, a renewed struggle for individual freedom sets in and gives the whole intellectual development, the progressive literature and the way of life of the younger generation the stamp of a fight for freedom. The intellectual disposition of the period shows hardly a feature which is independent of this fight against tradition and convention, puritanism and philistinism, barren utilitarianism and sentimental romanticism. Youth fights the older generation for the possession and enjoyment of life. Modernism becomes the aesthetic and moral slogan of youth 'knocking at the door' and demanding to be let in. Ibsen's ideal of self-realization, the will to give expression to one's own personality and to obtain recognition for it, becomes the aim and content of life. And unclarified as what is understood by this 'self-realization' usually remains, the moral security of the old bourgeois world collapses under the attack of the new generation. Until about 1875 youth confronts a generally speaking stable society, self-confident in its traditions and conventions and respected even by its opponents. One feels not only with a Jane Austen but even with a George Eliot that they face a social order which, if not exactly ideal and to be accepted unconditionally, is, at any rate, by no means negligible or simply replaceable, whereas now all the norms of social life suddenly cease to be recognized as valid; everything begins to waver, to become problematical and open to discussion.

The liberal tendency in the English literature and art of the 'eighties represents an unpolitical individualism, even though there is a close connection between the younger generation's quest for self-realization and its fight against the old superindividual forms and the new political and social situation.[247] This younger generation is absolutely hostile to the bourgeoisie, but it is, on the whole, by no means democratic or even socialistic. Its sensualism and hedonism, its aim of enjoying life and becoming enraptured with it, of turning every hour of this life into an unforgettable and irreplaceable experience, often assumes an antisocial and a-moral character. The anti-philistine movement is not directed against the capitalistic, but against the dull, art-despising bourgeoisie. In England the whole movement of modernism is dominated by this hatred for the philistine which, incidentally, becomes a new mechanical convention. Most of the changes which impressionism undergoes in this country are also conditioned by it. In France, impressionist art and literature was not expressly anti-bourgeois in character; the French had already finished with their fight against philistinism and the symbolists even felt a certain sympathy for the conservative middle class. The literature of decadence in England has, on the other hand, to undertake the work of undermining which had been carried out in France partly by the romantics, partly by the naturalists. The most striking feature of the English literature of the period, in contrast to the French, is the proneness to paradox, to a surprising, bizarre, deliberately shocking mode of expression, to an intellectual smartness, the coquettish complacency and utter lack of concern for truth of which seems in such bad taste today. It is obvious that this fondness for paradox is nothing but the spirit of contradiction and has its real origin in the desire to 'épater le bourgeois'.

All the peculiarities and mannerisms of language, thought, clothing and way of life of the rebels are to be regarded as a protest against the outlook of the dull, unimaginative, mendacious and hypocritical philistine. Their extravagant dandyism is as much a protest as the colourful language in which all the treasures of the impressionistic style are paraded. The English decadent movement has been rightly described as a fusion of Mayfair and Bohemia. In England we find neither a bohemianism as absolute as the French, nor such uncompromising, unapproachable ivory-tower existences as that of Mallarmé. The English middle class still has sufficient vigour to absorb them or to segregate them. Oscar Wilde is a successful bourgeois writer, so long as he seems endurable to the ruling class, but as soon as he begins to disgust them, he is mercilessly 'liquidated'. In England the dandy takes the place of the bohemian to some extent, just as he was already his counterpart in France. He is the bourgeois intellectual taken out of his proper class into a higher one, whilst the bohemian is the artist who has sunk down to the proletariat. The fastidious elegance and extravagance of the dandy fulfils the same function as the depravation and dissipation of the bohemians. They embody the same protest against the routine and triviality of bourgeois life, the only difference being that the English resign themselves to the sunflower in the buttonhole more easily than to the open neck. It is a well-known fact that the prototypes of Musset, Gautier, Baudelaire and Barbey d'Aurevilly were already Englishmen; Whistler, Wilde and Beardsley, on the other hand, take over the philosophy of dandyism from the French. For Baudelaire, the dandy is the living indictment of a standardizing democracy. He unites within himself all the gentlemanly virtues that are still possible today; he is a match for every situation and is never astonished at anything; he never becomes vulgar and always preserves the cool smile of the stoic. Dandyism is the last revelation of heroism in an age of decadence, a sunset, a last radiant beam of human pride.[248] The elegance of dress, the fastidiousness of manners, the mental austerity, are only the external discipline which the members of this higher order impose upon themselves in the trite world of today; what really matters is the inward superiority and independence, the practical aimlessness and disinterestedness of life and action.[249] Baudelaire places the dandy above the artist;[250] for the latter is still capable of enthusiasm, still strives, still works—is still banausic in the ancient meaning of the word. The cruelty of Balzac's vision is here surpassed: the artist not only destroys his work, he also destroys his claim to fame and honour. When Oscar Wilde ranks the work of art that he intends to make out of his life, the art with which he shapes his conversations, relationships and habits, above his literary works, he has Baudelaire's dandy in mind—the ideal of an absolutely useless, purposeless and unmotivated existence.

But how complacent and coquettish this forgoing of the artist's honour and fame is, is shown by the strange combination of dilettantism and aestheticism which typifies the English decadents. Art had really never been taken so seriously before as it was now; never had so much trouble been taken to write skilfully chiselled lines, a flawless prose, perfectly articulated and balanced sentences. Never had 'beauty', the decorative element, the elegant, the exquisite and the costly played a greater rôle in art; never had it been practised with so much preciosity and virtuosity. If painting was the model for poetry in France, then it was the goldsmith's art in England. It is not for nothing that Wilde speaks so enthusiastically of Huysmans' 'jewelled style'. Colours like the 'jade-green piles of vegetables' in Covent Garden are his personal contribution to the inheritance of the French. G. K. Chesterton remarks somewhere that the scheme of the Shavian paradox consists in the author saying 'light-green grapes' instead of 'white grapes'. Wilde, who, in spite of all the differences, has so much in common with Shaw, also bases his metaphors on the most obvious and trivial details, and it is precisely this combination of the trivial and the exquisite which is so characteristic of his style. It is as if he were trying to say that there is beauty in even the most commonplace reality, as he had learnt from Walter Pater. 'Not the fruit of experience, but experience itself, is the end . . . to maintain this ecstasy, is success in life,' as we read in the Conclusion of *The Renaissance*, and these sentences contain the whole programme of the aesthetic movement. Walter Pater completes the trend which begins with Ruskin and is continued in William Morris, but he is no longer interested in his predecessors' social aims; his only aim is hedonistic: the heightening of the intensity of the aesthetic experience. With him impressionism is no more than a form of epicureanism. Since 'everything is in flux' in the Heraclitean sense, and life roars past us with uncanny speed, there is only one truth for us —that of the moment—and only so much delight and pleasure as we can wrest from the moment. All we can do is not to let a moment pass without enjoying its own peculiar charm, its inner power and beauty.—One realizes best how far the aesthetic movement in England departed from French impressionism, if one thinks of such a phenomenon as Beardsley. It is impossible to imagine a more 'literary' art than his, or one in which psychology, the intellectual motif and the anecdote play a greater rôle. The most essential element of his style is the merely ornamental calligraphy that the French masters tried so painfully to avoid. And this calligraphy is the starting point of the whole development which leads to the fashionable illustrators and stage decorators so beloved by the semi-educated and well-placed bourgeoisie.

The intellectualism which, in spite of the strong intuitionistic current, forms the predominant trend in French literature, also represents the main characteristic of the new literature in England. Wilde not only accepts Matthew Arnold's view that it is the critic who determines the intellectual climate of a century,[251] and not only assents to Baudelaire's statement that every genuine artist must also be a critic, he even places the critic above the artist and tends to look at the world through the eyes of the critic. This explains the fact that his art, like that of his contemporaries, usually seems so dilettante. Everything they produce seems like the virtuoso playing of very gifted people who are not, however, professional artists. But that was, if one may believe them, precisely the impression they wanted to create. Meredith and Henry James move on the foundations of the same intellectualism, though on a much higher level. If there is a tradition in the English novel connecting George Eliot and Henry James,[252] then it lies without any doubt in this intellectualism. From a sociological point of view, a new phase in the history of English literature began with George Eliot—the rise of a new and more exacting reading public. But, although she represented an intellectual stratum high above the Dickens public, it was still possible for comparatively large sections of the public to enjoy George Eliot, whereas Meredith and Henry James are read only by a quite small stratum of the intelligentsia, the members of which no longer expect a novel to provide them with a thrilling plot and colourful characters, as did the public of Dickens and George Eliot, but above all with a faultless style and mature, discriminating judgements on life. What is usually sheer mannerism in Meredith is often a real intellectual obsession in Henry James, but both are the representatives of an art whose relations with reality are often rather abstract, and whose figures seem to move in a vacuum compared with the world of Stendhal, Balzac, Flaubert, Tolstoy and Dostoevsky.

Towards the end of the century impressionism becomes the predominant style throughout Europe. From now onwards a poetry of moods, of atmospherical impressions, of the declining seasons of the year and the fugitive hours of the day is to be found everywhere. People spend their time puzzling over lyrics which express fleeting, scarcely palpable sensations, indefinite, indefinable sensual stimuli, delicate colours and tired voices. The undecided, the vague, that which moves on the nethermost boundaries of sensual perception, becomes the main theme of poetry; it is, however, not objective reality with which the poets are concerned, but their emotions about their own sensitiveness and capacity for experience. This unsubstantial art of moods and atmosphere now dominates all forms of literature; they are all transformed into lyricism, into imagery and music, into timbres and nuances. The story is reduced to mere situations, the plot to lyrical scenes, the character drawing to the description of spiritual dispositions and trends. Everything becomes episodical, peripheral to a life without a centre.

In literature outside France the impressionistic features of the exposition are more strongly marked than the symbolistic. With only French literature in mind, one is easily tempted to identify impressionism with symbolism.[253] Thus even Victor Hugo called the young Mallarmé 'mon cher poète impressioniste'. But the differences are unmistakable on closer examination; impressionism is materialistic and sensualistic, however delicate its motifs, whereas symbolism is idealistic and spiritualistic, although its world of ideas is only a sublimated world of the senses. But the most fundamental difference is that whilst French symbolism, to which must also be added, above all, Belgian symbolism, together with its offshoots, that is to say, Bergson's vitalism, on the one hand, and the catholicism and royalism of the *Action française*, on the other, represents a tendency which is always about to turn into activism, the impressionism of the Viennese, the Germans, the Italians and the Russians, with Schnitzler, Hofmannsthal, Rilke, D'Annunzio and Chekhov as the leading personalities, expresses a philosophy of passivity, of complete surrender to the immediate environment and of unresisting absorption in the passing moment. But how deep the relations between impressionism and symbolism are, how easily the irrational factor gets the upper hand in both, and passivity turns into activism, is shown by the development of such poets as Stefan George and D'Annunzio. One would be quite prepared to connect the latter's lapses into bad taste, his chronic intoxication with life and his sumptuous verbal draperies with his fascist inclinations, if in Barrès and Stefan George the same political tendency were not connected with taste and literary manners of such greater quality.

The Viennese represent the purest form of the impressionism which forgoes all resistance to the stream of experience. Perhaps it is the ancient and tired culture of this city, the lack of all active national politics and the great part played in literary life by foreigners, especially Jews, which gives Viennese impressionism its peculiarly subtle and passive character. This is the art of the sons of rich bourgeois, the expression of the joyless hedonism of that 'second generation' which lives on the fruits of its fathers' work. They are nervous and melancholy, tired and aimless, sceptical and ironical about themselves, these poets of exquisite moods which evaporate in a trice and leave nothing behind but the feeling of evanescence, of having missed one's opportunities, and the consciousness of being unfit for life. The latent content of every kind of impressionism, the coincidence of the near and far, the strangeness of the nearest, most everyday things, the feeling of being for ever separated from the world, here becomes the basic experience.

> Wie kann das sein, dass diese nahen Tage
> fort sind, fuer immer fort und ganz vergangen?
>
> (How can it be that these recent days
> are gone, gone for ever and completely lost?)

asks Hofmannsthal, and this question contains almost all the others: the horror at the 'here and now, that is, at the same time, the beyond', the amazement at the fact that 'these things are different and the words we use different again', the consternation over the fact that 'all men go their own ways' and, finally, the last great question: 'When a man has passed on, he takes a secret with him: how it was possible for him, just him—to live in the spiritual sense of the word.' If one thinks of Balzac's 'Nous mourons tous inconnus', one sees how consistently the European outlook on life has developed since 1830. This outlook has one constant, always predominant and ever more profoundly rooted characteristic: the consciousness of estrangement and loneliness. It may sink down to the feeling of absolute god- and world-forsakenness or rise, in the moment of exuberance, which is often that of the greatest despair, to the idea of superhumanity; the superman feels just as lonely and unhappy in the rarified air of his mountain heights as the aesthete in his ivory tower.

The most curious phenomenon in the history of impressionism in Europe is its adoption by Russia and the emergence of a writer like Chekhov, who can be described as the purest representative of the whole movement. Nothing is more surprising than to meet such a personality in a country that not long before has lived in the intellectual atmosphere of the enlightenment and to which that aestheticism and decadentism which accompany the rise of impressionism in the West had been completely foreign. But in a technical century like the nineteenth, the spread of ideas proceeds rapidly and the adoption of the industrial forms of economy now creates conditions in Russia which lead to the rise of a social structure corresponding to that of the Western intelligentsia and of an outlook on life similar to that of *ennui*.[254] Gorky understood from the very beginning the decisive rôle that Chekhov was to play in Russian literature; he saw that with him a whole epoch had come to an end and that his style had an attraction for the new generation which they could no longer forgo. 'Do you know what you are doing?' he writes to him in 1900. 'You are slaying realism. . . . After any of your stories, however insignificant, everything appears crude, as if written not by a pen but by a cudgel.'[255]

As the apologist of inefficiency and failure, it is true that Chekhov has his predecessors in Dostoevsky and Turgenev, but they had not yet regarded lack of success and loneliness as the inevitable fate of the best. Chekhov's philosophy is the first to hinge on the experience of the unapproachable isolation of men, their inability to bridge the last gap that divides them, or, even if they do sometimes succeed in doing that, to persist in an intimate nearness to one another, which is so typical of the whole of impressionism. Chekhov's characters are filled with the feeling of absolute helplessness and hopelessness, of the incurable crippling of the will-power, on the one hand, and on the fruitlessness of all effort, on the other. This philosophy of passivity and indolence, this feeling that nothing in life reaches an end and a goal, has considerable formal consequences; it leads to stress being laid on the episodical nature and irrelevance of all external happenings, it brings about a renunciation of all formal organization, all concentration and integration, and prefers to express itself in an ex-centric form of composition in which the given framework is neglected and violated. Just as Degas moves important parts of the representation to the edge of the picture, and makes the frame overlap them, Chekhov ends his short stories and plays with an anacrusis, in order to arouse the impression of the inconclusiveness, abruptness and casual, arbitrary ending of the works. He follows a formal principle that is in every respect opposed to 'frontality', one in which everything is aimed at giving the representation the character of something overheard by chance, intimated by chance, something that has occurred by chance.

The feeling of the senselessness, insignificance and fragmentariness of external happenings leads in the drama to the reduction of the plot to an indispensable minimum and to the forgoing of the effects which were so characteristic of the 'pièce bien faite'. The effective stage drama owes its success fundamentally to the principles of classical form: to the uniformity, conclusiveness and well-proportioned arrangement of the plot. The poetic drama, that is, both the symbolical drama of Maeterlinck and the impressionistic drama of Chekhov, renounces these structural expedients in the interest of direct lyrical expression. Chekhov's dramatic form is perhaps the least theatrical in the whole history of the drama—a form in which 'coups de théâtre', the stage effects of surprise and tension, play the smallest rôle. There is no drama in which less happens, in which there is less dramatic movement, less dramatic conflict. The characters do not fight, do not defend themselves, are not defeated—they simply go under, founder slowly, are swallowed up by the routine of their eventless, hopeless lives. They endure their fate with patience, a fate that is consummated not in the form of catastrophes, but of disappointments.

Ever since the existence of this kind of play without action and without movements, doubts have been expressed as to its *raison d'être* and the question has been raised whether it is real drama and real theatre at all, that is to say, whether it will prove capable of surviving on the stage.

The 'pièce bien faite' was still a drama in the old sense which, although it had indeed assimilated certain elements of naturalism, still kept on the whole both to the technical conventions and heroic ideal of the classical and romantic drama. It is not until the 'eighties that naturalism conquers the stage, that is, at a time when naturalism in the novel is already on the decline. Henri Becque's *Les Corbeaux*, the first naturalistic drama, is written in the year 1882, and Antoine's 'Théâtre libre', the first naturalistic theatre, is founded in 1887. To begin with, the bourgeois public's attitude is absolutely negative, although Henri Becque and his direct successors merely turn to good account for the stage what Balzac and Flaubert had long since made common literary property. The naturalistic drama in the narrower sense comes into being outside France, in the Scandinavian countries, in Germany and Russia. The public gradually accepts its conventions and, as far as the plays of Ibsen, Brieux and Shaw are concerned, merely protests against the immoderately aggressive attacks on bourgeois morality. Finally, however, even the anti-bourgeois drama conquers the bourgeois public and even Gerhart Hauptmann's socialistic drama celebrates its earliest and greatest triumphs in the bourgeois West End of Berlin. The naturalistic theatre is merely the path leading to the intimate theatre, to the psychological differentiation of the dramatic conflict and to a more immediate contact between the stage and the public. It is true that the all too obvious expedients of stagecraft, the complicated intrigue and the artificial tension, the delays and surprises, the great scenes of conflict and the violent curtains, are held in honour for a longer period than the corresponding expedients in the novel, but they suddenly begin to seem ridiculous and have to be replaced or concealed by more subtle effects. Without the conquest of comparatively large sections of the public, the naturalistic drama would never have become a reality in the history of the theatre; for a volume of lyrical poetry can appear in a few hundred, a novel in one or two thousand copies, but a play must be seen by tens of thousands to pay. The new naturalistic drama had long since proved itself capable of surviving from this point of view, at a time when the critics and aesthetic theorists were still racking their brains about its admissibility. They found it impossible to emancipate themselves from the classicistic conception of the drama and even the most reasonable and those with the greatest taste for art among them considered the naturalistic theatre a 'contradiction in terms' [256] They found it impossible, in particular, to disregard the fact that the economy of the classical drama was being neglected, that unconstrained, free-and-easy conversation was being carried on on the stage, problems discussed, experiences described, no end of subjects thrashed out, as if the time of performance were unlimited and the play had never to come to an end. They criticized the naturalistic drama for not having arisen 'from a consideration of destiny, character and action, but from a detailed reproduction of reality';[257] in fact, nothing had happened, however, except that reality itself, with its concrete limitations, was felt to be heavy with destiny, and that 'characters' were no longer interpreted as clear-cut stage puppets, but as many-sided, complicated, inconsistent and, in the old sense of the word, 'unprincipled' people, who, as Strindberg explained in the Preface to *Miss Julia* in 1888, were the product of particular situations, of heredity, of the milieu, of education, of natural disposition, of the influences of place, season and chance, and whose decisions were conditioned not by a single but by a whole series of motives.

The preponderance in the drama of inwardness, mood, atmosphere and lyricism over the plot is, incidentally, the result of the same progressive elimination of the story element as in impressionist painting. The whole art of the period shows a tendency to the psychological and the lyrical, and the escape from the story, the replacement of external by internal movement, of the plot by a philosophy and interpretation of life, can be described as the really basic characteristic of the new trend in art which is everywhere coming to the fore. But whilst anecdotal painting had found hardly any advocates amongst the art critics, the dramatic critics protested most emphatically against the neglect of the plot in the drama. They speak, especially in Germany, of a fateful separation of the drama from the theatre, of the decisive rôle played by suitability for the stage in theatrical experience, of the mass character of this experience and the fundamental absurdity of the intimate theatre. The motives inspiring the opposition to the naturalistic drama were of many kinds; the reactionary political tendency did not always play the chief part and often found expression only in a roundabout way; of more decisive importance was the toying with the idea of the 'monumental theatre', which was played off, again above all in Germany, against the intimate theatre, that is to say, against the really topical form of theatre, and the ambition to create a theatre for the masses which certainly existed, but did not constitute a theatre public. It was typical of the whole confusion of ideas that the classicism of the old aristocracy and bourgeoisie was alleged to be the style suitable for the future people's theatre as against the naturalism rooted in the democratic outlook on life.

The most serious reproach levelled against the new drama was on account of the determinism and relativism which are inseparable from the naturalistic outlook. It was pointed out that where internal and external freedom, absolute values and objective, universally acknowledged, unquestionable moral laws are non-existent, no real, that is, no tragic drama is possible either. The determinism of moral norms and the appreciation of antithetical moral points of view made a real dramatic conflict impossible from the very outset, so it was said. When one can understand and forgive everything, then the hero fighting at the risk of his life must ultimately seem like a stubborn fool, the conflict must lose its inevitability and the drama acquire a tragicomic and pathological character.[258] The whole train of thought teems with a confusion of ideas, with pseudo-problems and sophisms. First of all, the tragic drama is here identified with the drama as such or, at any rate, represented as its ideal form, a preconception which is in itself very relative, because historically and sociologically conditioned. In reality, not only the non-tragic, but also the drama without a clear-cut conflict is a legitimate form of theatre, which is, therefore, perfectly compatible with a relativisitic outlook on life. But even if one considers conflict an indispensable element of the drama, it is difficult to see why shattering conflicts should take place only when absolute values are at stake. Is it not just as shattering when men are fighting for their ideologically conditioned moral principles? And even if their struggle were necessarily tragi-comic, is not tragi-comedy one of the strongest dramatic effects in an age of rationalism and relativism? But the presupposition of the whole argument, that is to say, the assumption that lack of freedom and moral relativism make tragedy impossible, is open to question. It is by no means an established fact that only absolutely free, socially independent people, kings and generals, for instance, are the most suitable heroes in tragedy. Is not the fate of Hebbel's Meister Anton, Ibsen's Gregers Werle, Hauptmann's Fuhrmann Henschel, tragic? Even if one admits without qualification that tragic and sad are not one and the same thing. It would be 'undemocratic', to say the least, to maintain with Schiller that there can be nothing tragic about the theft of silver spoons. Whether a situation is tragic or not depends solely on the measure of power with which irreconcilable moral principles are found in a human soul. For a tragic impression to be made, it is not even necessary that a public that believes in absolute values should see these questioned, and even less so with a public that has lost the belief in such values.

The central figure in the history of the modern drama is Ibsen, not merely because he is the greatest theatrical talent of the century, but also because he gives the most intense dramatic expression to the moral problems of his age. His settlement of accounts with aestheticism, the crucial problem of his generation, marks the beginning and the end of his artistic development. He writes to Björnson as early as 1865: 'If I were to tell at this

201

moment what has been the chief result of my stay abroad, I should say that it consisted in my having driven out of myself the aestheticism which had a great power over me—an isolated aestheticism with a claim to independent existence. Aestheticism of this kind seems to me now as great a curse to poetry as theology is to religion.'[259] To all appearances, Ibsen achieves his mastery of this problem under the influence of Kierkegaard, who may have played a very important rôle in his development, even though, as he himself admits, he did not understand much of the philosopher's teaching.[260] Kierkegaard, with his categorical 'Either-Or', will have given the decisive impulse to the development of Ibsen's moral austerity.[261] Ibsen's ethical passion, the consciousness of having to choose and decide for oneself, his conception of art as 'passing sentence on oneself', all that has its roots in Kierkegaardian ideas. It has often been observed that Brand's 'All or Nothing' corresponds to Kierkegaard's 'Either-Or', but Ibsen owes more than that to the uncompromisingness of his teacher—he owes him his whole unromantic and totally unaesthetic concept of the ethical attitude. The short-sightedness of the romantics consisted above all in the fact that they saw all the things of the mind in terms of aesthetics and that all values had a more or less genius-like character in their eyes. Kierkegaard was the first to emphasize, in opposition to romanticism, that religious and ethical experience has nothing to do with beauty and genius, and that a religious martyr is absolutely different from a poet or philosopher. Apart from him, there was no one in the post-romantic West who had grasped the limitations of the aesthetic and who would have been capable of influencing Ibsen in this direction. How far Ibsen was otherwise influenced by Kierkegaard in his criticism of romanticism is hard to say. The unreality of romanticism represented a general problem of the age and he certainly did not need a particular stimulus to set him grappling with it. The whole of French naturalism hinged on the conflict between the ideal and reality, between poetry and truth, poetry and prose, and all the important thinkers of the century recognized the lack of a sense of reality as the curse of modern culture. In this respect Ibsen merely continued the struggle of his predecessors and stood at the end of a long succession in which the opponents of romanticism were united. The fatal blow which he struck at the enemy consisted in his exposure of the tragi-comedy of romantic idealism. It is true that there had been nothing absolutely new about that since the appearance of *Don Quixote*, but Cervantes had still treated his hero with a good deal of sympathy and forbearance, whereas Ibsen completely destroys his Brand, Peer Gynt and Gregers Werle. The 'ideal demands' of his romantics are revealed as pure egoism, the harshness of which is scarcely mitigated by the artlessness of the egoists themselves. Don Quixote asserted his ideals above all against his own interests, whereas Ibsen's idealists are merely distinguished by their intolerance towards others.

Ibsen owed his European fame to the social message of his plays, which was reducible, in the final analysis, to a single idea, the duty of the individual towards himself, the task of self-realization, the enforcement of one's own nature against the narrow-minded, stupid and out-of-date conventions of bourgeois society. It was his gospel of individualism, his glorification of the sovereign personality and his apotheosis of the creative life, that is, once again a more or less romantic ideal, that made the deepest impression on the younger generation, and that was not only akin to Nietzsche's ideal of the superman and Bergson's vitalism, but also found an echo in Shaw's idea of the 'life-force'. Ibsen was fundamentally an anarchistic individualist, who regarded personal freedom as life's supreme value, and based his whole thought on the idea that the free individual, independent of all external ties, can do very much for himself, whereas society can do very little for him. His idea of self-realization had in itself a very far-reaching social significance, but the 'social problem' as such hardly worried him at all. 'I have really never had a strong feeling for solidarity,' he writes to Brandes in 1871.[262] His thinking revolved around private ethical problems; society itself was for him merely the expression of the principle of evil. He saw in it nothing but the rule of stupidity, of prejudice and force. Finally, he attained that aristocratically conservative master morality, to which he gave the clearest expression in *Rosmersholm*. In Europe he was regarded, as a result of his modernism, his anti-philistinism and his embittered struggle against all conventions, as a thoroughly progressive mind, but in his own country, where his political views were seen in a more adequate context, he was considered, in contrast to Björnson the radical, the great conservative writer. Outside Norway, however, his historical importance was assessed more accurately. There he was looked upon as one of the few representative personalities of the age—if not the only one who could be compared with Tolstoy. He too, like Tolstoy himself, owed his reputation and influence not so much to his literary work, as to his activity as a teacher and an agitator. He was honoured, above all, as the great moral preacher, the passionate accuser and the fearless champion of the truth, for whom the stage was merely the means to a higher end. But Ibsen had nothing positive to say to his contemporaries as a politician. His whole outlook on life was shot through with a profound contradiction: he fought against conventional morality, bourgeois prejudices and the prevailing society on behalf of an idea of freedom in the realizability of which he himself did not believe. He was a crusader without a faith, a revolutionary without a social ideal, a reformer who finally turned out to be a sad fatalist.

In the end he stopped precisely at the point where Balzac's Frenhofer or Rimbaud and Mallarmé had stopped: Rubek, the hero of his last play, the purest embodiment of his idea of the artist, disowns his work and feels what more or less every artist had felt since the romantic movement, that he had lost life itself by living only for art. 'A summer night on the Vidda! With thee! With thee! Ah, Irene, that could have been our life!' This exclamation contains a judgement on the whole of modern art. From the apotheosis of the 'summer nights' of life there has developed an unsatisfying substitute and an opiate, which blunts the senses and makes men incapable of enjoying life itself.

Shaw is Ibsen's only real disciple and successor—the only one to continue the fight against romanticism effectively and to deepen the great European discussion of the century. The unmasking of the romantic hero, the shattering of the belief in the great, theatrical and tragic gesture, is consummated by him. Everything purely decorative, grandiosely heroic, sublime and idealistic becomes suspect; all sentimentality and refusal to face reality is revealed as humbug and fraud. The psychology of self-deception is the source of his art and he is not merely one of the bravest and most uncompromising, but also one of the most buoyant and amusing unmaskers of the self-deceivers. He can in no way deny his descent from the enlightenment, the origin of his whole legend-destroying and fiction-revealing thought, but through his philosophy of history, which has its roots in historical materialism, he is at the same time the most progressive and the most modern writer of his generation. He shows that the angle from which people see the world and themselves, the lies that they proclaim as the truth or allow to prevail as such and for which they are in certain circumstances capable of doing anything, are ideologically conditioned, that is, by economic interests and social aspirations. The worst thing is not that they think irrationally—they often think only too rationally—but that they have no sense of reality, that they refuse to admit facts as facts. Hence it is realism and not rationalism that is the object of Shaw's striving, and the will, not the reason, that is the *faculté maîtresse* of his heroes.[263] That also partly explains why he became a dramatist and found the most adequate medium for his ideas in the most dynamic literary genre.

Shaw would not have been the perfect representative of his age, if he had not shared its intellectualism. In spite of the stirring dramatic life that pulses in them, in spite of their effectiveness on the stage, which often reminds us of the 'pièce bien faite', and their somewhat crude melodramatics, his plays have an essentially intellectualistic character; they are plays of ideas to an even higher degree than the plays of Ibsen. The hero's self-recollection and the intellectual tussles between the dramatis personae are not peculiar to the modern drama; the dramatic conflict demands rather, if it is to achieve an appropriate intensity and significance, the full consciousness in the persons involved in the struggle of what is happening to them. No really dramatic, above all no tragic, effect is possible without this intellectuality of the characters. Shakespeare's most artless and impulsive heroes becomes geniuses in the moment in which their fate is to be decided. The 'dramatic debates', as Shaw's plays have been called, seemed indigestible merely because they were preceded by the meagre intellectual diet of the successful plays of entertainment of the time, so that the critics and the public first had to get used to the new fare. Shaw kept more strictly to the intellectual quality of the dramatic dialogue than his predecessors, but, surely, no public was more fitted to find pleasure in such an offering than the theatre-goers at the turn of the century. And they enjoyed, in fact, without the slightest restraint even the most daring intellectual acrobatics presented to them, as soon as they were convinced that Shaw's attacks on bourgeois society were nothing like so dangerous as they seemed, and, above all, that he had no desire to take their money from them. In the end, it turned out that he felt fundamentally at one with the bourgeoisie, and that he was merely the mouthpiece of that self-criticism that had always been part of the intellectual make-up of this class.

The psychology which determines the direction of the outlook on life at the turn of the century is a 'psychology of exposure'. Both Nietzsche and Freud start out from the assumption that the manifest life of the mind, that is to say, what men know or pretend to know about the motives of their behaviour, is often merely a concealment and distortion of the real motives of their feelings and actions. Nietzsche attributes the fact of this falsification to the decadence that has been discernible since the advent of Christianity and to the attempt to represent the weakness and resentments of degenerate humanity as ethical values, as altruistic and ascetic ideals. Freud interprets the phenomenon of self-deception, which Nietzsche exposes with the aid of his historical criticism of civilization, through individual psychological analysis, and establishes that the unconscious stands behind human consciousness as the real motor of human attitudes and actions, and that all conscious thinking is only the more or less transparent cloak masking the instincts which form the content of the unconscious. Now, whatever Nietzsche and Freud knew and thought of Marx, when they were developing their theories, they followed the same technique of analysis in their revelations as had first been used in historical materialism. Marx also emphasizes that human consciousness is distorted and corrupt and that it sees the world from a false angle. The concept of 'rationaliza-

206

tion' in psycho-analysis corresponds exactly to what Marx and Engels understand by the formation of ideology and 'false consciousness'. Engels[264] and Jones[265] define the two concepts in the same sense. Men not only act, they also motivate and justify their actions in accordance with their particular, sociologically or psychologically determined approach. Marx is the first to point out that, driven by their class interests, they not only commit isolated mistakes, falsifications and mystifications, but that their whole thinking and their whole world-view is crooked and false, and that they cannot see and judge except in accordance with the presuppositions contained in the facts of their economic and social circumstances. The doctrine on which he bases his whole philosophy of history is that in a society differentiated and riven by class distinctions, correct thinking is impossible from the very outset.[266] The recognition that it is chiefly a matter of self-deception, and that the separate individuals are by no means always aware of the motives conditioning their actions, was of basic importance for the further development of psychology.

But historical materialism with its technique of exposure was itself a product of that bourgeois-capitalistic outlook on life the background of which Marx wanted to expose. Before economics had achieved its primacy in the life of Western man, such a theory would have been unthinkable. The decisive experience of the post-romantic age was the dialectic of everything that comes to pass, the antithetical nature of being and consciousness, the ambivalence of feelings and intellectual relationships. The basic principle of the new technique of analysis was the suspicion that behind all the manifest world is hidden a latent world, behind all consciousness an unconscious and behind all apparent uniformity a conflict. In view of the commonness of this approach, it was by no means necessary for all the individual thinkers and scholars to be conscious of their dependence on the method of historical materialism; the idea of the unmasking technique of thought and the psychology of exposure was part of the property of the century and Nietzsche was not so much dependent on Marx, Freud not so much on Nietzsche, as all were dependent on the general atmosphere of crisis which marked the whole age. They discovered, each in his own way, that the self-determination of the mind was a fiction and that we are the slaves of a power working inside us and often against us. The doctrine of historical materialism was, like later that of psycho-analysis, though with a more optimistic upshot, the expression of a frame of mind n which the Western world had lost its exuberant belief in itself.

Even the most rationalistic and self-conscious thinkers by no means always take the ultimate philosophical presuppositions of their thinking as the starting point in the development of their theories. They often only become aware of them later and, in some cases, never at all. Freud, too, did not recollect the experience in which the problems of his psycho-analysis were rooted until he had reached a comparatively advanced stage in his development. This experience, which was the origin of every pertinent intellectual and artistic utterance at the turn of the century, was described by Freud himself as the 'sense of discomfort with civilization' (*das Unbehagen in der Kultur*). This expressed the same feeling of estrangement and loneliness as the romanticism and aestheticism of the age, the same anxiety, the same loss of confidence in the meaning of culture, the same concern at being surrounded by unknown, unfathomable and indefinable dangers. Freud traced back this uneasiness, this feeling of an unstable and precarious balance, to the injury that had been inflicted on the life of the instincts, especially the erotic impulses, thereby completely leaving out of account the part played by economic insecurity, lack of social success and political influence. Now, there is no doubt that neuroses are part of the price we have to pay for our civilization, but they are only a part and often only a secondary form of our tribute to society. As a consequence of his strictly scientific outlook, Freud is unable to appreciate the sociological factors in man's spiritual life, and although he discerns in the super-ego the judicial representative of society, he denies that social developments can bring about essential changes in our biological and instinctive constitution. In his view, cultural forms are not historical and sociological products, but the more or less mechanical expressions of the instincts. In bourgeois-capitalistic society analerotic instincts are expressed, wars are the work of the death-instinct, the discomfort of living in a civilized society is attributable to the suppression of the libido. Even the theory of sublimation, which is one of the greatest achievements of psycho-analysis, leads to a dangerous simplification and coarsening of the concept of culture, when the sexual instinct is made the sole or even the most important source of creative intellectual work. The Marxists are right to reproach psycho-analysis for moving in a vacuum with its a-historical and unsociological method and for retaining in its idea of a constant human nature a remnant of conservative idealism. Their objection, on the other hand, that psycho-analysis is the creation of the decadent bourgeoisie and must perish with that class, is all the more dogmatic. What living intellectual values do we possess —including historical materialism—that are not the creation of this 'decadent' society? If psycho-analysis is a decadent phenomenon, then the whole naturalistic novel and the whole of impressionist art are too—then everything that bears the marks of the discord of the nineteenth century is decadent.

Thomas Mann points out that Freud is deeply involved in the irrationalism of the beginning of the new century because of the nature of the material of his enquiry, the unconscious, passions, instincts and dreams.[267] But Freud is really connected not only with this neo-romantic movement, in which the subterranean regions of the life of the mind are the central point of interest, but at the same time with the beginning and origins of the whole aspect of romantic thought which goes back to the pre-civilized and the pre-rational. There is still an abundant share of Rousseauism in the pleasure with which he describes the freedom of the uncivilized man of instinct. And even though he does not assert, for instance, that the natural man who slew his father and enjoyed cohabiting with the women members of his family can be called 'good' in Rousseau's sense of the term, at any rate, he doubts whether man has become much better or even happier in the course of the process of civilization. The real danger of irrationalism consists, for psycho-analysis, not in its choice of material and in its sympathy for the primitive man unmolested by culture, but in the foundation of its theory on mere instinct and nature. All undialectic concepts of man based on the assump-

209

tion that human nature is an historically unchangeable constant contain an element of irrationalism and conservatism. Whoever does not believe in man's capacity for development usually does not want man, and society with him, to change. Pessimism and conservatism here condition each other reciprocally. But Freud is no more a real pessimist than he is a conservative or even an irrationalist. In spite of all its questionable factors, his work bears the unmistakable evidence of a spontaneous affection for mankind and of a progressive mind. It is not necessary to prove this, but there is no lack of proof. Freud certainly has doubts in the power of the reason over the instincts, but he emphasizes that we have no other means of controlling them but our intelligence. And that is not a statement quite without hope. 'The voice of the intellect is a soft one,' he says, 'but it does not rest until it has gained a hearing. . . . This is one of the few points in which one may be optimistic about the future of mankind, but in itself it signifies not a little. And one can make it a starting point for yet other hopes. The primacy of the intellect certainly lies in the far, far, but still probably not infinite distance.'[268]

Freud resists the evils of his age, he fights against the dark irrational forces to which it has sold its soul, but he is and remains tied by innumerable threads to both its achievements and its limitations. The principle of his psychology of exposure itself, in which individual differences play so much greater a part than in Marx, is most intimately connected with the impressionistic outlook on life and the relativistic philosophy of the age. The concept of deception, which is rooted in the experience that our feelings and impressions, moods and ideas are always changing, that reality makes itself known to us in ever varying, never stable forms, that every impression we receive from it is knowledge and illusion at the same time, is an impressionistic idea, and the corresponding Freudian notion, that men spend their lives concealed from themselves and others, would have been hardly conceivable before the advent of impressionism. Impressionism is the style in which both the thinking and the art of the period are expressed. The whole philosophy of the last decades of the century is dependent on it. Relativism, subjectivism, psychologism, historicism, anti-systematism, the principle of the atomization of the world of mind and the doctrine of the perspective nature of truth are elements common to the theories of Nietzsche, Bergson, the pragmatists and all the philosophical trends independent of German academic idealism.

Nietzsche says: 'Truth has never yet hung on the arm of an absolute.' Science as an end in itself, truth without presuppositions, disinterested beauty, selfless morality, are fictions for him and his contemporaries. What we call truths are, he asserts, in reality nothing more than life-promoting, power-increasing lies and deceptions which are necessary for life to continue,[269] and, in essentials, pragmatism adopts this activistic and utilitarian concept of truth. Truth is what is effective, useful and profitable, what stands the test of time and 'pays', as William James says. It is impossible to imagine a theory of cognition more in harmony with impressionism. Every truth has a certain actuality; it is valid only in quite definite situations. An assertion can be true in itself, and yet absolutely meaningless in certain circumstances, because without relation to anything else. If to the question, 'How old are you?', someone replies, 'The earth turns round the sun', then these words, in spite of the possible truth of the statement, represent a perfectly irrelevant and meaningless assertion in the given situation. Reality is an unanalysable subject-object relationship, the individual components of which are quite unascertainable and unthinkable independently of one another. We change and the world of objects changes with us. Statements about natural and historical happenings, which may have been true a hundred years ago, are no longer true today, for reality, like ourselves, is involved in a process of constant movement, development and change, it is the sum-total of ever new, unexpected, chance phenomena, and can never be considered finished. The whole pragmatic school of thought springs from the artist's impressionistic experience of reality; for here, in the sphere of art, the relation to truth is, in fact, exactly what this philosophy assumes it to be for the whole of experience. The Shakespeare of Dr. Johnson, Coleridge, Hazlitt and Bradley no longer exists; the great dramatist's works are no longer the same as they were. The words may still be the same; works of literature do not consist, however, merely of words, but also of the meaning of words, and this meaning changes from one generation to another.

Impressionistic thinking finds its purest expression in the philosophy of Bergson, above all in his interpretation of time—the medium which is the vital element of impressionism. The uniqueness of the moment, which has never existed before and will never be repeated, was the basic experience of the nineteenth century, and the whole naturalistic novel, especially that of Flaubert, was the description and analysis of this experience. But the main difference between Flaubert's philosophy and Bergson's was that he still saw time as an element of disintegration by which the ideal substance of life is destroyed. The change in our conception of time and hence of the whole of our experience of reality took place step by step, first in impressionist painting, then in Bergson's philosophy, and finally, most explicitly and significantly of all, in the work of Proust. Time is no longer the principle of dissolution and destruction, no longer the element in which ideas and ideals lose their value, and life and mind their substance, it is rather the form in which we obtain possession and become aware of our spiritual life, our living nature, which is the antithesis of dead matter and rigid mechanics. What we are, we become not only in time but through time. We are not merely the sum-total of the individual moments of our life, but the result of the ever-changing aspect which they acquire through each new moment. Time that is past does not make us poorer; it is this very time that fills our lives with content. The justification of Bergson's philosophy is the Proustian novel; it is here that Bergson's conception of time first becomes really creative. Existence acquires actual life, movement, colour, an ideal transparency and a spiritual content from the perspective of a present that is the result of our past. There is no other happiness but that of remembrance and the revival, resuscitation and conquest of time that is past and lost; for, as Proust says, the real paradises are the lost paradises. Since romanticism, art had been made responsible for the loss of life, and Flaubert's 'dire' and 'avoir' had been regarded as a tragic alternative; Proust is the first to see in contemplation, in remembrance and in art not only one possible form but the only possible form in which we can possess life. The new conception of time does not, it is true, alter the aestheticism of the age, it merely gives it a more conciliatory appearance—and nothing but the appearance of conciliation; for Proust's philosophy is merely the self-consolation and self-deception of a sick man, of a man already buried alive.

CHAPTER II

THE FILM AGE

THE 'twentieth century' begins after the first world war, that is to say, in the 'twenties, just as the 'nineteenth century' did not begin until about 1830. But the war marks a turning point in the development only in so far as it provides an occasion for a choice between the existing possibilities. All three main trends in the art of the new century have their predecessors in the foregoing period: cubism in Cézanne and the neoclassicists, expressionism in Van Gogh and Strindberg, surrealism in Rimbaud and Lautréamont. The continuity of the artistic development corresponds to a certain steadiness in the economic and social history of the same period. Sombart limits the lifetime of high capitalism to a hundred and fifty years and makes it end with the outbreak of the war. He wants to interpret the system of cartels and trusts of the years 1895–1914 itself as a phenomenon of old age and as an omen of the impending crisis. But in the period before 1914 only the socialists speak of the collapse of capitalism, in bourgeois circles people are certainly aware of the socialist danger, but believe neither in the 'internal contradictions' of the capitalist economy, nor in the impossibility of overcoming its occasional crises. In these circles there is no thought of a crisis in the system itself. The generally speaking confident frame of mind even continues in the first years after the end of the war and the atmosphere in the bourgeoisie is, apart from the lower middle class, which has to struggle against fearful odds, by no means hopeless. The real economic crisis begins in 1929 with the crash in America which brings the war and post-war boom to an end and unmistakably reveals the consequences of the lack of international planning of production and distribution. Now people suddenly begin to talk everywhere about the crisis of capitalism, the failure of the free economy and liberal society, about an imminent catastrophe and the threat of revolution. The history of the 'thirties is the history of a period of social criticism, of realism and activism, of the radicalization of political attitudes and the increasingly widespread conviction that only a radical solution can be of any help, in other words, that the moderate parties have had their day. But there is nowhere a greater awareness of the crisis through which the bourgeois way of life is passing than in the bourgeoisie itself, and nowhere is there so much talk of the end of the bourgeois epoch. Fascism and bolshevism are at one in considering the bourgeois a living corpse and in turning with the same uncompromisingness against the principle of liberalism and parliamentarianism. On the whole, the intelligentsia takes its stand alongside the authoritarian forms of government, demands order, discipline, dictatorship, is inspired with enthusiasm for a new Church, a new scholasticism and a new Byzantinism. The attraction of fascism for the enervated literary stratum, confused by the vitalism of Nietzsche and Bergson, consists in its illusion of absolute, solid, unquestionable values and in the hope of being rid of the responsibility that is connected with all rationalism and individualism. From communism the intelligentsia promises itself a direct contact with the broad masses of the people and the redemption from its isolation in society.

In this precarious situation the spokesmen of the liberal bourgeoisie can think of nothing better than to stress the characteristics that fascism and bolshevism have in common, and to discredit one by the other. They point to the unscrupulous realism peculiar to both and they find in a ruthless technocracy the common denominator to which their forms of organization and government can be reduced.[1] They wilfully neglect the ideological differences between the various authoritarian forms of government and represent them as mere 'techniques', that is, as the province of the party expert, the political administrator, the engineer of the social machine, in a word, of the 'managers'. There is, no doubt, a certain analogy between the different forms of social regulation, and if one proceeds from the mere fact of technicism and the standardization connected with it, one can even discern a likeness between Russia and America.[2] No state machinery today can wholly dispense with the 'managers'. They exercise political power on behalf of the more or less broad masses, just as the technicians manage their factories and the artists paint and write for them. The question is always merely in whose interest power is being exerted. No ruler in the world today dares to admit that he has not the interests of the people exclusively at heart. From this point of view, we are, in fact, living in a mass society and a mass democracy. The broad masses have, at any rate, a share in political life in so far as the powers that be are forced to take pains to lead them astray.

Nothing is more typical of the prevailing philosophy of culture of the period than the attempt to make this 'revolt of the masses'[3] responsible for the alienation and degradation of modern culture and the attack which is made on it in the name of the mind and spirit. Most of the extremists profess a belief in the usually somewhat confused cultural criticism which underlies this philosophy. It is true that the two parties take it as meaning absolutely different things and wage their war against the 'soulless' scientific world-view with positivism in mind, on the one side, and capitalism, on the other. But the way the intelligentsia is divided into the two camps is very unequal right up to the 'thirties. The majority are consciously or unconsciously reactionary and prepare the way for fascism under the spell of the ideas of Bergson, Barrès, Charles Maurras, Ortega y Gasset, Chesterton, Spengler, Keyserling, Klages and the rest. The 'new Middle Ages', the 'new Christendom', the 'new Europe', are all the old romantic land of counter-revolution, and the 'revolution in science', the mobilization of the 'spirit' against the mechanism and determinism of the natural sciences, nothing but 'the beginning of the great world reaction against the democratic and social enlightenment'.[4]

In this period of 'mass democracy' there is an attempt to make pretensions and demands in the name of ever larger groups, so that, in the end, Hitler does the trick of ennobling the overwhelming majority of his people. The new 'democratic' process of aristocratization begins by playing off the West against the

East, against Asia and Russia. West and East are contrasted as representing order and chaos, authority and anarchy, stability and revolution, disciplined rationalism and unbridled mysticism respectively,[5] and post-war Europe under the spell of Russian literature is emphatically warned that with its cult of Dostoevsky and its Karamazovism it is treading the path to chaos.[6] At the time of Vogüé, Russia and Russian literature were by no means 'Asiatic', they were, on the contrary, the representatives of the genuine Christianity which was set up as a model for the pagan West. At that time there was, however, still a Czar in Russia. The new crusaders do not, incidentally, really believe that the West can be saved at all and they clothe the hopelessness of their political outlook in a general shroud of pessimism. They are determined to bury the whole of Western civilization along with their political hopes and, as the genuine heirs of decadence, they accept the 'decline of the West'.

The great reactionary movement of the century takes effect in the realm of art as a rejection of impressionism—a change which, in some respects, forms a deeper incision in the history of art than all the changes of style since the Renaissance, leaving the artistic tradition of naturalism fundamentally unaffected. It is true that there had always been a swinging to and fro between formalism and anti-formalism, but the function of art being true to life and faithful to nature had never been questioned in principle since the Middle Ages. In this respect impressionism was the climax and the end of a development which had lasted more than four hundred years. Post-impressionist art is the first to renounce all illusion of reality on principle and to express its outlook on life by the deliberate deformation of natural objects. Cubism, constructivism, futurism, expressionism, dadaism and surrealism turn away with equal determination from nature-bound and reality-affirming impressionism. But impressionism itself prepares the ground for this development in so far as it does not aspire to an integrating description of reality, to a confrontation of the subject with the objective world as a whole, but marks rather the beginning of that process which has been called the 'annexation' of reality by art.[7] Post-impressionist art can no longer be called in any sense a reproduction of nature; its relationship to nature is one of violation. We can speak at most of a kind of magic naturalism, of the production of objects which exist alongside reality, but do not wish to take its place. Confronted with the works of Braque, Chagall, Rouault, Picasso, Henri Rousseau, Salvador Dali, we always feel that, for all their differences, we are in a second world, a super-world which, however many features of ordinary reality it may still display, represents a form of existence surpassing and incompatible with this reality.

Modern art is, however, anti-impressionistic in yet another respect: it is a fundamentally 'ugly' art, forgoing the euphony, the fascinating forms, tones and colours of impressionism. It destroys pictorial values in painting, carefully and consistently executed images in poetry and melody and tonality in music. It implies an anxious escape from everything pleasant and agreeable, everything purely decorative and ingratiating. Debussy already plays off a coldness of tone and a pure harmonic structure against the sentimentality of German romanticism, and this anti-romanticism is intensified in Stravinsky, Schoenberg and Hindemith into an anti-*espressivo*, which forswears all connection with the music of the sensitive nineteenth century. The intention is to write, paint and compose from the intellect, not from the emotions; stress is laid sometimes on purity of structure, at others on the ecstasy of a metaphysical vision, but there is a desire to escape at all costs from the complacent sensual aestheticism of the impressionist epoch. Impressionism itself had no doubt already been well aware of the critical situation in which modern aesthetic culture finds itself, but post-impressionist art is the first to stress the grotesqueness and mendacity of this culture. Hence the fight against all voluptuous and hedonistic feelings, hence the gloom, depression and torment in the works of Picasso, Kafka and Joyce. The aversion to the sensualism of the older art, the desire to destroy its illusions, goes so far that artists now refuse to use even its means of expression and prefer, like Rimbaud, to create an artificial language of their own. Schoenberg invents his twelve-tone system, and it has been rightly said of Picasso that he paints each of his pictures as if he were trying to discover the art of painting all over again.

The systematic fight against the use of the conventional

means of expression and the consequent break up of the artistic tradition of the nineteenth century begins in 1916 with dadaism, a war-time phenomenon, a protest against the civilization that had led to the war and, therefore, a form of defeatism.[8] The purpose of the whole movement consists in its resistance to the allurements of ready-made forms and the convenient but worthless, because worn-out, linguistic clichés, which falsify the object to be described and destroy all spontaneity of expression. Dadaism, like surrealism, which is in complete agreement with it in this respect, is a struggle for directness of expression, that is to say, it is an essentially romantic movement. The fight is aimed at that falsification of experience by forms, of which, as we know, Goethe had already been conscious and which was the decisive impulse behind the romantic revolution. Since romanticism the whole development in literature had consisted in a controversy with the traditional and conventional forms of language, so that the literary history of the last century is to some extent the history of a renewal of language itself. But whereas the nineteenth century always seeks merely for a balance between the old and the new, between traditional forms and the spontaneity of the individual, dadaism demands the complete destruction of the current and exhausted means of expression. It demands entirely spontaneous expression, and thereby bases its theory of art on a contradiction. For how is one to make oneself understood—which at any rate surrealism intends to do—and at the same time deny and destroy all means of communication?—The French critic Jean Paulhan differentiates between two distinct categories of writers, according to their relationship to language.[9] He calls the language-destroyers, that is to say, the romantics, symbolists and surrealists, who want to eliminate the commonplace, conventional forms and ready-made clichés from language completely and who take refuge from the dangers of language in pure, virginal, original inspiration, the 'terrorists'. They fight against all consolidation and coagulation of the living, fluid, intimate life of the mind, against all externalization and institutionalization, in other words, against all 'culture'. Paulhan links them up with Bergson and establishes the influence of intuitionism and the theory of the 'élan vital' in their attempt to preserve the directness and originality of the spiritual experience. The other camp, that is, the writers who know perfectly well that commonplaces and clichés are the price of mutual understanding and that literature is communication, that is to say, language, tradition, 'worn-out' and, precisely on that account, unproblematical, immediately intelligible form, he calls the 'rhetoricians', the oratorical artists. He regards their attitude as the only possible one, since the consistent administration of the 'terror' in literature would mean absolute silence, that is, intellectual suicide, from which the surrealists can only save themselves by constant self-deception. For there is actually no more rigid and narrow-minded convention than the doctrine of surrealism and no more insipid and monotonous art than that of the sworn surrealists. The 'automatic method of writing' is much less elastic than the rationally and aesthetically controlled style, and the unconscious—or at least as much of it as is brought to light—much poorer and simpler than the conscious mind. The historical importance of dadaism and surrealism does not consist, however, in the works of their official representatives, but in the fact that they draw attention to the blind alley in which literature found itself at the end of the symbolist movement, to the sterility of a literary convention which no longer had any connection with real life.[10] Mallarmé and the symbolists thought that every idea that occurred to them was the expression of their innermost nature; it was a mystical belief in the 'magic of the word' which made them poets. The dadaists and the surrealists now doubt whether anything objective, external, formal, rationally organized is capable of expressing man at all, but they also doubt the value of such expression. It is really 'inadmissible'—they think—that a man should leave a trace behind him.[11] Dadaism, therefore, replaces the nihilism of aesthetic culture by a new nihilism, which not only questions the value of art but of the whole human situation. For, as it is stated in one of its manifestos, 'measured by the standard of eternity, all human action is futile'.[12]

But the Mallarmé tradition by no means comes to an end. The 'rhetoricians' André Gide, Paul Valéry, T. S. Eliot and the later Rilke continue the symbolist trend in spite of their affinity to surrealism. They are the representatives of a difficult and

exquisite art, they believe in the 'magic of the word', their poetry·
is based on the spirit of language, of literature and tradition.
Joyce's *Ulysses* and T. S. Eliot's *The Waste Land* appear simultaneously, in the year 1922, and strike the two keynotes of the
new literature; the one work moves in an expressionistic and surrealistic, the other in a symbolistic and formalistic direction. The
intellectualistic approach is common to both, but Eliot's art
springs from the 'experience of culture', Joyce's from the 'experience of pure, prime existence', as defined by Friedrich Gundolf,
who introduces these concepts in the preface to his book on
Goethe, thereby expressing a typical thought-pattern of the
period.[13] In one case historical culture, intellectual tradition and
the legacy of ideas and forms is the source of inspiration, in the
other the direct facts of life and the problems of human existence.
With T. S. Eliot and Paul Valéry the primary foundation is
always an idea, a thought, a problem, with Joyce and Kafka an
irrational experience, a vision, a metaphysical or mythological
image. Gundolf's conceptual distinction is the record of a dicho-
tomy which is being carried through in the whole field of
modern art. Cubism and constructivism, on the one side, and
expressionism and surrealism, on the other, embody strictly
formal and form-destroying tendencies respectively which now
appear for the first time side by side in such sharp contradiction. The situation is all the more peculiar as the two opposing
styles display the most remarkable hybrid forms and combina-
tions, so that one often acquires more the impression of a split
consciousness than that of two competing trends. Picasso, who
shifts from one of the different stylistic tendencies to the other
most abruptly, is at the same time the most representative artist
of the present age. But to call him an eclectic and a 'master of
pastiche',[14] to maintain that he only wants to show to what an
extent he has command of the rules of art against which he is in
revolt,[15] to compare him with Stravinsky and to recall how he,
too, changes his models and 'makes use of' Bach, then Pergolesi,
then again Tchaikovsky for the purposes of modern music,[16] is
not to tell the whole story. Picasso's eclecticism signifies the
deliberate destruction of the unity of the personality; his imita-
tions are protests against the cult of originality; his deformation

of reality, which is always clothing itself in new forms, in order the more forcibly to demonstrate their arbitrariness, is intended, above all, to confirm the thesis that 'nature and art are two entirely dissimilar phenomena'. Picasso turns himself into a conjurer, a juggler, a parodist, out of opposition to the romantic with his 'inner voice', his 'take it or leave it', his self-esteem and self-worship. And he disavows not only romanticism, but even the Renaissance, which, with its concept of genius and its idea of the unity of work and style, anticipates romanticism to some extent. He represents a complete break with individualism and subjectivism, the absolute denial of art as the expression of an unmistakable personality. His works are notes and commentaries on reality; they make no claim to be regarded as a picture of a world and a totality, as a synthesis and epitome of existence. Picasso compromises the artistic means of expression by his indiscriminate use of the different artistic styles just as thoroughly and wilfully as do the surrealists by their renunciation of traditional forms.

The new century is full of such deep antagonisms, the unity of its outlook on life is so profoundly menaced, that the combination of the furthest extremes, the unification of the greatest contradictions, becomes the main theme, often the only theme, of its art. Surrealism, which, as André Breton remarks, at first revolved entirely round the problem of language, that is, of poetic expression, and which, as we should say with Paulhan, sought to be understood without the means of understanding, developed into an art which made the paradox of all form and the absurdity of all human existence the basis of its outlook. Dadaism still pleaded, out of despair at the inadequacy of cultural forms, for the destruction of art and for a return to chaos, that is to say, for romantic Rousseauism in the most extreme meaning of the term. Surrealism, which supplements the method of dadaism with the 'automatic method of writing',[17] thereby already expresses its belief that a new knowledge, a new truth and a new art will arise from chaos, from the unconscious and the irrational, from dreams and the uncontrolled regions of the mind. The surrealists expect the salvation of art, which they forswear as such just as much as the dadaists and are only prepared to accept it at all as a vehicle of irrational knowledge, from a plunging into the unconscious, into the pre-rational and the chaotic, and they take over the psycho-analytical method of free association, that is, the automatic development of ideas and their reproduction without any rational, moral and aesthetic censorship,[18] because they imagine they have discovered therein a recipe for the restoration of the good old romantic type of inspiration. So, after all, they still take their refuge in the rationalization of the irrational and the methodical re-production of the spontaneous, the only difference being that their method is incomparably more pedantic, dogmatic and rigid than the mode of creation in which the irrational and the intuitive are controlled by aesthetic judgement, taste and criticism, and which makes reflection and not indiscrimination its guiding principle. How much more fruitful than the surrealists' recipe was the procedure of Proust, who likewise put himself into a kind of somnambulistic condition and abandoned himself to the stream of memories and associations with the passivity of a hypnotic medium,[19] but who remained at the same time a disciplined thinker and in the highest degree a consciously creative artist.[20] Freud himself seems to have seen through the trick perpetrated by surrealism. He is said to have remarked to Salvador Dali, who visited him in London shortly before his death: 'What interests me in your art is not the unconscious, but the conscious.' [21] Must he not have meant by that: 'I am not interested in your simulated paranoia, but in the method of your simulation.'

The basic experience of the surrealists consists in the discovery of a 'second reality', which, although it is inseparably fused with ordinary, empirical reality, is nevertheless so different from it that we are only able to make negative statements about it and to point to the gaps and cavities in our experience as evidence for its existence. Nowhere is this dualism expressed more acutely than in the works of Kafka and Joyce, who, although they have nothing to do with surrealism as a doctrine, are surrealists in the wider sense, like most of the progressive artists of the century. It is also this experience of the double-sidedness of existence, with its home in two different spheres, which makes the surrealists aware of the peculiarity of dreams

223

and induces them to recognize in the mixed reality of dreams their own stylistic ideal. The dream becomes the paradigm of the whole world-picture, in which reality and unreality, logic and fantasy, the banality and sublimation of existence, form an indissoluble and inexplicable unity. The meticulous naturalism of the details and the arbitrary combination of their relationships which surrealism copies from the dream, not only express the feeling that we live on two different levels, in two different spheres, but also that these regions of being penetrate one another so thoroughly that the one can neither be subordinated to[22] nor set against the other as its antithesis.[23]

The dualism of being is certainly no new conception, and the idea of the 'coincidentia oppositorum' is quite familiar to us from the philosophy of Nicholas of Cusa and Giordano Bruno, but the double meaning and the duplicity of existence, the snare and the seduction for the human understanding which lies hidden in every single phenomenon of reality, had never been experienced so intensively as now. Only mannerism had seen the contrast between the concrete and the abstract, the sensual and the spiritual, dreaming and waking in a similarly glaring light. The emphasis which modern art lays not so much on the coincidence of the opposites themselves, as on the fancifulness of this coincidence, is also reminiscent of mannerism. The sharp contrast, in the work of Dali, between the photographically faithful reproduction of the details and the wild disorder of their grouping corresponds, on a very humble level, to the fondness for paradox in the Elizabethan drama and the lyric poetry of the 'metaphysical poets' of the seventeenth century. But the difference of level between the style of Kafka and Joyce, in which a sober and often trivial prose is combined with the most fragile transparency of ideas, and that of the manneristic poets of the sixteenth and seventeenth centuries is no longer so great. In both cases the real subject of the representation is the absurdity of life, which seems all the more surprising and shocking the more realistic the elements of the fantastic whole are. The sewing machine and the umbrella on the dissecting table, the donkey's corpse on the piano or the naked woman's body which opens like a chest of drawers, in brief, all the forms of juxtaposition and simultaneity into which the non-simultaneous and the incompatible are pressed, are only the expression of a desire to bring unity and coherence, certainly in a very paradoxical way, into the atomized world in which we live. Art is seized by a real mania for totality.[24] It seems possible to bring everything into relationship with everything else, everything seems to include within itself the law of the whole. The disparagement of man, the so-called 'dehumanization' of art, is connected above all with this feeling. In a world in which everything is significant or of equal significance, man loses his pre-eminence and psychology its authority.

The crisis of the psychological novel is perhaps the most striking phenomenon in the new literature. The works of Kafka and Joyce are no longer psychological novels in the sense that the great novels of the nineteenth century were. In Kafka, psychology is replaced by a kind of mythology, and in Joyce, although the psychological analyses are perfectly accurate, just as the details in a surrealistic picture are absolutely true to nature, there are not only no heroes, in the sense of a psychological centre, but also no particular psychological sphere in the totality of being. The de-psychologization of the novel already begins with Proust,[25] who, as the greatest master of the analysis of feelings and thoughts, marks the summit of the psychological novel, but also represents the incipient displacement of the soul in the balance of reality. For, since the whole of existence has become merely the content of the consciousness and things acquire their significance purely and simply through the spiritual medium by which they are experienced, there can no longer be any question here of psychology as understood by Stendhal, Balzac, Flaubert, George Eliot, Tolstoy or Dostoevsky. In the novel of the nineteenth century, the soul and character of man are seen as the opposite pole to the world of physical reality, and psychology as the conflict between the subject and object, the self and the non-self, the human spirit and the external world. This psychology ceases to be predominant in Proust. He is not concerned so much with the characterization of the individual personality, although he is an ardent portraitist and caricaturist, as with the analysis of the spiritual mechanism as an ontological phenomenon. His work is a

'Summa' not merely in the familiar sense of containing a total picture of modern society, but also because it describes the whole spiritual apparatus of modern man with all his inclinations, instincts, talents, automatisms, rationalisms and irrationalisms. Joyce's *Ulysses* is therefore the direct continuation of the Proustian novel; we are here confronted literally with an encyclopaedia of modern civilization, as reflected in the tissue of the motifs which make up the content of a day in the life of a great city. This day is the protagonist of the novel. The flight from the plot is followed by the flight from the hero. Instead of a flood of events, Joyce describes a flood of ideas and associations, instead of an individual hero a stream of consciousness and an unending, uninterrupted inner monologue. The emphasis lies everywhere on the uninterruptedness of the movement, the 'heterogeneous continuum', the kaleidoscopic picture of a disintegrated world. The Bergsonian concept of time undergoes a new interpretation, an intensification and a deflection. The accent is now on the simultaneity of the contents of consciousness, the immanence of the past in the present, the constant flowing together of the different periods of time, the amorphous fluidity of inner experience, the boundlessness of the stream of time by which the soul is borne along, the relativity of space and time, that is to say, the impossibility of differentiating and defining the media in which the mind moves. In this new conception of time almost all the strands of the texture which form the stuff of modern art converge: the abandonment of the plot, the elimination of the hero, the relinquishing of psychology, the 'automatic method of writing' and, above all, the montage technique and the intermingling of temporal and spatial forms of the film. The new concept of time, whose basic element is simultaneity and whose nature consists in the spatialization of the temporal element, is expressed in no other genre so impressively as in this youngest art, which dates from the same period as Bergson's philosophy of time. The agreement between the technical methods of the film and the characteristics of the new concept of time is so complete that one has the feeling that the time categories of modern art altogether must have arisen from the spirit of cinematic form, and one is inclined to consider the film itself as the stylistically most representative, though qualitatively perhaps not the most fertile genre of contemporary art.

The theatre is in many respects the artistic medium most similar to the film; particularly in view of its combination of spatial and temporal forms, it represents the only real analogy to the film. But what happens on the stage is partly spatial, partly temporal; as a rule spatial and temporal, but never a mixture of the spatial and the temporal, as are the happenings in a film. The most fundamental difference between the film and the other arts is that, in its world-picture, the boundaries of space and time are fluid—space has a quasi-temporal, time, to some extent, a spatial character. In the plastic arts, as also on the stage, space remains static, motionless, unchanging, without a goal and without a direction; we move about quite freely in it, because it is homogeneous in all its parts and because none of the parts presupposes the other temporally. The phases of the movement are not stages, not steps in a gradual development; their sequence is subject to no constraint. Time in literature—above all in the drama—on the other hand, has a definite direction, a trend of development, an objective goal, independent of the spectator's experience of time; it is no mere reservoir, but an ordered succession. Now, these dramaturgical categories of space and time have their character and functions completely altered in the film. Space loses its static quality, its serene passivity and now becomes dynamic; it comes into being as it were before our eyes. It is fluid, unlimited, unfinished, an element with its own history, its own scheme and process of development. Homogeneous physical space here assumes the characteristics of heterogeneously composed historical time. In this medium the individual stages are no longer of the same kind, the individual parts of space no longer of equal value; it contains specially qualified positions, some with a certain priority in the development and others signifying the culmination of the spatial experience. The use of the close-up, for example, not only has spatial criteria, it also represents a phase to be reached or to be surpassed in the temporal development of the film. In a good film the close-ups are not distributed arbitrarily and capriciously. They are not cut in independently of the inner development of the scene, not at any time and anywhere, but only where their potential energy can and should make itself felt. For a close-up is not a cut-out picture with a frame; it is always merely part of a picture, like, for instance, the repoussoir figures in baroque painting which introduce a dynamic quality into the picture similar to that created by the close-ups in the spatial structure of a film.

But as if space and time in the film were interrelated by being interchangeable, the temporal relationships acquire an almost spatial character, just as space acquires a topical interest and takes on temporal characteristics, in other words, a certain element of freedom is introduced into the succession of their moments. In the temporal medium of a film we move in a way that is otherwise peculiar to space, completely free to choose our direction, proceeding from one phase of time into another, just as one goes from one room to another, disconnecting the individual stages in the development of events and grouping them, generally speaking, according to the principles of spatial order. In brief, time here loses, on the one hand, its uninterrupted continuity, on the other, its irreversible direction. It can be brought to a standstill: in close-ups; reversed: in flash-backs; repeated: in recollections; and skipped across: in visions of the future. Concurrent, simultaneous events can be shown successively, and temporally distinct events simultaneously—by double-exposure and alternation; the earlier can appear later, the later before its time. This cinematic conception of time has a thoroughly subjective and apparently irregular character compared with the empirical and the dramatic conception of the same medium. The time of empirical reality is a uniformly progressive, uninterruptedly continuous, absolutely irreversible order, in which events follow one another as if 'on a conveyor belt'. It is true that dramatic time is by no means identical with empirical time—the embarrassment caused by a clock showing the correct time on the stage comes from this discrepancy—and the unity of time prescribed by classicistic dramaturgy can even be interpreted as the fundamental elimination of ordinary time, and yet the temporal relationships in the drama have more points of contact with the chronological order of ordinary experience than the order of time in a film. Thus in the drama, or at least in one and the same act

228

of a drama, the temporal continuity of empirical reality is preserved intact. Here too, as in real life, events follow each other according to the law of a progression which permits neither interruptions and jumps, nor repetitions and inversions, and conforms to a standard of time which is absolutely constant, that is, undergoes no acceleration, retardation or stoppages of any kind within the several sections (acts or scenes). In the film, on the other hand, not only the speed of successive events, but also the chronometric standard itself is often different from shot to shot, according as to whether slow or fast motion, short or long cutting, many or few close-ups, are used.

The dramatist is prohibited by the logic of scenic arrangement from repeating moments and phases of time, an expedient that is often the source of the most intensive aesthetic effects in the film. It is true that a part of the story is often treated retrospectively in the drama, and the antecedents followed backwards in time, but they are usually represented indirectly—either in the form of a coherent narrative or of one limited to scattered hints. The technique of the drama does not permit the playwright to go back to past stages in the course of a progressively developing plot and to insert them *directly* into the sequence of events, into the dramatic present—that is, it is only recently that it has begun to permit it, perhaps under the immediate influence of the film, or under the influence of the new conception of time, familiar also from the modern novel. The technical possibility of interrupting any shot without further ado suggests the possibilities of a discontinuous treatment of time from the very outset and provides the film with the means of heightening the tension of a scene either by interpolating heterogeneous incidents or assigning the individual phases of the scene to different sections of the work. In this way the film often produces the effect of someone playing on a keyboard and striking the keys ad libitum, up and down, to right and left. In a film we often see the hero first at the beginning of his career as a young man, later, going back to the past, as a child; we then see him, in the further course of the plot, as a mature man and, having followed his career for a time, we, finally, may see him still living after his death, in the memory of one of his relations or friends. As a result of the discontinuity of time, the retrospective development of the plot is combined with the progressive in complete freedom, with no kind of chronological tie, and through the repeated twists and turns in the time-continuum, mobility, which is the very essence of the cinematic experience, is pushed to the uttermost limits. The real spatialization of time in the film does not take place, however, until the simultaneity of parallel plots is portrayed. It is the experience of the simultaneity of different, spatially separated happenings that puts the audience into that condition of suspense, which moves between space and time and claims the categories of both orders for itself. It is the simultaneous nearness and remoteness of things—their nearness to one another in time and their distance from one another in space—that constitutes that spatio-temporal element, that two-dimensionality of time, which is the real medium of the film and the basic category of its world-picture.

It was discovered in a comparatively early stage in the history of the film that the representation of two simultaneous sequences of events is part of the original stock of cinematic forms. First this simultaneity was simply recorded and brought to the notice of the audience by clocks showing the same time or by similar direct indications; the artistic technique of the intermittent treatment of a double plot and the alternating montage of the single phases of such a plot only developed step by step. But later on we come across examples of this technique at every turn. And whether we stand between two rival parties, two competitors or two doubles, the structure of the film is dominated in any case by the crossing and intersecting of the two different lines, by the bilateral character of the development and the simultaneity of the opposing actions. The famous finish of the early, already classical Griffith films, in which the upshot of an exciting plot is made to depend on whether a train or a car, the intriguer or the 'king's messenger on horseback', the murderer or the rescuer, reaches the goal first, using the then revolutionary technique of continuously changing pictures, flashing and vanishing like lightning, became the pattern of the dénouement since followed by most films in similar situations.

The time experience of the present age consists above all in an awareness of the moment in which we find ourselves: in an awareness of the present. Everything topical, contemporary, bound together in the present moment is of special significance and value to the man of today, and, filled with this idea, the mere fact of simultaneity acquires new meaning in his eyes. His intel-elctual world is imbued with the atmosphere of the immediate present, just as that of the Middle Ages was characterized by an other-worldly atmosphere and that of the enlightenment by a mood of forward-looking expectancy. He experiences the great-ness of his cities, the miracles of his technics, the wealth of his ideas, the hidden depths of his psychology in the contiguity, the interconnections and dovetailing of things and processes. The fascination of 'simultaneity', the discovery that, on the one hand, the same man experiences so many different, unconnected and irreconcilable things in one and the same moment, and that, on the other, different men in different places often experience the same things, that the same things are happening at the same time in places completely isolated from each other, this universal-ism, of which modern technics have made contemporary man conscious, is perhaps the real source of the new conception of time and of the whole abruptness with which modern art describes life. This rhapsodic quality, which distinguishes the modern novel most sharply from the older novel, is at the same time the characteristic accountable for its most cinematic effects. The discontinuity of the plot and the scenic development, the sudden emersion of the thoughts and moods, the relativity and the inconsistency of the time-standards, are what remind us in the works of Proust and Joyce, Dos Passos and Virginia Woolf of the cuttings, dissolves and interpolations of the film, and it is simply film magic when Proust brings two incidents, which may lie thirty years apart, as closely together as if there were only two hours between them. The way in which, in Proust, past and present, dreams and speculation join hands across the intervals of space and time, the sensibility, always on the scent of new tracks, roams about in space and time, and the boundaries of space and time vanish in this endless and boundless stream of interrela-tions: all this corresponds exactly to that mixture of space and time in which the film moves. Proust never mentions dates and

231

ages; we never know exactly how old the hero of his novel is, and even the chronological relationships of the events often remain rather vague. The experiences and happenings do not cohere by reason of their proximity in time and the attempt to demarcate and arrange them chronologically would be all the more nonsensical from his point of view as, in his opinion, every man has his typical experiences which recur periodically. The boy, the youth and the man always experience fundamentally the same things; the meaning of an incident often does not dawn on him until years after he has experienced and endured it; but he can hardly ever distinguish the deposit of the years that are past from the experience of the present hour in which he is living. Is one not in every moment of one's life the same child or the same invalid or the same lonely stranger with the same wakeful, sensitive, unappeased nerves? Is one not in every situation of life the person capable of experiencing this and that, who possesses, in the recurring features of his experience, the one protection against the passage of time? Do not all our experiences take place as it were at the same time? And is this simultaneity not really the negation of time? And this negation, is it not a struggle for the recovery of that inwardness of which physical space and time deprive us?

Joyce fights for the same inwardness, the same directness of experience, when he, like Proust, breaks up and merges well-articulated, chronologically organized time. In his work, too, it is the interchangeability of the contents of consciousness which triumphs over the chronological arrangement of the experiences, for him, too, time is a road without direction, on which man moves to and fro. But he pushes the spatialization of time even further than Proust, and shows the inner happenings not only in longitudinal but also in cross-sections. The images, ideas, brain-waves and memories stand side by side with sudden and absolute abruptness; hardly any consideration is paid to their origins, all the emphasis is on their contiguity, their simultaneity. The spatialization of time goes so far in Joyce, that one can begin the reading of *Ulysses* where one likes, with only a rough knowledge of the context—not necessarily only after a first reading, as has been said, and almost in any sequence one cares to choose. The

232

medium in which the reader finds himself, is in fact wholly spatial, for the novel describes not only the picture of a great city, but also adopts its structure to some extent, the network of its streets and squares, in which people stroll about, walking in and out and stopping when and where they like. It is supremely characteristic of the cinematic quality of this technique that Joyce wrote his novel not in the final succession of the chapters, but— as is the custom in the production of films—made himself independent of the sequence of the plot and worked at several chapters at the same time.

We meet the Bergsonian conception of time, as used in the film and the modern novel—though not always so unmistakably as here—in all the genres and trends of contemporary art. The 'simultanéité des états d'âmes' is, above all, the basic experience connecting the various tendencies of modern painting, the futurism of the Italians with the expressionism of Chagall, and the cubism of Picasso with the surrealism of Giorgio de Chirico or Salvador Dali. Bergson discovered the counterpoint of spiritual processes and the musical structure of their interrelationships. Just as, when we listen properly to a piece of music, we have in our ears the mutual connection of each new note with all those that have already sounded, so we always possess in our deepest and most vital experiences everything that we have ever experienced and made our own in life. If we understand ourselves, we read our own souls as a musical score, we resolve the chaos of the entangled sounds and transform them into a polyphony of different parts.—All art is a game with and a fight against chaos; it is always advancing more and more dangerously towards chaos and rescuing more and more extensive provinces of the spirit from its clutch. If there is any progress in the history of art, then it consists in the constant growth of these provinces wrested from chaos. With its analysis of time, the film stands in the direct line of this development: it has made it possible to represent visually experiences that have previously been expressed only in musical forms. The artist capable of filling this new possibility, this still empty form, with real life has not yet arrived, however.

The crisis of the film, which seems to be developing into a chronic illness, is due above all to the fact that the film is not finding its writers or, to put it more accurately, the writers are not finding their way to the film. Accustomed to doing as they like within their own four walls, they are now required to take into account producers, directors, script-writers, cameramen, art-directors and technicians of all kinds, although they do not acknowledge the authority of this spirit of co-operation, or indeed the idea of artistic co-operation at all. Their feelings revolt against the idea of the production of works of art being surrendered to a collective, to a 'concern', and they feel that it is a disparagement of art that an extraneous dictate, or at best a majority, should have the last word in decisions of the motives of which they are often unable to account for themselves. From the point of view of the nineteenth century, the situation with which the writer is asked to come to terms is quite unusual and unnatural. The atomized and uncontrolled artistic endeavours of the present now meet for the first time with a principle opposed to their anarchy. For the mere fact of an artistic enterprise based on co-operation is evidence of an integrating tendency of which—if one disregards the theatre, where it is in any case more a matter of the reproduction than the production of works of art—there had really been no perfect example since the Middle Ages, and, in particular, since the masons' lodge. How far removed film production still is, however, from the generally accepted principle of an artistic co-operative group, is shown not only by the inability of most writers to establish a connection with the film, but also by such a phenomenon as Chaplin, who believes that he must do as much as possible in his films on his own: the acting of the main part, the direction, the script, the music. But even if it is only the beginning of a new method of organized art production, the, for the present, still empty framework of a new integration, nevertheless, here too, as in the whole economic, social and political life of the present age, what is being striven for is the comprehensive planning without which both our cultural and material world threaten to go to pieces. We are confronted here with the same tension as we find throughout our social life: democracy and dictatorship, specialization and integration, rationalism and irrationalism, colliding with each other. But if even in the field of economics and politics planning cannot always be solved by

234

imposing rules of conduct, it is all the less possible in art, where all violation of spontaneity, all forcible levelling down of taste, all institutional regulation of personal initiative, are involved in great though certainly not such mortal dangers as is often imagined.

But how, in an age of the most extreme specialization and the most sophisticated individualism, are harmony and an integration of individual endeavours to be brought about? How, to speak on a practical level, is the situation to be brought to an end in which the most poverty-stricken literary inventions sometimes underlie the technically most successful films? It is not a question of competent directors against incompetent writers, but of two phenomena belonging to different periods of time—the lonely, isolated writer dependent on his own resources and the problems of the film which can only be solved collectively. The co-operative film-unit anticipates a social technique to which we are not yet equal, just as the newly invented camera anticipated an artistic technique of which no one at the time really knew the range and power. The reunion of the divided functions, first of all the personal union of the director and the author, which has been suggested as a way to surmount the crisis, would be more an evasion of the problem than its solution, for it would prevent but not abolish the specialization that has to be overcome, would not bring about but merely avoid the necessity of the planning which is needed. Incidentally, the monistic-individual principle in the discharge of the various functions, in place of a collectively organized division of labour, corresponds not merely externally and technically to an amateurish method of working, but it also involves a lack of inner tension which is reminiscent of the simplicity of the amateur film. Or may the whole effort to achieve a production of art based on planning only have been a temporary disturbance, a mere episode, which is now being swept away again by the torrent of individualism? May the film be perhaps not the beginning of a new artistic era, but merely the somewhat hesitant continuation of the old individualistic culture, still full of vitality, to which we owe the whole of post-medieval art?—Only if this were so, would it be possible to solve the film crisis by the personal union of certain functions, that is, by partly surrendering the principle of collective labour.

The film crisis is, however, also connected with a crisis in the public itself. The millions and millions who fill the many thousands of cinemas all over the world from Hollywood to Shanghai and from Stockholm to Cape Town daily and hourly, this unique world-embracing league of mankind, have a very confused social structure. The only link between these people is that they all stream into the cinemas, and stream out of them again as amorphously as they are pumped in; they remain a heterogeneous, inarticulate, shapeless mass with the only common feature of belonging to no uniform class or culture. This mass of cinema-goers can hardly be called a 'public' proper, for only a more or less constant group of patrons can be described as such, one which is able to some extent to guarantee the continuity of production in a certain field of art. Public-like agglomerations are based on mutual understanding; even if opinions are divided, they diverge on one and the same plane. But with the masses who sit together in the cinemas and who have undergone no previous common intellectual formation of any kind, it would be futile to look for such a platform of mutual understanding. If they dislike a film there is such a small chance of agreement amongst them as to the reasons for their rejection of the film that one must assume that even general approval is based on a misunderstanding.

The homogeneous and constant public units which, as mediators between the art producers and the social strata with no real interest in art, had always discharged a fundamentally conserving function were, as we know, dissolved with the advancing democratization of the enjoyment of art. The bourgeois subscription audiences of the state and municipal theatres of the last century still formed a more or less uniform, organically developed body, but with the end of the repertory theatre even the last remains of this public were scattered and since then an integrated audience has come into being only in particular circumstances, though in some cases the size of such audiences has been bigger than ever before. It was on the whole identical with the casual cinema-going public which has to be caught by new and original attractions every time and over and over again. The repertory theatre, the serial performance theatre and the cinema mark the successive stages in the democratization of art and the gradual

236

loss of the festive character that was formerly more or less the property of every form of theatre. The cinema takes the final step on this road of profanation, for even to attend the modern metropolitan theatre showing some popular play or other still demands a certain internal and external preparation—in most cases seats have to be booked in advance, one has to keep to a fixed time and to prepare for an occupation that will fill the whole evening—whereas one attends the cinema *en passant*, in one's everyday clothes and at any time during the continuous performance. The everyday point of view of the film is in perfect accordance with the improvisation and unpretentiousness of cinema-going.

The film signifies the first attempt since the beginning of our modern individualistic civilization to produce art for a mass public. As is known, the changes in the structure of the theatre and reading public, connected at the beginning of the last century with the rise of the boulevard play and the feuilleton novel, formed the real beginning of the democratization of art which reaches its culmination in mass attendance of cinemas. The transition from the private theatre of the princes' courts to the bourgeois state and municipal theatre and then to the theatre trusts, or from the opera to the operetta and then to the revue, marked the separate phases of a development characterized by the effort to capture ever wider circles of consumers, in order to cover the costs of the growing investments. The outfit for an operetta could still be sustained by a medium-sized theatre, that of a revue or a large ballet had already to travel from one big city to the next; in order to amortise the invested capital, the cinema-goers of the whole world have to contribute to the financing of a big film. But it is this fact that determines the influence of the masses on the production of art. By their mere presence at theatrical performances in Athens or the Middle Ages they were never able to influence the ways of art directly, only since they have come on the scene as consumers and paid the full price for their enjoyment, have the terms on which they hand over their shillings become a decisive factor in the history of art.

There has always been an element of tension between the quality and the popularity of art, which is not by any means to say that the broad masses of the people have at any time taken a

237

stand against qualitatively good art in favour of inferior art on principle. Naturally, the appreciation of a more complicated art presents them with greater difficulties than the more simple and less developed, but the lack of adequate understanding does not necessarily prevent them from accepting this art—albeit not exactly on account of its aesthetic quality. Success with them is completely divorced from qualitative criteria. They do not react to what is artistically good or bad, but to impressions by which they feel themselves reassured or alarmed in their own sphere of existence. They take an interest in the artistically valuable, provided it is presented so as to suit their mentality, that is, provided the subject-matter is attractive. The chances of success of a good film are from this point of view better from the very outset than those of a good painting or poem. For, apart from the film, progressive art is almost a closed book today for the uninitiated; it is intrinsically unpopular, because its means of communication have become transformed in the course of a long and self-contained development into a kind of secret code, whereas to learn the newly developing idiom of the film was child's play for even the most primitive cinema public. From this happy constellation one would be inclined to draw far-reaching optimistic conclusions for the future of the film, if one did not know that that kind of intellectual concord is nothing more than the state of a paradisian childhood, and is probably repeated as often as new arts arise. Perhaps all the cinematic means of expression will no longer be intelligible even to the next generation, and certainly the cleft will sooner or later arise that even in this field separates the layman from the connoisseur. Only a young art can be popular, for as soon as it grows older it is necessary, in order to understand it, to be acquainted with the earlier stages in its development. To understand an art means to realize the necessary connection between its formal and material elements; as long as an art is young, there is a natural, unproblematical relation between its content and its means of expression, that is to say, there is a direct path leading from its subject-matter to its forms. In the course of time these forms become independent of the thematic material, they become autonomous, poorer in meaning, and harder to interpret, until they become accessible only to a

238

quite small stratum of the public. In the film this process has hardly begun, and a great many cinema-goers still belong to the generation which saw the birth of the film and witnessed the full significance of its forms. But the process of estrangement already makes itself felt in the present-day director's forgoing of most of the so-called 'cinematic' means of expression. The once so popular effects produced by different camera-angles and manoeuvrings, changing distances and speeds, by the tricks of montage and printing, the close-ups and the panoramas, the cut-ins and the flash-backs, the fade-ins, fade-outs and dissolves, seem affected and unnatural today, because the directors and cameramen are concentrating their attention, under the pressure of a second, already less film-minded generation, on the clear, smooth and exciting narration of a story and believe they can learn more from the masters of the 'pièce bien faite' than from the masters of the silent film.

It is inconceivable that, in the present stage of cultural development, an art could begin all over again, even though, like the film, it has completely new means at its disposal. Even the simplest plot has a history and bears within it certain epic and dramatic formulae of the older periods of literature. The film, whose public is on the average level of the petty bourgeois, borrows these formulae from the light fiction of the upper middle class and entertains the cinema-goers of today with the dramatic effects of yesterday. Film production owes its greatest successes to the realization that the mind of the petty bourgeois is the psychological meeting place of the masses. The psychological category of this human type has, however, a wider range than the sociological category of the actual middle class; it embraces fragments of both the upper and the lower classes, that is to say, the very considerable elements who, where they are not engaged in a direct struggle for their existence, join forces unreservedly with the middle classes, above all in the matter of entertainment. The mass public of the film is the product of this equalizing process, and if the film is to be profitable, it has to base itself on that class from which the intellectual levelling proceeds. The middle class, especially since the 'new middle class', with its army of 'employees', minor civil servants and private officials,

239

commercial travellers and shop-assistants, has come into being, has hovered 'between the classes' and has always been used to bridge the gaps between them.[26] It has always felt menaced from above and below, but has preferred to give up its real interests rather than its hopes and alleged prospects. It has wanted to be reckoned as part of the bourgeois upper class, although in reality it shared the lot of the lower class. But without a clear-cut and clarified social position no coherent consciousness and consistent outlook on life is possible, and the film producer has been able to rely quite safely on the disorientation of these rootless elements of society. The petty bourgeois attitude to life is typified by a thoughtless, uncritical optimism. It believes in the ultimate un-importance of social differences and, accordingly, wants to see films in which people simply walk out of one social stratum into another. For this middle class the cinema gives the fulfilment to the social romanticism which life never realizes and the lending libraries never realize so deceptively as the film with its illu-sionism. 'Everyone is the architect of his own fortune', that is its supreme belief and climbing the basic motif of the wish-fantasies which entice it into the cinema. Will Hays, the one-time 'film czar', was well aware of that when he included in his directions for the American film industry the instruction, 'to show the life of the upper classes'.

The development of moving photography to the film as an art was dependent on two achievements: the invention of the close-up—attributed to the American director D. W. Griffith—and a new method of interpolation, discovered by the Russians, the so-called short cutting. The Russians did not, however, invent the frequent interruption of the continuity of a scene, the Ameri-cans had long had this means of producing excited atmospheres or dramatic accelerations at their disposal; but the new factor in the Russian method was the restriction of the flashes to close-ups —forgoing the insertion of informative long-shots—and the shortening, pushed to the limits of perceptibility, of the indi-vidual shots. The Russians thereby succeeded in finding an expressionistic film style for the description of certain agitated moods, nervous rhythms and tearing speeds, which made possible quite new effects, unattainable in any other art. The

240

revolutionary quality of this montage technique consisted, however, less in the shortness of the cutting, in the speed and rhythm of the change of shots and in the extension of the boundaries of the cinematically feasible, than in the fact that it was no longer the phenomena of a homogeneous world of objects, but of quite heterogeneous elements of reality, that were brought face to face. Thus Eisenstein showed the following sequence in *The Battleship Potemkin*: men working desperately, engine-room of the cruiser; busy hands, revolving wheels; faces distorted with exertion, maximum pressure of the manometer; a chest soaked with perspiration, a glowing boiler; an arm, a wheel; a wheel, an arm; machine, man; machine, man; machine, man. Two utterly different realities, a spiritual and a material, were joined together here, and not only joined but identified, in fact, the one proceeding from the other. But such a conscious and deliberate trespassing presupposed a philosophy which denies the autonomy of the individual spheres of life, as surrealism does, and as historical materialism has done from the very beginning.

That it is not simply a question of analogies but of equations, and that the confrontation of the different spheres is not merely metaphorical, becomes even more obvious when the montage no longer shows two interconnected phenomena but only one and, instead of the one to be expected from the context, a substituted one. Thus, in the *End of St. Petersburg*, Pudovkin shows a trembling crystal chandelier for the shattered power of the bourgeoisie; a steep, endless staircase on which a small human figure is laboriously climbing up for the official hierarchy, its thousands of intermediary stages and its unattainable summit. In Eisenstein's *October*, the twilight of the Czars is represented by dark equestrian statues on leaning pedestals, quivering statues of the Buddha used as knick-knacks and shattered negro idols. In the *Strike*, executions are replaced by slaughter-house scenes. Throughout things take the place of ideas; things which expose the ideological character of ideas. A social-historical situation has hardly ever found a more direct expression in art than the crisis of capitalism and the Marxist philosophy of history in this montage technique. A tunic covered with decorations but without a head signifies the automatism of the war machine in these

Russian films; new, strong soldiers' boots, the blind brutality of military power. Thus, in *Potemkin*, we see again and again only these heavy, indestructible and merciless boots, instead of the steadily advancing Cossacks. Good boots are the precondition of military power, that is the meaning of this 'pars pro toto'-montage, just as the meaning of the earlier example from *Potemkin* was that the victorious masses are nothing but the personification of the triumphant machine. Man, with his ideas, faith, and hope is merely a function of the material world in which he lives; the doctrine of historical materialism becomes the formal principle of the art of the Russian film. One must not forget, however, how far the film's whole method of presentation, especially its technique of the close-up, which favours the description of the material requisites from the outset and is calculated to give them an important motivating rôle, comes to meet this materialism half-way. On the other hand, the question whether the whole of this technique, in which the properties are put in the foreground, is not itself already a product of materialism cannot simply be dismissed. For the fact that the film is the creation of the historical epoch which has witnessed the exposure of the ideological basis of human thought is no more pure coincidence than the fact that the Russians have been the first classical exponents of this art.

Film directors throughout the world, irrespective of national and ideological divergences, have adopted the stock forms of the Russian film and thereby confirmed that as soon as the content has been translated into form, form can be taken over and used as a purely technical expedient, without the ideological background from which it has emerged. The paradox of historicity and timelessness in art, to which Marx refers in his *Introduction to the Critique of Political Economy*, is rooted in this capacity of form to become autonomous: 'Is Achilles conceivable in an era of powder and lead?' he asks. 'Or for that matter the *Iliad* at all in these days of printing-press and press-jacks? Do not song and legend and muse necessarily lose their meaning in the age of the Press? But the difficulty is not that Greek art and epic are connected with certain forms of social development, but rather that they still give us aesthetic satisfaction today, that in a sense they act as a norm, as an unattainable paragon.'—The works of Eisenstein and Pudovkin are in some respects the heroic epics of the cinema; the fact that they are regarded as models, independent of the social conditions which made their realization possible, is no more surprising than the fact that Homer still gives us supreme artistic satisfaction.

The film is the only art in which Soviet Russia has important achievements to its credit. The affinity between the young communist state and the new form of expression is obvious. Both are revolutionary phenomena moving along new paths, without a historical past, without binding and crippling traditions, without presuppositions of a cultural or routine nature of any kind. The film is an elastic, extremely malleable, unexhausted form which offers no inner resistance to the expression of the new ideas. It is an unsophisticated, popular means of communication, making a direct appeal to the broad masses, an ideal instrument of propaganda the value of which was immediately recognized by Lenin. Its attraction as an irreproachable, that is to say, historically uncompromised, entertainment was so great from the point of view of communist cultural policy from the very outset, its picture-book-like style so easy to grasp, the possibility of using it to propagate ideas to the uneducated so simple, that it seemed to have been specially created for the purposes of a revolutionary art. The film is, moreover, an art evolved from the spiritual foundations of technics and, therefore, all the more in accordance with the problems in store for it. The machine is its origin, its medium and its most suitable subject. Films are 'fabricated' and they remain tied to an apparatus, to a machine in a narrower sense than the products of the other arts. The machine here stands both between the creative subject and his work and between the receptive subject and his enjoyment of art. The motory, the mechanical, the automatically moving, is the basic phenomenon of the film. Running and racing, travelling and flying, escape and pursuit, the overcoming of spatial obstacles is the cinematic theme par excellence. The film never feels so much in its element as when it has to describe movement, speed and pace. The wonders and mischievous tricks of instruments, automata and vehicles are among its oldest and most effective subjects. The old film comedies expressed sometimes naïve admiration, at others arrogant contempt for technics, but they were in most cases the self-teasing of man caught in the wheels of a mechanized world. The film is above all a 'photograph' and is already as such a technical art, with mechanical origins and aiming at mechanical repetition,[27] in other words, thanks to the cheapness of its reproduction, a popular and fundamentally 'democratic' art. It is perfectly comprehensible that it suited bolshevism with its romanticism of the machine, its fetishism of technics and its admiration for efficiency. Just as it is also comprehensible that the Russians and the Americans, as the two most technically-minded peoples, were partners and rivals in the development of this art. The film was, however, not only in accord with their technicism, but also with their interest in the documentary, the factual and the authentic. All the more important works of Russian film art are to some extent documentary films, historical documents of the building up of the new Russia, and the best we owe to the American film consists in the documentary reproduction of American life, of the everyday routine of the American economic and administrative machine, of the skyscraper cities and the Middle West farms, the American police and the gangster world. For a film is the more cinematic, the greater the share extra-human, material facts have in its description of reality, in other words, the closer the connection in this description between man and the world, the personality and the milieu, the end and the means.

This tendency to the factual and the authentic—to the 'document'—is evidence not only of the intensified hunger for reality characteristic of the present age, of its desire to be well informed about the world, with an activistic ulterior motive, but also of that refusal to accept the artistic aims of the last century which is expressed in the flight from the story and from the individual, psychologically differentiated hero. This tendency, which is tied up, in the documentary film, with an escape from the professional actor, again signifies not only the desire that is always recurring in the history of art, to show the plain reality, the unvarnished truth, unadulterated facts, that is, life 'as it really is', but very often a renunciation of art altogether. In our age the prestige of the aesthetic is being undermined in many ways. The documentary film, photography, newspaper reports, the reportage novel, are no longer art in the old sense at all. Moreover, the most intelligent and the most gifted representatives of these genres do not in any way insist that their products should be described as 'works of art'; they rather take the view that art has always been a by-product and arose in the service of an ideologically conditioned purpose.

In Soviet Russia it is regarded wholly as a means to an end. This utilitarianism is, of course, conditioned above all by the need to place all available means in the service of communist reconstruction and to exterminate the aestheticism of bourgeois culture which, with its 'l'art pour l'art', its contemplative and quietistic attitude to life, implies the greatest possible danger for the social revolution. It is the awareness of this danger that makes it impossible for the architects of communist cultural policy to do justice to the artistic developments of the last hundred years and it is the denial of this development which makes their views on art seem so old-fashioned. They would prefer to put back the historical standing of art to the level of the July monarchy, and it is not only in the novel that they have in mind the realism of the middle of the last century, in the other arts, particularly in painting, they encourage the same tendency. In a system of universal planning and in the midst of a struggle for mere existence, art cannot be left to work out its own salvation. But regimentation of art is not without risks even from the point of view of the immediate aim; in the process it must also lose much of its value as an instrument of propaganda.

It is certainly correct that art has produced many of its greatest creations under compulsion and dictation, and that it had to conform to the wishes of a ruthless despotism in the Ancient Orient and to the demands of a rigid authoritarian culture in the Middle Ages. But even compulsion and censorship have a different meaning and effect in the different periods of history. The main difference between the situation today and that of former ages is that we find ourselves at a point in time after the French Revolution and nineteenth-century liberalism and that every idea that we think, every impulse that we feel, is permeated by this liberalism. One might well argue that Christianity also had to destroy a very advanced and comparatively liberal civilization and that medieval art sprang from very modest beginnings; one must not forget, however, that early Christian art did in fact make an almost completely fresh start, whereas Soviet Russian art starts out from a style which was historically already highly developed, although it is much behind the times today. But even if one were willing to assume that the sacrifices demanded are the price of a new 'Gothic', there is no kind of guarantee that this 'Gothic' would not again become, as in the Middle Ages, the exclusive possession of a comparatively small cultured élite.

The problem is not to confine art to the present-day horizon of the broad masses, but to extend the horizon of the masses as much as possible. The way to a genuine appreciation of art is through education. Not the violent simplification of art, but the training of the capacity for aesthetic judgement is the means by which the constant monopolizing of art by a small minority can be prevented. Here too, as in the whole field of cultural policy, the great difficulty is that every arbitrary interruption of the development evades the real problem, that is, creates a situation in which the problem does not arise, and therefore merely postpones the task of finding a solution. There is today hardly any practicable way leading to a primitive and yet valuable art. Genuine, progressive, creative art can only mean a complicated art today. It will never be possible for everyone to enjoy and appreciate it in equal measure, but the share of the broader masses in it can be increased and deepened. The preconditions of a slackening of the cultural monopoly are above all economic and social. We can do no other than fight for the creation of these preconditions.

NOTES

I. NATURALISM AND IMPRESSIONISM

1. HENRI GUILLEMIN: *Le Jocelyn de Lamartine* (1936), p. 59.
2. Cf. for the following JEAN-PAUL SARTRE: 'Qu'est-ce que la littérature?' *Les Temps Modernes*, 1947, II, pp. 971 ff.—Also in· *Situations*, II, 1948.
3. Ibid., p. 976.
4. Ibid., p. 981.
5. S. CHARLÉTY: 'La Monarchie de Juillet'. In E. Lavisse, *Hist. de France contemporaine*, V, 1921, pp. 178–9.
6. WERNER SOMBART: *Der moderne Kapitalismus*, III/1, pp. 35–8, 82, 657–61.
7. WERNER SOMBART: *Der Bourgeois*, 1913, p. 220.
8. Cf. LOUIS BLANC: *Histoire de dix ans*, III, 1843, pp. 90–2.—WERNER SOMBART: *Die deutsche Volkswirtschaft des 19. Jahrhunderts*, 7th edit., 1927, pp. 399 ff.
9. EMIL LEDERER: 'Zum sozialpsych. Habitus der Gegenwart'. *Archiv fuer Sozialwiss. u. Sozialpolit.*, 1918, vol. 46, pp. 122 ff.
10. PAUL LOUIS: *Hist. du socialisme en France de la Révolution à nos jours*, 1936, 3rd edit., pp. 64, 97.—J. LUCAS-DUBRETON: *La Restauration et la Monarchie de Juillet*, 1937, pp. 160–1.
11. PAUL LOUIS, op. cit., pp. 106–7.
12. FRIEDRICH ENGELS: *Die Entwicklung des Sozialismus von der Utopie zur Wissenschaft*, 4th edit., 1891, p. 24.
13. ROBERT MICHELS: 'Psychologie der antikapitalistischen Massenbewegungen'. *Grundriss der Sozialoekon.*, IX/1, 1926, pp. 244–6, 270.
14. W. SOMBART: *Die deutsche Volkswirtsch.*, p. 471.
15. SAINTE-BEUVE: 'De la littérature industrielle'. *Revue des Deux Mondes*, 1839. Also in: *Portraits contemporains*, 1847.
16. JULES CHAMPFLEURY: *Souvenirs et portraits*, 1872, p. 77.
17. EUGÈNE GILBERT: *Le Roman en France pendant le 19e siècle*, 1909, p. 209.
18. NORA ATKINSON: *Eugène Sue et le roman-feuilleton*, 1929, p. 211.— ALFRED NETTEMENT: *Études critiques sur le feuilleton-roman*, 1845, I, p. 16.
19. Cf. MAURICE BARDÈCHE: *Stendhal romancier*, 1947.
20. ANDRÉ BRETON: *Le Roman français au 19e siècle*, I, 1901, pp. 6–7, 73.—MAURICE BARDÈCHE: *Balzac romancier*, 1947, pp. 2–8, 12–13.
21. CH.-M. DES GRANGES: *La Presse littéraire sous la Restoration*, 1907, p. 22.

I

22. H. J. Hunt: *Le Socialisme et le romantisme en France*, 1935, pp. 195, 340.

23. Ibid., pp. 203–4.—Albert Cassagne: *Le Théorie de l'art pour l'art en France*, 1906, pp. 61–71.

24. Cf. Edmond Estève: *Byron et le romantisme franç.*, 1907, p. 228.

25. Cf. Pierre Moreau: *Le Classicisme des romantiques*, 1932, pp. 242 ff.

26. Charles Rémusat's article of March 12 1825.—Quoted by A. Cassagne, op. cit., p. 37.

27. A. Cassagne, ibid.

28. José Ortega y Gasset: *La Deshumanización del Arte*, 1925, p. 19.

29. H. J. Hunt, op. cit., pp. 157–8.

30. Ibid., p. 174.

31. Georg Lukács: *Goethe und seine Zeit*, 1947, pp. 39–40.

32. M. Bardèche: *Balzac romancier*, pp. 3, 7.

33. Quoted by Jules Marsan: *Stendhal* (1932), p. 141.

34. M. Bardèche: *Stendhal romancier*, p. 424.

35. Albert Thibaudet: *Stendhal*, 1931.—Henri Martineau: *L'Œuvre de Stendhal*, 1945, p. 198.

36. Cf. Jean Mélia: 'Stendhal et Taine'. *La Nouvelle Revue*, 1910, p. 392.

37. Pierre Martineau: *Stendhal*, 1934, p. 302.

38. H. Martineau, op. cit., p. 470.

39. Émile Faguet: *Politiques et moralistes*, III, 1900, p. 8.

40. M. Bardèche: *Stendhal romancier*, p. 47.

41. Sainte-Beuve: *Port-Royal*, 1888, 5th edit., VI, pp. 266–7.

42. Émile Zola: *Les Romanciers naturalistes*, 1881, 2nd edit., p. 124.

43. Cf. Paul Bourget: *Essais de psychologie contemp.*, 1885, p. 282.

44. André de Breton: *Balzac*, 1905, pp. 70–3.

45. M. Bardèche: *Balzac romancier*, p. 285.

46. Bernard Guyon: *La Pensée politique et sociale de Balzac*, 1947, p. 432.

47. V. Grib: *Balzac*. Critics Group Series, 5, 1937, p. 76.

48. Marie Bor: *Balzac contre Balzac*, 1933, p. 38.

49. E. Buttke: *Balzac als Dichter des modernen Kapitalismus*, 1932, p. 28.

50. Balzac: *Correspondance*, 1876, I, p. 433.

51. Ernest Seillière: *Balzac et la morale romantique*, 1922, p. 61.

52. André Bellessort: *Balzac et son œuvre*, 1924, p. 175.

53. Karl Marx and Frederick Engels: *Literature and Art*, 1947, pp. 42–3.—Also in *International Literature*, July, 1933, No. 3, p. 114.

54. Marcel Proust: *La Prisonnière*, I.

55. E. Preston: *Recherches sur la technique de Balzac*, 1926, pp. 5, 222.

56. Thomas Mann: *Die Forderung des Tages*, 1930, pp. 273 ff.

NOTES

57. HUGO VON HOFMANNSTHAL: *Unterhaltungen ueber literarische Gegenstaende* (1904), p. 40.

58. A. CERFBERR-J. CHRISTOPHE: *Répertoire de la Comédie humaine*, 1887.

59. TAINE: *Nouveaux essais de critique et d'histoire*, 1865, pp. 104–13.

60. Cf. TOCQUEVILLE's speech in the National Assembly quoted by P. LOUIS, op. cit., II, p. 191.

61. Ibid., pp. 200–1.

62. Ibid., p. 197.

63. PIERRE MARTINO: *Le Roman réaliste sous le second Empire*, 1913, p. 85.

64. ALBERT THIBAUDET: *Hist. de la litt. franç. de 1789 à nos jours*, 1936, p. 361.

65. ÉMILE BOUVIER: *La Bataille réaliste*, 1913, p. 237.

66. JULES COULIN: *Die sozialistische Weltanschauung i. d. franz. Mal.* (1909), p. 61.

67. ÉMILE ZOLA: *La République et la litt.*, 1879.

68. OLIVER LARKIN: 'Courbet and his Contemporaries'. *Science and Society*, 1939, III/1, p. 44.

69. E. BOUVIER, op. cit., p. 248.

70. Cf. LÉON ROSENTHAL: *La Peinture romant.* (1903), pp. 267–8.—HENRI FOCILLON: *La Peinture aux XIXᵉ et XXᵉ siècles*, 1928, pp. 74–101.

71. H. J. HUNT, op. cit., pp. 342–4.

72. Vide i.a. the letter to Victor Hugo of 15th July 1853: FLAUBERT, *Correspondance*, edited by Conrad, 1910, III, p. 6.

73. Ibid., II, pp. 116–17, 366.

74. Ibid., III, pp. 120, 390.

75. E. and J. DE GONCOURT: *Journal*. The entry of 29th January 1863. Édit. Flammarion-Fasquelle, II, p. 67.

76. FLAUBERT: *Corresp.*, III, pp. 485, 490, 508.—*Éducation sentimentale*, II/3.—ERNEST SEILLIÈRE: *Le Romantisme des réalistes: Gustave Flaubert*, 1914, p. 257.—EUGEN HAAS: *Flaubert und die Politik*, 1931, p. 30.

77. Letter to Mlle Leroyer de Chantepie of 18th May 1857. *Corresp.*, III, p. 119.

78. E. GILBERT, op. cit., p. 157.

79. *Corresp.*, III, pp. 157, 448, etc.

80. *Le Moniteur*, 4th May 1857.—*Causeries de Lundi*, XIII.

81. ÉMILE ZOLA: *Les Romanciers naturalistes*, 1881, 2nd edit., pp. 126–9.

82. *Corresp.*, II, p. 182; III, p. 113.

83. Ibid., II, p. 112.

84. A. THIBAUDET: *Gustave Flaubert*, 1922, p. 12.

85. *Corresp.*, II, p. 155.

86. GEORG LUKÁCS: 'Theodor Storm oder die Buergerlichkeit und l'art pour l'art'. *Die Seele und die Formen*, 1911.—THOMAS MANN: *Betrachtungen eines Unpolitischen*, 1918, pp. 69–70.

NOTES

87. GEORG KEFERSTEIN: *Buergertum und Buergerlichkeit bei Goethe,* 1933, pp. 126–223.
88. *Corresp.,* I, p. 238, Sept. 1851.
89. Ibid., IV, p. 244, Dec. 1875.
90. Ibid., III, p. 119.
91. ÉMILE FAGUET: *Flaubert,* 1913, p. 145.
92. *Corresp.,* II, p. 237.
93. Ibid., III, p. 190.
94. Ibid., III, p. 446.
95. Ibid., II, p. 70.
96. Ibid., II, p. 137.
97. Ibid., III, p. 440.
98. Ibid., II, pp. 133, 140–1, 336.
99. JULES DE GAULTIER: *Le Bovarysme,* 1902.
100. ÉDOUARD MAYNIAL: *Flaubert* (1943), pp. 111–12.
101. PAUL BOURGET: *Essais de psych. contempt.,* 1885, p. 144.
102. *Corresp.,* I, p. 289.
103. GEORG LUKÁCS: *Die Theorie des Romans,* 1920, p. 131.
104. ÉMILE ZOLA: *La Roman experimental,* 1880, 2nd edit., pp. 24, 28.
105. CHARLES-BRUN: *Le Roman social en France au 19ᵉ siècle,* 1910, p. 158.
106. ANDRÉ BELLESSORT: 'La Société française sous le second Empire'. *Revue hebdomaire,* 1932, No. 12, pp. 290, 292.
107. FRANCISQUE SARCEY: *Quarante ans de théâtre,* I, 1900, pp. 120, 122.
108. Ibid., pp. 209–12.
109. J.-J. WEISS: *Le Théâtre et les mœurs,* 1889, pp. 121–2.—Cf. RENAN: *Preface to the Drames philosophiques,* 1888.
110. A. THIBAUDET, op. cit., pp. 295 ff.
111. SARCEY, op. cit., V, p. 94.
112. Ibid., p. 286.
113. Cf. JULES LEMAÎTRE: *Impressions de théâtre,* I, 1888, p. 217.
114. SARCEY, op. cit., VI, 1901, p. 180.
115. S. KRACAUER: *Jacques Offenbach und das Paris seiner Zeit,* 1937, p. 349.
116. Ibid., p. 270.
117. Cf. FLEURY-SONOLET: *La Société du second Empire,* III, 1913, p. 387.
118. PAUL BEKKER: *Wandlungen der Oper.,* 1934, p. 86.
119. LIONEL DE LAURENCIE: *Le Goût musical en France,* 1905, p. 292.— WILLIAM L. CROSTEN: *French Grand Opera,* 1948, p. 106.
120. ALFRED EINSTEIN: *Music in the Romantic Era,* 1947, p. 231.
121. FRIEDRICH NIETZSCHE: *Der Fall Wagner,* 1888.—*Nietzsche contra Wagner,* 1888.
122. Cf. THOMAS MANN: *Betrachtungen eines Unpolitischen,* 1918, p. 75. —*Leiden und Groesse der Meister,* 1935, pp. 145 ff.

250

NOTES

123. A. PAUL OPPÉ: 'Art'. In *Early Victorian England*, edited by G. M. Young, 1934, II, p. 154.

124. RUSKIN: *Stones of Venice*, III.—*Works*, 1904, XI, p. 201.

125. H. W. SINGER: *Der Praeraffaelismus in England*, 1912, p. 51.

126. Cf. A. CLUTTON-BROCK: *William Morris. His Work and Influence*, 1914, p. 9.

127. D. C. SOMERWELL: *English Thought in the 19th Century*, 1947, 5th edit., p. 153.

128. CHRISTIAN ECKERT: 'John Ruskin'. *Schmollers Jahrbuch.*, 1902, XXVI, p. 362.

129. E. BATHO-B. DOBRÉE: *The Victorians and After*, 1938, p. 112.

130. A. CLUTTON-BROCK, op. cit., p. 150.

131. Ibid., p. 228.

132. WILLIAM MORRIS: *Art under Plutocracy*, 1883.

133. LOUIS CAZAMIAN: *Le Roman social en Angleterre* (1830–1850), II, 1935, pp. 250–1.

134. Ibid., I, 1934, pp. 11–12, 163.

135. W. L. CROSS: *The Development of the English Novel*, 1899, p. 182.

136. L. CAZAMIAN, op. cit., I, p. 8.

137. A. H. THORNDIKE: *Literature in a Changing Age*, 1920, pp. 24–5.

138. Cf. Q. D. LEAVIS: *Fiction and the Reading Public*, 1939, p. 156.

139. G. K. CHESTERTON: *Charles Dickens*, 1917, 11th edit., pp. 79, 84.

140. AMY CRUSE: *The Victorians and their Books*, 1936, 2nd edit., p. 158.

141. OSBERT SITWELL: *Dickens*, 1932, p. 15.

142. Cf. L. CAZAMIAN, op. cit., I, pp. 209 ff.

143. T. S. JACKSON: *Charles Dickens*, 1937, pp. 22–3.

144. HUMPHREY HOUSE: *The Dickens World*, 1941, p. 219.

145. Cf. the speech Dickens made in Birmingham on 27th September 1869.

146. Cf. HUMPHREY HOUSE, op. cit., p. 209.

147. TAINE: *Hist. de la litt. angl.*, 1864, IV, p. 66.

148. O. SITWELL, op. cit., p. 16.

149. Q. D. LEAVIS, op. cit., pp. 33–4, 42–3, 158–9, 168–9.

150. M. L. CAZAMIAN: *Le Roman et les idées en Angleterre*, I, 1923, p. 138.—ELIZABETH S. HALDANE: *George Eliot and her Times*, 1927, p. 292.

151. P. BOURL'HONNE: *George Eliot*, 1933, pp. 128, 135.

152. ERNEST A. BAKER: *History of the English Novel*, VIII, 1937, pp. 240, 254.

153. E. BATHO-B. DOBRÉE, op. cit., pp. 78–9, 91–2.

154. *Middlemarch*, XV.

155. M. L. CAZAMIAN, op. cit., p. 108.

156. J. W. CROSS: *George Eliot's Life as related in her Letters and Journals*, 1885, p. 230.

157. F. R. LEAVIS: *The Great Tradition*, 1948, p. 61.

NOTES

158. ALFRED WEBER: 'Die Not der geistigen Arbeiter'. *Schriften des Vereins fuer Sozialpolitik*, 1920.

159. GEORG LUKÁCS: 'Moses Hess und die Probleme der idealistischen Dialektik'. *Archiv f.d. Gesch. d. Sozialismus u. die Arbeiterbewegung*, 1926, XII, p. 123.

160. KARL MANNHEIM: *Ideology and Utopia*, 1936, pp. 136 ff.—*Man and Soc. in an Age of Reconstruction*, 1940, pp. 79 ff.

161. Cf. HANS SPEIER: 'Zur Soziologie der buergerl. Intelligenz in Deutschland'. *Die Gesellschaft*, 1929, II, p. 71.

162. D. S. MIRSKY: *Contemp. Russian Lit.*, 1926, pp. 42–3.

163. D. S. MIRSKY: *A Hist. of Russian Lit.*, 1927, pp. 321, 322.

164. M. N. POKROVSKY: *Brief Hist. of Russia*, I, 1933, p. 144.

165. D. S. MIRSKY: *Russia. A Social History*, 1931, p. 199.

166. JANKO LAVRIN: *Pushkin and Russian Lit.*, 1947, p. 198.

167. D. S. MIRSKY: *A Hist. of Russian Lit.*, pp. 203–4.

168. Ibid., p. 204.

169. Ibid., p. 282.

170. TH. G. MASARYK: *The Spirit of Russia*, 1919, I, p. 148.

171. Turgenev in a letter to Herzen of 8th November 1862.

172. E. H. CARR: *Dostoevsky*, 1931, p. 268.

173. NICOLAS BERDIAEFF: *L'Esprit de Dostoievski*, 1946, p. 18.

174. D. S. MIRSKY: *A Hist. of Russian Lit.*, p. 219.

175. E. H. CARR, op. cit., pp. 281 ff.

176. Ibid., pp. 267–8.

177. DOSTOEVSKY: *An Author's Diary*, February 1877.

178. EDMUND WILSON: *The Wound and the Bow*, 1941, p. 50.—REX WARNER: *The Cult of Power*, 1946, p. 41.

179. DMITRI MEREJKOWSKI: *Tolstoi as Man and Artist*, 1902, p. 251.

180. VLADIMIR POZNER: 'Dostoievski et le roman d'aventure'. *Europe*, XXVII, 1931.

181. Ibid., pp. 135–6.

182. Cf. LEO SCHESTOW: *Dostojewski und Nietzsche*, 1924, pp. 90–1.

183. THOMAS MANN: 'Goethe und Tolstoi'. In *Bemuehungen*, 1925, p. 33.

184. N. LENIN: 'L. N. Tolstoi' (1910). In N. LENIN-G. PLECHANOW: *L. N. Tolstoi im Spiegel des Marxismus*, 1928, pp. 42–4.

185. D. S. MIRSKY: *Contemp. Russian Lit.*, p. 8.

186. Ibid., p. 9.—JANKO LAVRIN: *Tolstoy*, 1944, p. 94.

187. D. S. MERESCHKOWSKI, op. cit., p. 213.

188. LUKÁCS GYÖRGY: *Nagy orosz realisták*, Budapest, 1946, p. 92.

189. TOLSTOY: *What is Art?*, XVI.

190. Cf. THOMAS MANN: *Die Forderung des Tages*, 1930, p. 283.

191. MAXIM GORKY: *Literature and Life*, 1946, p. 74.

192. THOMAS MANN: *Die Forderung des Tages*, p. 278.

NOTES

193. ANDRÉ BELLESSORT: *Les Intellectuels et l'avènement de la troisième République*, 1931, p. 24.

194. PAUL LOUIS: *Hist. du socialisme en France*, pp. 236–7.

195. A. BELLESSORT, op. cit., p. 39.

196. WERNER SOMBART: *Der mod. Kapit.*, III/1, pp. xii/xiii.

197. PAUL LOUIS, op. cit., pp. 242, 216–7.

198. Cf. HENRY FORD: *My Life and My Work*, 1922, p. 155.

199. W. SOMBART: *Der mod. Kapit.*, III/2, pp. 603–7.—*Die deutsche Volkswirtschaft*, pp. 397–8.

200. Cf. PIERRE FRANCASTEL: *L'Impressionnisme*, 1937, pp. 25–6, 80.

201. GEORG MARZYNSKI: 'Die impressionistische Methode'. *Zeitschr. f. Aesth. u. allg. Kunstwissenschaft*, XIV, 1920.

202. GEORGES RIVIÈRE: 'L'Exposition des Impressionnistes'. In *L'Impressioniste. Journal d'Art*, 6th April 1877.—Reprinted in L. VENTURI: *Les Archives de l'Impressionnisme*, 1939, II, p. 309.

203. ANDRÉ MALRAUX: 'The Psychology of Art'. *Horizon*, 1948, No. 103, p. 55.

204. G. MARZYNSKI, loc. cit., p. 90.

205. Ibid., p. 91.

206. JOHN REWALD: *The History of Impressionism*, 1946, pp. 6–7.

207. ALBERT CASSAGNE: *La Théorie de l'art pour l'art en France*, 1906, p. 351.

208. E. and J. DE GONCOURT: *Journal*. 1st May 1869, III, p. 221.

209. HENRI FOCILLON: *La Peinture aux 19e et 20e siècles*, 1928, p. 200.

210. PAUL BOURGET, op. cit., p. 25.

211. CHARLES SEIGNOBOS: 'L'Évolution de la troisième République'. In E. LAVISSE: *Hist. de la France contempt.*, VIII, 1921, pp. 54–5.

212. HENRY BÉRENGER: *L'Aristocratie intellectuelle*, 1895, p. 3.

213. A. THIBAUDET: *Hist de la litt. franç.*, p. 430.

214. E. R. CURTIUS: *Maurice Barrès*, 1921, p. 98.

215. JULES HURET: *Enquête sur l'évolution litt.*, 1891, pp. xvi–xvii.

216. E. and J. DE GONCOURT: *Idées et sensations*, 1866.

217. NIETZSCHE: *Menschliches Allzumenschliches*, 155.

218. BAUDELAIRE: *Richard Wagner et Tannhaeuser à Paris*, 1861.

219. BAUDELAIRE: *Le Peintre de la vie moderne*, 1863. Reprinted in BAUDELAIRE: *L'Art moderne*, edited by E. Raynaud, 1931, p. 79.

220. VILLIERS DE L'ISLE-ADAM: *Contes cruels*, 1883, pp. 13 ff.

221. ÉMILE TARDIEU: *L'Ennui*, 1903, pp. 81 ff.

222. E. VON SYDOW: *Die Kultur der Dekadenz*, 1921, p. 34.

223. PETER QUENNELL: *Baudelaire and the Symbolists*, 1929, p. 82.

224. MAX NORDAU: *Entartung*, 1896, 3rd edit., II, p. 102.

225. BAUDELAIRE: *Journaux intimes*, edited by Ad. van Bever, 1920, p. 8.

226. THOMAS MANN: 'Kollege Hitler'. *Das Tagebuch*, edited by Leopold Schwarzschild, 1939.

253

NOTES

227. Cf. René Dumesnil: *L'Époque réaliste et naturaliste*, 1945, pp. 31 ff.—Ernest Raynaud: *Baudelaire et la religion du dandysme*, 1918, pp. 13–14.

228. Baudelaire: *Œuvres posthumes*, edited by J. Crépet, I, pp. 223 ff.

229. Chekhov: *The House with the Mezzanine. A Painter's Story*, translated by S. S. Koteliansky, Everyman's Library.

230. *Le Figaro*, 18th September 1886.

231. A. Thibaudet: *Hist de la litt. franç.*, p. 485.

232. Ibid., p. 489.

233. J. Huret, op. cit., p. 60.

234. Cf. Ernest Raynaud: *La Mêlée symboliste*, 1920, II, p. 163.

235. John Charpentier: *Le Symbolisme*, 1927, p. 62.

236. Charles Mauron: Introduction to Roger Fry's translation of Mallarmé's poems, 1936, p. 14.

237. Georges Duhamel: *Les Poètes et la poésie*, 1914, pp. 145–6.

238. Cf. Roger Fry: *An Early Introduction to Mallarmé's Poems*, 1936, pp. 296, 302, 304–6.

239. Henri Bremond: *La Poésie pure*, 1926, pp. 16–20.

240. E. and J. de Goncourt: *Journal*. 23rd February 1893, IX, p. 87.

241. J. Huret, op. cit., p. 297.

242. Cf. C. M. Bowra: *The Heritage of Symbolism*, 1943, p. 10.

243. G. M. Turnell: 'Mallarmé'. *Scrutiny*, 1937, V, p. 432.

244. J. Huret, op. cit., p. 23.

245. H. M. Lynd: *England in the Eighteen-Eighties*, 1945, p. 17.

246. Ibid., p. 8.

247. Bernhard Fehr: *Die engl. Lit. des 19. u. 20. Jahrhunderts*, 1931, p. 322.

248. Baudelaire: *Le Peintre de la vie moderne*, loc. cit., pp. 73–4.

249. J.-P. Sartre: *Baudelaire*, 1947, pp. 166–7.

250. Baudelaire: *Le Peintre de la vie mod.*, p. 50.

251. M. L. Cazamian: *Le Roman et les idées en Angleterre* (1880–1900), 1935, p. 167.

252. F. R. Leavis: *The Great Tradition*, 1948, passim.

253. H. Hatzfeld: *Der franzoesische Symbolismus*, 1923, p. 140.

254. Cf. D. S. Mirsky: *Modern Russian Lit.*, 1925, pp. 84–5.

255. Janko Lavrin: *An Introduction to the Russian Novel*, 1942, p. 134.

256. Thomas Mann: 'Versuch ueber das Theater'. In *Rede und Antwort*, 1916, p. 55.

257. Paul Ernst: *Ein Credo*, 1912, I, p. 227.

258. Paul Ernst: *Der Weg zur Form*, 1928, 3rd edit., pp. 42 ff.

259. Ibsen: *Correspondence*, edited by Mary Morison, 1905, p. 86.

260. Halvdan Koht: *The Life of Ibsen*, 1931, p. 63.

261. M. C. Bradbrook: *Ibsen*, 1946, pp. 34–5.

262. Ibsen: *Corresp.*, p. 218.

263. Holbrook Jackson: *The Eighteen-Nineties*, 1939 (1913), p. 177.

NOTES

264. Letter to Mehring of 14th July 1893. MARX-ENGELS: *Correspondence*, 1934, pp. 511–12.

265. ERNEST JONES: 'Rationalism in Everyday Life'. Read at the First Internat. Psycho-Analytic Congress, 1908. In *Papers on Psycho-Analysis*, 1913.

266. KARL MANNHEIM: *Ideology and Utopia*, 1936, pp. 61–2.

267. THOMAS MANN: 'Die Stellung Freuds in der modernen Geistesgeschichte'. In *Die Forderung des Tages*, 1930, pp. 201 ff.

268. S. FREUD: *The Future of an Illusion*, translated by W. D. Robson-Scott, 1928, p. 93.

269. NIETZSCHE: *Werke*, 1895 ff., XVI, p. 19.

II. THE FILM AGE

1. HERMANN KEYSERLING: *Die neuentstehende Welt*, 1926.—JAMES BURNHAM: *The Managerial Revolution*, 1941.

2. M. J. BONN: *The American Experiment*, 1933, p. 285.

3. JOSÉ ORTEGA Y GASSET: *The Revolt of the Masses*, 1932.

4. ERNST TROELTSCH: 'Die Revolution in der Wissenschaft'. *Gesammelte Schriften*, IV, 1925, p. 676.

5. HENRI MASSIS: *La Défense de l'Occident*, 1927.

6. HERMANN HESSE: *Blick ins Chaos*, 1923.

7. ANDRÉ MALRAUX: *Psychologie de l'art*, 1947.

8. ANDRÉ BRETON: *What is Surrealism?*, 1936, pp. 45 ff.

9. JEAN PAULHAN: *Les Fleurs de Tarbes*, 1941.

10. JACQUES RIVIÈRE: 'Reconnaissance à Dada'. *Nouvelle Revue Française*, 1920, XV, pp. 231 ff.—MARCEL RAYMOND: *De Baudelaire au surréalisme*, 1933, p. 390.

11. ANDRÉ BRETON: *Les Pas perdus*, 1924.

12. TRISTAN TZARA: *Sept manifestes dada*, 1920.

13. FRIEDRICH GUNDOLF: *Goethe*, 1916.

14. MICHAEL AYRTON: 'A Master of Pastiche'. *New Writing and Daylight*, 1946, pp. 108 ff.

15. RENÉ HUYGHE-GERMAIN BAZIN: *Hist. de l'art contemp.*, 1935, p. 223.

16. CONSTANT LAMBERT: *Music ho!*, 1934.

17. EDMUND WILSON: *Axel's Castle*, 1931, p. 256.

18. ANDRÉ BRETON: *(Premier) Manifeste du surréalisme*, 1924.

19. LOUIS REYNAUD: *La Crise de notre littérature*, 1929, pp. 196–7.

20. Cf. CHARLES DU BOS: *Approximations*, 1922.—BENJAMIN CRÉMIEUX: *XXᵉ siècle*, 1924.—JACQUES RIVIÈRE: *Marcel Proust*, 1924.

21. J. TH. SOBY: *Salvador Dali*, 1946, p. 24.

22. ANDRÉ BRETON: *What is Surrealism?* p. 67.

23. ANDRÉ BRETON: *Second Manifeste du surréalisme*, 1930.—MAURICE NADEAU: *Histoire du surréalisme*, 1945, 2nd edit., p. 176.

24. JULIEN BENDA: *La France byzantine*, 1945, p. 48.

NOTES

25. Cf. E. R. Curtius: *Franzoesischer Geist im neuen Europa*, 1925, pp. 75–6.

26. Cf. Emil Lederer-Jakob Marschak: 'Der neue Mittelstand'. *Grundriss der Sozialoekonomik*, IX/1, 1926, pp. 121 ff.

27. Walter Benjamin: 'L'Œuvre d'art à l'époque de sa reproduction mécanisée'. *Zeitschrift fuer Sozialforschung*, 1936, V/1, p. 45.

INDEX

INDEX

INDEX

265